Te Ata

Chickasaw Storyteller, American Treasure

Te Ata

Chickasaw Storyteller, American Treasure

RICHARD GREEN

Afterword by Rayna Green and John Troutman

University of Oklahoma Press • Norman

Publication of this book is made possible through the generosity of Edith Kinney Gaylord.

Library of Congress Cataloging-in-Publication Data

Green, Richard (Richard Walter)
    Te Ata, Chickasaw storyteller, American treasure / Richard Green ; afterword by Rayna Green and John Troutman.
        p.   cm.
    Includes bibliographical references and index.
    ISBN 0-8061-3411-9 (hardcover : alk. paper)
        1. Ata, Te. 2. Chickasaw Indians—Biography. 3. Storytellers—United States—Biography.   I. Title

E99.C55 A725 2002
976.004'973—dc21

                                                              2001055700

1   2   3   4   5   6   7   8   9   10

FRONTISPIECE:
Te Ata, London, 1930

To my wife, Gail Fites, who made this book possible

CONTENTS

ILLUSTRATIONS

All photographs are from the family collection, courtesy of Helen Cole, unless otherwise indicated.

INTRODUCTION

At the White House on April 22, 1933, President Franklin D. Roosevelt and his wife, Eleanor, hosted the first official State Dinner of his administration. Some sixty-two guests filed into the Blue Room to honor the visiting prime minister of Great Britain, the honorable Ramsey MacDonald. In accordance with the usual pomp and protocol, many toasts were made to Anglo-American friendship and a splendid banquet was served on the official White House dinner service. Afterward, in the East Room, Eleanor Roosevelt introduced the evening's entertainment.

She told the audience that the featured performer, Te Ata, was a member of the Chickasaw tribe and a longtime friend. Te Ata, she announced, would be presenting a "delightful" program of Indian folklore. But as the audience would soon realize, these were not mere recitations but artistic presentations, imbued with drama, rhythm, pathos, and occasional humor. This blending of authentic folklore with artistry is what made Te Ata's performance unique. Like her, many other Indian entertainers crisscrossed the American landscape for portions of the period from the 1920s to the postwar years. Bit players were killed off daily in Wild West shows; relatively anonymous singers, dancers, and actors performed for the masses in burlesque theaters; very few actors (most notably Will Rogers, one-fourth Cherokee) starred in successful movies but not as Indians; a number of accomplished musicians performed in concert halls but normally playing show tunes or opera; a few others made small circuits presenting Indian folklore—but none had Te Ata's appeal and artistry.

Te Ata's stunning appearance captured the East Room audience's attention before she uttered a word. Wearing an elegant white buckskin Sioux dress, Te Ata, at age 37, was five feet seven, slender, and beautiful. Her voice was strong, full, and somewhat deep for a woman. At times she accompanied herself by shaking a gourd rattle or beating a drum. Throughout her performance, she moved sparingly but always with grace and fluidity. Without a change of dress, she assumed widely disparate roles as she moved through her program. From a bumptious young brave to an old woman at the end of her trail, Te Ata modulated voice and gesture to be in character and complement the stories and songs.

As with all great performers, the seeming effortlessness of her performance was illusory. She learned her first Indian stories from her father, a Chickasaw tribal official before Oklahoma became a state in 1907. Her college drama teacher refined her talent and contributed to the poise and judgment she needed to launch her career in the 1920s. Apart from her talent as an dramatist, she needed vision, commitment, and grit to control her shyness and to break through the social mores holding that a woman's proper place was in the home.

Te Ata's husband, Clyde Fisher, a curator at the American Museum of Natural History in New York, certainly did not think she should give up her career. He immediately recognized that she was an extraordinary artist, and even before their marriage in 1933, he promoted her among his many circles of friends and associates. Fisher, seventeen years her senior, was a highly respected scientist whose scholarly appearance was crowned with billowing white hair. They made a striking and attractive couple. By virtue of their exalted status both individually and perhaps still more as a couple, they were bona fide members of New York's intellectual and cultural elite. But they were often apart during their seventeen-year marriage and wrote hundreds of letters to one another, a main source of material for this book.

Te Ata's career took her all over America in venues of all kinds, from great stages to school auditoriums to Indian reservations. But no matter the quality of the facility or the degree of education or sophistication of the audience or that she was sometimes exhausted or ill, Te Ata's performance was never less than inspired. She never compromised her integrity or her material. Her mission was to entertain and educate, to enlighten and inspire, and she gladly accepted this honor and responsibility during the decades when the dominant white society was not nearly as receptive to minorities as it is today.

Introduction

During the first thirty years of her career, the great majority of Americans scarcely knew or cared that Indians still existed. Moreover, many of the tribes and their traditional cultures had been weakened, some to the point of extinction, by federal programs designed to abolish tribal governments and force members to blend into the American melting pot.

When a grassroots movement to revitalize her own tribal government was building in the mid-1950s, she appeared as the star of the tribe's constitutional centennial celebration in 1955 in her hometown, Tishomingo. She said this honor rivaled that of being invited to entertain at the White House or at Stratford-on-Avon. Two years later she was inducted into the Oklahoma Hall of Fame and later was the third inductee into the Chickasaw Hall of Fame.

Te Ata continued to tour for another twenty years—into the modern era of tribal self-determination. She helped bring this era about, not politically, but by presenting the beauty and wisdom of tribal folklore to thousand of Americans, many of whom never forgot her.

Some of her admirers in her home state, such as Betty Price, executive director of the Oklahoma Arts Council, eventually were in a position to demonstrate their appreciation in a unique and permanent way. With Te Ata in mind, Price led the effort to establish the Oklahoma Treasure, patterned after a tradition in Japan, which names exalted artists as national treasures.

In 1987, when Te Ata was 92 years old, she was named Oklahoma's first official State Treasure. Since then, through the efforts of Price and various state officials, the east oval of the State Capitol has been designated as the Te Ata Garden to honor all official Oklahoma Treasures (eight so far). A sculpture of Te Ata will be commissioned for the landscaped garden.

Te Ata
Chickasaw Storyteller, American Treasure

Prologue

According to the tribal migration legend, Chickasaws and Choctaws arose from common ancestors. Following an upheaval of some sort, the people were told by Ubabeneli, the Great Spirit, to migrate to a new home. They were led by two brothers, Chikasah and Chatah, who guided them by means of a sacred pole. Every night the pole was placed upright into the ground; every morning it was leaning, indicating the direction of the day's travel. The brothers separated sometime after crossing the great river they called the *misha sipokni*, meaning "beyond all age" (later known as the Mississippi).

At this point, versions of the migration legend diverge as to how the people got separated into the two tribes that eventually became the Chickasaws and Choctaws. Whether the breakup was accidental or acrimonious, many more people followed Chatah, which accounts for the Choctaws' three- to four-to-one numerical superiority. At any rate, the two tribes settled in the Southeast as contiguous but often unfriendly neighbors.[1]

Before contact with Europeans, the Chickasaws were never a large tribe, with a population that ranged between thirty-five hundred and forty-five hundred. They controlled, however, a vast amount of hunting lands—comprising most of present-day northern Mississippi and parts of northwestern Alabama, western Tennessee, and western Kentucky.[2]

In the eighteenth century the tribe was weakened by almost continuous warfare with other tribes, notably the Choctaws, and their allies, the French colonialists. Although the Chickasaws fought fiercely and skillfully, battlefield casualties and morbidity and mortality from European-borne diseases seriously decreased their ranks as the number of white encroachers mushroomed.

After President Thomas Jefferson bought the Louisiana Territory in 1803, the U.S. government forced Indians located east of the Mississippi to sell their lands and migrate to new homes in the West. Initially, the Chickasaws resisted all talk of moving from their land. But they became indebted to colonial traders, and the tribe was compelled three times in the early nineteenth century to sell part of its land to the government. Then President Andrew Jackson signed the Indian Removal Act of 1830, which expressed the government's purpose of moving the Southeastern tribes beyond the frontier. The die was cast; as the Chickasaws viewed it, they could fight a disastrous war with no chance of winning, liquidate and become citizens of Mississippi, or move to the West.[3] The Chickasaws were among the last of the Southeastern tribes to travel the Trail of Tears to Indian Territory, emigrating in both large and small groups by steamship and overland between 1837 and 1850. As in all removal treaties with the federal government, the Chickasaws were given a solemn guarantee that the new land would be theirs in perpetuity and that they would never be subjugated by another government without their consent.[4]

Although the physical journey for most of them was relatively mild compared to the horrors inflicted on the Cherokees and Choctaws, the majority of Indians suffered in spiritual ways that few whites could understand, much less appreciate. According to the late historian Grant Foreman, "They cherished a passionate attachment for the earth that held the bones of their ancestors and relatives. The trees that shaded their homes, the cooling spring that ministered to every family, familiar trails, busk [ceremonial] grounds and council houses were their property and their friends; these simple possessions filled their lives; their loss was cataclysmic."[5]

The Chickasaws paid $530,000 to the Choctaws for about one-third of their land in Indian Territory; it was designated the Chickasaw district of the Choctaw Nation. For the most part, the Chickasaws lived in poverty and misery among the Choctaws until after 1844, when the federal government finally started paying the annuity to tribal members from the sale of their former homeland. Although the

Chickasaws theoretically had equal rights with the Choctaws under their government, the Chickasaws were never happy with the relationship and several sources of friction resulted in a treaty of separation, executed in Washington, D.C., in 1855. Accordingly, the Chickasaws purchased clear title to their land by paying $150,000 to the Choctaws. Although the nations were separate and distinct, the treaty included provisions that amounted to conferring on one another a "most favored nation" status, including a joint undivided interest in much of the tribal domains.[6] After the treaty was signed, the Chickasaws met at Good Spring (later Tishomingo) and immediately promulgated their own constitution, democratic government, and laws. Impressive strides in tribal government were made until the Civil War broke out in 1861.

In a way the Civil War was the beginning of the end for many tribal governments. The Chickasaw Nation and the Choctaw Nation signed treaties to support the Confederacy, and being on the losing side cost both tribes dearly. They supported the Confederacy for two main reasons. First, when hostilities broke out, U.S. troops garrisoned in Indian Territory to protect the citizens of the Indian nations were ordered out by the federal government. The Confederates moved in, taking military possession of the Indian nations and leaving the Chickasaws and Choctaws little choice but to join them. Second, many of the tribal leaders had an economic interest to protect. They were members of well-to-do mixed-blood families who owned slaves; they had brought their slaves with them during removal and put them to work in the cotton fields and cornfields.[7]

After the war the Chickasaws and Choctaws had to negotiate a new treaty with the U.S. government. Besides the abolition of slavery and emancipation of the slaves, the treaty provided the railroads with rights-of-way through the Indian nations, thus greatly facilitating and accelerating intrusion by non-Indians. Into the 1880s both major Chickasaw political parties were committed to preserving the Chickasaw way of life and trying to control the flood of non-Indians into their nation. But within a few years external political and economic forces had destroyed tribal unity and the federal government had done little to enforce the tribe's attempts to control non-Indian emigration.[8] According to the 1890 census, the population of the Chickasaw Nation was approximately 57,000. Less than 3,000 were Chickasaw;

about 5,000 belonged to other tribes or were freedmen (former slaves); and more than 47,000 were white. Just a decade later, in 1900, the number of white noncitizens had tripled.[9]

Since Chickasaw laws and courts had jurisdiction only over members of the tribe and U.S. marshals were in short supply in Indian Territory, violence and crime kept pace with the population of intruders. Those who favored abolishing the Indian governments often cited lawlessness to support their argument. The federal government's solution to its Indian problem was the Dawes Act of 1887, a plan for transforming Indian communal lands into individual land allotments. Although the Chickasaw and other so-called civilized tribes (Choctaw, Creek, Seminole, and Cherokee) were excluded from the act, the Dawes Commission was established by Congress in 1893 to negotiate with the five tribes for the termination of their tribal titles to the land.[10]

At first the Chickasaws flatly refused to discuss land allotment with members of the Dawes Commission. In 1894 the Chickasaw Nation consisted of a constitutional government of three branches, county governments, a complete school system—including day and boarding schools—and $1.2 million held in trust by the federal government from the sale of the Southeastern lands.[11] But in 1895 Congress appropriated funding to survey tribal lands in Indian Territory and gave the Dawes Commission the go-ahead to prepare individual tribal rolls. Fearing that the government would enroll whites and freedmen, in July 1895 the Chickasaws agreed to meet with the Dawes Commission. But the Chickasaw governor and legislature failed to appear. The commissioners then declared that they were finished coming to the Chickasaws. Henceforth it would have to be the other way around.[12]

It was clearly a time of transition for the tribe. But toward what? Into this emotional cauldron of conflict, confusion, despair, and hope, Te Ata was born on December 3, 1895.

CHAPTER 1

Listening to the Corn Grow

As a child, Te Ata learned tribal folklore from her father, Thomas Benjamin Thompson, a Chickasaw emblematic of tribal members facing the final phase of acculturation at the turn of the century. A natural storyteller, Thompson loved entertaining his children. But, as a man working hard to be successful in business in white society, he passed on little else about the tribe's heritage or his own Indian ancestors. If he had schooled his children in such matters, Te Ata would have recorded it, for she sopped up his stories like a sponge. But in the voluminous amount of material she amassed on her life and times, there are only a few scraps of paper containing names of a handful of her Indian ancestors. Since virtually no details exist, these people, including her paternal grandfather and great-grandfather, were nothing more than disembodied figures in her mind.[1] In her unpublished memoir, "Te Ata: As I Remember It," none of her ancestors except her parents is named. In fact, her only reference to earlier ancestors was indirect: she wrote that both Chickasaw and Choctaw blood ran in her veins.[2] Moreover, Te Ata told some interviewers that her mother, Bertie, had a little Osage blood, but the claim was undocumented and therefore not recognized by either tribal or federal authorities.[3]

A chart in Te Ata's papers identifies Thomas Jacob Thompson as her paternal great-grandfather.[4] Thompson lived in the old Chickasaw Nation in what is now northeastern Mississippi. He apparently was married twice. He may have had Choctaw-Chickasaw blood, as Te Ata's family believes, but it is said that he was adopted into the Chickasaw tribe, likely because one of his wives was Chickasaw.[5] He did not join the tribe's forced migration to Indian Territory but stayed behind and fathered four sons. One of them, Thomas Jefferson Thompson, born in 1840, was Te Ata's grandfather. When he and a brother were teenagers, they decided to join the tribe in the west.[6] Subsequently, their father joined them and then died in Indian Territory, the year unrecorded.

Thomas Jefferson enrolled at the Chickasaw Manual Labor Academy, which in 1851 had become the first tribally established boarding school in the Chickasaw Nation, located near present-day Tishomingo. After he graduated his flair for numbers landed him a job teaching mathematics at the academy. On Christmas Day, 1863, he married Millenium Bynum, an eighteen-year-old Chickasaw woman.[7] The couple's first child, Thomas Benjamin (Te Ata's father), was born on May 20, 1865, near Emet, about eight miles from Tishomingo, the capital of the Chickasaw Nation. Almost nothing is known of Millenium (Te Ata's grandmother) except that she was a direct descendant of James Logan Colbert, a Scotsman who settled in the old Chickasaw Nation in 1729 and started, with the help of three Chickasaw wives, one of the tribe's leading mixed-blood families.[8] Millenium died giving birth to Mary Frances in 1867, when Thomas Benjamin was just 2 years old.[9]

Soon after Millenium's death Thomas Jefferson married Loisina Harkins, and they had two sons. Thomas Jefferson was named clerk of a local Chickasaw court and was later elevated to clerk of the Chickasaw Nation's supreme court. He died inexplicably at the age of 35 in 1875. His eldest son, Thomas Benjamin, was 10 years old. The boy was taken from his stepmother by his maternal grandmother, Lucinda Bynum, who placed him in a tribal boarding school for secondary students, the Lebanon Orphan School. He later attended the Harley Institute in Tishomingo. One year before graduating he went to work for a prominent judge, Sobe Love, in Marietta, near the Red River. Surely the Bynums arranged the situation with Judge Love, to steer him toward a career in the law, as they might have done earlier for his father.

A turning point in the boy's life occurred in 1881 when Nellie Bynum, from his grandmother's side of the family, married Douglas

Te Ata: Chickasaw Storyteller, American Treasure

Johnston, who in 1898 would be elected governor of the Chickasaw Nation. As Thomas Benjamin was just 16, it was arranged that he should live with the young couple; Nellie was 21 and Douglas 25. There is no record of how long Thomas stayed with the couple, probably only a year or two, but in 1884 Johnston became superintendent of Bloomfield Academy, a Chickasaw boarding school for girls that was located at Achille, about three miles north of the Red River. Two years later Nellie died in childbirth. Although the formal Thompson link to Johnston was then severed, the two men continued to feel kinship, and from this bond their relationship expanded in the years ahead.

In the 1880s Thomas learned merchandising by working in a Tishomingo general store. He married a Choctaw, Belle Gardner, in 1888, and they established a home in Emet, near his birthplace. That same year he was elected permit collector and the following year followed in his father's footsteps by being appointed clerk of the Chickasaw Supreme Court. In 1890 Thomas helped to conduct the Chickasaw tribal census, he had seventy-five acres of fertile land under cultivation and Belle was pregnant with the couple's first child.[10] Then Thomas's world turned upside down. Belle died in childbirth, but the baby, Selena, lived. In the matrilineal tradition of the Chickasaws and Choctaws, the baby went to live with her maternal grandparents.

In 1893 Thomas and Douglas Johnston opened a general store in Emet. Johnston's job at Bloomfield made him a partner in absentia; that Thomas was able to operate the store while holding down his court job probably was due to the help of his new wife, Lucy Alberta "Bertie" Freund, whom he had married on April 16, 1893.[11]

Bertie was born on March 25, 1870, one of six children of tenant-farmer parents who settled in Texas. At times the family lived off the land, but through hard work and trusting in the Lord, the Freunds held together. They gradually accumulated some livestock and a little money, but they never owned land. Bertie learned how to read and write by attending school for parts of four years, as time and circumstances permitted. As Bertie suggested in her unpublished memoir, handwritten in 1939, most of her childhood was spent at hard labor: "I had to get up very early for I had to milk 6 cows, feed 4 head of horses, had to cut and carry green corn for nearly a half mile to feed

Te Ata's mother, Bertie, about the time she married "her Indian," Thomas Thompson.

them twice a day. . . . On Saturdays I had to stay home and wash and iron." In season, she picked cotton all day long.

Although Bertie's parents, Daniel and Mary Freund, were impoverished and never stayed in one place long enough to make friends, they always cared for their neighbors in need. If a family needed clothes, Bertie sewed for them. If someone was sick, Mary or her daughter administered natural preparations of their own making. Bertie wrote, "In those days, we had the only sewing machine near us and Ma would make me sew for all the neighbors." For one family of eight, Bertie had to "make shirts for three men and all the underwear for the whole family, dresses, bonnets, aprons for the women." She was paid with a fifty-pound sack of flour. "Ma thought it was all right. When she loved her neighbors, she would do anything for

Te Ata: Chickasaw Storyteller, American Treasure

them." The Freunds' reputation got around: "Every Saturday evening you would see a wagon load of people drive up and stop. They had come to stay the night and until Sunday evening, maybe six or eight in the family. Their [*sic*] were six of us at this time. We would make pallets all over the floor."

Because the land was more fertile and game more abundant north of the Red River, the Freunds moved to Indian Territory, near Willis. Bertie wrote, "The wild grass was thick and as high as your head. So we could let our stock all run out and they cost us very little to feed them. The country was sure wild and we had lots of deer, turkey, prairie chickens and wild hogs and horses. Rabbits, quail and squirrels were nearly as thick as blackbirds. I have gone with my brother to kill squirrels and killed twenty many a time and was not out of sight of our house." The family moved near Emet in 1892. After about a year, during which the family planted and harvested about fifty acres of corn, Bertie wrote that she "found [her] Indian." She met Thomas Benjamin Thompson at a spelling bee held every Friday night in an abandoned house that had been fixed up by some of the competitors. After attending a few such matches, Thomas worked up the courage to ask Bertie if he could walk her home. She consented, and he began walking her home every Friday evening and seeing her on Sundays.

Bertie termed their courtship "peculiar." Thomas was "very reserved," Bertie wrote. "He never taken my arm and he walked on his side of the road and I on mine. He would come home with me but when we got to the porch he said good night and I didn't see him again till Sunday." Still, the couple was compatible: "It seemed that everything I liked he did [too] and we agreed on everything. We never did disagree on things before our marriage and a very few times afterward. A wife never had a more affectionate husband though he never told me he loved me till we was married. He proposed to propose on a Friday and proposed the following Sunday. He always laughed afterwards and said I answered: 'Yes, and thank you Mr. Thompson.' But I did not."[12]

Mary Freund was dead set against her daughter marrying an Indian. (If Bertie had Osage blood, as she told her children, it evidently must have been a vanishingly small amount.) Bertie was prepared to honor her mother's wishes until she found that her mother had

Thomas Thompson was the last treasurer of the Chickasaw Nation before Oklahoma's statehood. He told his daughter, Mary, that Indian stories were like ragweed. Though the branches spread out this way and that, they all come from the same root.

unlocked her trunk and read Thomas's love letters.[13] Angry, she told her mother that the wedding would take place after all. Mrs. Freund threatened to jump in the water tank and drown. Bertie told her to go ahead. Meanwhile, Bertie, having no money, was forced to pick cotton to earn enough to buy four yards of satin and calico for a wedding dress. One shoe had a hole in it, so she cut out a piece of tongue from an even more dilapidated shoe, slipped it between the leather and lining, and blackened it with soot. She spent two weeks plowing and planting a field of corn and got married the day after the job was finished.

The marriage license in the Chickasaw Nation cost $50 but conferred on Bertie all the citizenship rights of the nation, including the right to receive annuity payments from the federal government. Thomas's monthly salary as clerk of the supreme court was $50. After paying the fee, the couple was left with $1.50. Fortunately, they were married by Thomas's uncle, Judge Joe Bynum, who waived his fee.[14] Bertie's mother sent word that her daughter had disgraced the family by marrying an Indian. But six weeks later, on a Sunday, Mrs. Freund suddenly showed up and spent the day with the couple as though nothing had ever been wrong.

Three months after the wedding Douglas Johnston and Thomas opened the general store in Emet. After four months, Thomas took $400 he had made and bought the lumber for a new five-room, L-shaped frame house, which he built near the store. Bertie's parents moved into the Thompsons' former home, a small log house. A fire destroyed the general store in November. Johnston wanted to resume the partnership, but the younger man declined because he no longer needed Johnston's money to run a business. Soon after their marriage Thomsas learned, to his amazement, that Bertie owned twenty-eight head of cattle, which she had accumulated over the years as payment for various kinds of work. With her permission, he put them up as collateral on a bank loan to buy the rebuilt store's first inventory.[15]

The frame house was built to accommodate the large family the Thompsons' expected to have. But until the rooms were needed, the ever resourceful Bertie turned part of the house into what she called a hotel. She provided room and board to peddlers and other traveling salesmen who gravitated to the new population centers that sprang up with the mass immigration of non-Indians into the nations of the Indian Territory. What Thomas, as a Chickasaw and an official of the Chickasaw Nation, thought of accommodating these largely illegal aliens is not known, but by 1893 it was obvious that there was no turning back the tidal wave of non-Indian intruders.[16]

At any rate, many of the "hotel guests" doted on the Thompsons' first child, Eugene Ross, who was born on March 13, 1894. One drummer used to get the baby out of his crib and put him in his high chair next to him at mealtimes. Then, in a custom of the time that Bertie "could hardly stand," the drummer would prechew the baby's food for him. The hotel business was good. Often she had six overnight guests, each of whom paid twenty-five cents for the bed and twenty-five cents per meal. Her net profit for the first year was $400.[17] Although it was probably not yet apparent to Bertie, she had much more business acumen than her husband. Though she must have realized this in time, she always deferred to him and his business ventures; as a result, the family would struggle financially. Te Ata never said so, but she probably learned the value of self-reliance in reverse from her parents' example. Once on her own, she would never subjugate her talents the way her mother had.

Near the end of 1895 Bertie was again about to deliver, but the baby, who would be called Te Ata, awaited a "blue norther." She was born on December 3, on what Bertie said was the coldest night she had ever experienced: "I thought we would all freeze to death." The heat from the fireplace scarcely reached into the room before being smothered by the intense cold. The baby girl was born in a bed with a high walnut headboard that was given to the Thompsons by Douglas Johnston. Thomas took the baby from Bertie, wrapped her in blankets, and held her against his body throughout the night. Thomas and Bertie named the baby Mary Frances, the same name as Thomas's sister who had died in infancy. "Coincidence," said Te Ata, who wrote in her memoir that she was named for her father's aunt Mary Harkins.[18]

Although too little is known about Thomas Thompson's ancestry to be precise about his Indian blood quantum, he was enrolled as one-fourth Chickasaw on the roll of 1897.[19] This was probably part guesswork and part calculation. Many enrolled Chickasaws underreported their Indian blood because federal restrictions on an individual's land allotment were tied to blood quantum. Persons with less Indian blood had more control over their land, including the right to sell it. The degree of Thomas's Indian blood, whether it was one-fourth or as much as one-half, was irrelevant; in his mind and heart

Te Ata: Chickasaw Storyteller, American Treasure

he was Chickasaw. He spoke Chickasaw and knew something about tribal lore and passed it along to his children. He also frequently reminded them, "You can never trust a white man." At the same time, he had a white wife who was no shrinking violet; Bertie had at least as much influence on her children as Thomas did. Moreover, in 1897, in the relatively short span of Thomas's thirty-three years, he had seen the weakening and dissolution of tribal ways and believed the Chickasaws were going to be totally assimilated into the American mainstream. He had a foot in each world: even while he held an office with the tribe, he was practicing capitalism by running his general store. He wanted his children to be prepared to compete in American society, and for that they would need a solid liberal arts education, free of such cultural baggage as the Chickasaw language. As a game or diversion, he taught the children to count to ten in Chickasaw but refused Mary's entreaties to teach her more of the language.

The stork visited the family about every eighteen months. Gladys arrived in 1897, Thomas Bynum in 1899, Iona in 1900, Jewel in 1903 and Avis in 1904. Jewel lived just six months and Thomas Bynum only seven months.[20] Only Jewel's death is noted in Te Ata's memoir. While writing about her childhood preoccupation with angels, she mentioned that she once saw three angels gliding in the sky and that one of them was Jewel. Gladys developed diptheria and nearly died. A new antitoxin was administered, which may have done more harm than good, and in fact Te Ata and other family members later speculated that either the disease or the cure may have had a deleterious effect on her mental stability. Selena, Thompson's daughter by his first wife, lived with her maternal grandparents until she was school age. Then she came to live with the Thompsons and, according to Bertie and Te Ata, was immediately accepted into the family.[21] Selena came into a stable and loving environment. Thomas and Bertie seldom disagreed and rarely squabbled; they did not show much outward affection but were clearly devoted to one another and to their children. While Thomas was by no means a workaholic, he had plenty to occupy him and seemed to be relatively successful for most of the first decade of the twentieth century. He had the only general store in a radius of twelve miles, farmed rich and productive land in the Emet area, and in 1904 was appointed tribal treasurer by Chickasaw governor Douglas Johnston. In a turn-of-the-century book on Indian

It is likely that these clothes worn by the Thompson children were made by Bertie from material at one of their father's general stores, which he ran successfully for a short time. The portrait, probably taken in Tishomingo about 1906, includes, from left, Gladys, Mary (Te Ata), Selena, Avis, Eugene, and Iona.

Territory leaders, Thomas was described as "a man of forceful individuality, strong purpose, indomitable enterprise and good judgment." He also was "deeply interested in everything pertaining to the welfare of the community and his efforts [were] of great benefit in promoting public advancement."[22] For example, Thomas donated land to the community so that a school and church could be built.

Like her parents, Bertie worked steadily from sunup until she closed her eyes at night. While most of her housework and farmwork

Te Ata: Chickasaw Storyteller, American Treasure

was tedious or laborious, she regarded all work as good if it was done well. While she worked, she sang or whistled, mainly hymns. Even after dinner as she sat by the fire, she was always sewing or darning. She said she had restless hands.[23] Taking after her mother, Bertie would do anything to help her neighbors. If they lacked food or medicine, she supplied it. Once she tended the critically ill infant of a man whom she learned had been swindling her husband in his mercantile business. Bertie practiced Christianity unconditionally.

The Thompsons' little girl was called by her given name, Mary, by everyone except the man she referred to as uncle, Douglas Johnston. He called the child Aiukla Ohoyo, which he understood to be Chickasaw for "Handsome Woman." Mary liked the sound of the Indian name but never used it because she was too embarrassed to tell white people its meaning. Another time, an elderly aunt, probably Mary Harkins, gave the little girl a different Indian name in a special ceremony she conducted in a high, quavering voice. This name was Te Ata, which she said meant "Bearer of the Dawn." Modern Chickasaw speakers report that the words have no meaning in their language. But the little girl liked the name so well that she took to introducing herself as Te Ata to her family during impromptu performances of singing, dancing, and improvised narratives, such as how she escaped from pursuing bears.[24]

On occasion, when exasperated, Mary's mother called her by her full name, Mary Frances. Those occasions resulted not from disobedience or rebelliousness but from the fact that Mary was constitutionally high-strung, curious, and adventurous. Tall for her age and reed thin, she had an athletic nimbleness and grace. As her mother said, "Mary never walks but she runs and never steps but she jumps." Her playmates were mainly boys, with whom she more than held her own; she could jump higher and run faster and was just as daring. The big elm tree near the family's yard satisfied two of her innate needs. She liked to climb the tree and spring from one branch to the next. Sometimes, she climbed up near the top to be alone; there, hidden by the leaves, Mary would sit enjoying the view and the solitude for an hour or more. A generation later while living at Loon Island in New Hampshire, she often thought of her childhood arbor perch as she looked out the windows of her third-floor room at the treetops almost within reach. When Mary got hungry, she would eat the food out of the basket she had carried up into the tree with her. Mary's being in the tree did not bother Bertie unduly, but when she saw her daughter leaping about twenty or thirty feet above the ground, she warned her sternly to desist. Mary meant to stop but found the activity too exhilarating. After repeated warnings, Bertie had the elm tree cut down.[25] Afterward, Mary found the solitude she needed in the woods and fields. Once Bertie discovered her little girl sitting in the middle of a cornfield and asked what she was doing. She replied with a solemnity that belied her young age, "I am listening to the corn grow."

Mary chafed at being inside for long. Wisely, Bertie assigned her mostly outdoor chores. Actually, Bertie had always preferred the outdoors herself, and mother and daughter spent quite a bit of time together on nature walks, during which Bertie gathered plants she would use to prepare medicines. Although Te Ata thought these were tribal medicines, they were more likely pioneer nostrums that Bertie had learned about from her mother. She administered most of them to Indian neighbors and relatives. At any rate, Bertie was much in demand: "I have done my share of waiting on the sick. Dad would keep the babies and I would often be gone all night." She was also called to minister to the dying and prepare the body for the funeral. "I was the one to wash them and lay them out and make the shroud," she explained.[26]

On their walks, Mary learned to identify a great variety of plants, and thirty years later, on nature walks with her husband, Clyde Fisher, she amazed and delighted this Ph.D. in botany and expert naturalist with her great breadth of plant knowledge. Bertie also taught Mary how to use certain plants for one thing or another. They dug up fragrant sassafras roots and made tea. They collected twigs from the winged elm and frayed them for use as toothbrushes. They boiled bitter broomweed and combined it with honey to make a cough syrup. They used willow bark as an analgesic and parts of the tamarisk tree in various medicinal preparations. They even made chewing gum from sunflowers and stretchberries.[27]

During the long, cold winter nights when Mary was very young, she and her brother, Eugene, whom everyone called Snake, were entertained by their father's string tricks, shadow puppets, and Indian stories. Just how large and varied his repertoire was Te Ata did not

Te Ata: Chickasaw Storyteller, American Treasure

specify. Some were instructional: what tree to use in making a durable bow or foods that are good or bad for you. Other stories were informative and entertaining: how the Cherokees long ago tied down the four corners of the earth, and if people do wrong, a corner could loosen and "we can all slip off the edge and into the big water." When they asked why it was the Cherokees and not the Chickasaws, he said, "Stories are like this old ragweed. See all the fine branches? They all come from the same root, but they spread out, this way, that way; they are all a little bit different."

Years later, when Te Ata began telling some of these stories to her high school and college classmates and they would ask for a story's origin, she could only say that she had heard it from her father. The truth was her father had never considered it important to trace the origin of the stories, and she tended to agree with him. What was important to her—if not always to her father—was why the story was made up in the first place and why it had been perpetuated. One of Mary's favorite stories from her father described how different races came to be. It was simple, humorous, and conjured up rich and vivid imagery. In these racially sensitive times, the story might be thought of as crude or insulting. But when it was told by an Indian with great presence, like Thomas Thompson and, later, Te Ata, it seemed to fit the context of the times. At any rate, it became a permanent part of her children's repertoire and she delighted audiences across America with it for decades.

Sometime around the turn of the century, Thomas Thompson sat in a rocker near the fireplace and held up his hands to quiet Snake and Mary who were imploring him to tell them a story. He began:

> Long time ago, after the Earth was made, first water, then land, then animals and plants for food, Old Man Earthmaker got tired sitting up in Sky all by himself. He had worked hard making all those animals. He had asked each one how it wanted to be made. Some had chosen feathers, some fur, some scaly skin. Now he began to think he guess he make somebody to talk with and to walk on the earth. He wanted someone to keep him company, and he decide to make Man, and to make Man his way.
>
> He saw a hemlock tree; it had been torn up by the roots, and earth was clinging to all those little roots. So he picked up some of

the sandy soil and mixed it with water, and he began to shape it into Man. He made the head, arms, body, the legs. Then he fix a big oven and put this Man in to bake. Earthmaker was all excited, and he pulled out Man too quick, half baked and hairy from the hemlock needles. That was White Man. Old Man Earthmaker looked at him from behind hemlock tree. He breathed the breath of life into him, but he was displeased, so he took that Man by the leg and threw him across big body of water, out of his sight. Ever since, poor White Man has been pale and sickly-looking, with lots of hair.

Earthmaker didn't want give up first time, so he decided to try again to make perfect Man. He walked along and saw a beautiful black walnut tree. The earth was rich and dark, so Earthmaker decided to make another Man. He scooped up some soil from under that big black walnut tree, he mixed it with water to make a nice clay, and he shaped it into Man. He placed this Man in that oven to bake. Earthmaker did not want to take Man out too soon again, so he leave this one in a long time. Too long. When Earthmaker took him out he was very black. Earthmaker did not like him much better than the white Man, but he breathed the breath of life into him. Then he took him by the leg and threw him across another body of water, and out of sight.

Earthmaker decided he would try one more time. This time he would be very careful. So he walked along until he came to a beautiful sugar maple tree. He scooped up some soil from under that tree, he mixed it with water to make a nice clay, and he shaped it into a Man. He put him into the oven to bake, and he watched that oven very carefully. He pulled him out when he was a beautiful golden brown—just right, a perfect Man. And that is how our people came to be.[28]

From tribal elders, the children heard stories of tribal practices that had passed or were passing from the scene. One was the Green Corn Dance, or busk, an ancient ceremony held when the corn was ripening to thank the Great Spirit for a bountiful harvest. Because of the pervasive influence of Christian missionaries and the rise of mixed-bloods to tribal leadership, this ceremony had been falling into disuse even before the Chickasaws and Choctaws were forced to leave their ancestral homes in the Southeast. Few Chickasaws alive in 1900 had seen one, but some of the elders were at least still telling the story. Years later Te Ata incorporated pieces of the celebration into some of her programs and once wrote an authoritative article on it for the prestigious publication, *Natural History*.

Integral to the ceremony was a large rectangular court with a figure eight drawn in the center. Inside one circle a tall pole was driven into the ground and a cow or horse skull was placed on top. In the center of the other circle was a sacred ceremonial fire from which all household fires would be started for the new year ahead. The ceremonial fire had been kindled by the Tat-ko-hi-ah, the medicine chief. He had rubbed two sticks together, and the flame, it was believed, had come down from the eternal fire of the Great Spirit. A large cooking pot containing herbs and willow root was placed over the fire, and the boiling brew produced a strong emetic. Each dancer drank a cup and then ran outside the circle to vomit, as a rite of purification. Dancing began after several maidens entered the dance ground rhythmically shaking pebble-filled tortoise shells strapped to their legs. The dancing lasted two to three days.[29]

Indians living in the Emet area occasionally had what they called stomp dances, but these were more social than religious in nature. Only once when Mary was 5 or 6 was she exposed to a traditional religious ceremony. This one, called a Pashofa, was for healing. A neighbor of the Thompsons was very sick and the family called for a medicine man. Traditionally, neighbors, friends, and family participated in a Pashofa, usually as dancers. What Te Ata remembered most about the ceremony was getting in trouble. A dance ground had been fashioned in the front yard of the sick man's house. In the center a large fire was started, and the medicine man prayed over it to receive the blessing of the Great Spirit. Then the medicine man went inside to be with the sick person. Mary recalled, "We children knew better than to go between the sacred fire and the medicine man." But as they were playing tag, Mary got carried away: "Suddenly, one of the grown-ups grabbed me by one arm and whirled me around—just in time to keep me from running through that forbidden area." She was fortunate indeed, because had she crossed the invisible line, Mary would have been taken inside to the medicine man who would have doused her head with the sludgelike medicine. Otherwise, the healing ceremony might have been in vain.[30]

Christian missionaries and preachers condemned such ceremonies as sacrilegious, and by the time young Mary Thompson attended that Pashofa ceremony, the rite was dying out. By 1900 most of the Indians living in the Chickasaw Nation were Christians. Instead of celebrating the busk festival, they attended weeklong revivals, which included remnants and symbols of their former traditional culture. Outwardly and superficially these campground meetings resembled traditional Chickasaw and Choctaw meetings. Families built arbors around a large rectangular court, cooked up big pots of cracked corn and pork called *pashofa* (which had been included in the healing ceremony of the same name), and in between the praying and preaching and mealtimes they played an attenuated version of stickball, a game indigenous to the Southeastern tribes that had been so arduous and violent that it had been played to keep warriors in fighting trim. But the core of these camp meetings was Christianity.[31]

Another powerful force for change in the lives of young Chickasaws was the tribe's educational system, consisting of boarding and neighborhood schools. Since the system was created and run by Christian missionaries, the curriculum was designed to accomplish their goal of providing a quality education while thoroughly Christianizing and Americanizing their young wards. Mary began her formal education in a one-room tribal school but after two years seemed to have learned little or nothing. Bertie wondered if her daughter might be somewhat slow-witted academically. But the teacher, saddled with several students ranging from six to early teens, could not motivate this little girl to learn how to read. Even Bertie herself, trying to teach Mary the alphabet, made no progress until she thought to make a game of it. The Thompsons, disappointed and dismayed at their daughter's lack of academic progress, decided that she should follow in the footsteps of her older half sister, Selena, and attend a tribal boarding school for girls, the Bloomfield Academy.[32]

By the time Mary Thompson was enrolled there, Bloomfield was a half century old, having been founded by Methodist missionaries for the tribe in 1852. It had a widespread reputation in Indian Territory for producing cultured and educated young women. Playing the pivotal role in that development was its superintendent from 1884 to 1898, Douglas Johnston. The Thompsons had always been influenced by Johnston and his family. Since they were neighbors in Emet and considered each other family, the Thompsons visited the Johnstons fairly often in their imposing eight-room house, called the

Te Ata: Chickasaw Storyteller, American Treasure

Te Ata, upper right, was one of about seventy girls attending Bloomfield Academy, a Chickasaw boarding school in 1905. She was homesick, chafed under the rigid rules, and was an ordinary student. But she also felt a strong urge to excel.

"White House" by Chickasaws after Johnston was elected tribal governor in 1898. The Johnstons liked to read or recite literature and poetry, play musical instruments, and have dances featuring live music or recordings. Among their children, Douglas Jr. was a budding musician and Juanita aspired to be an actress. In the Johnston home Mary saw her first volume of Shakespeare, and before she could even begin to understand the plays and sonnets she longed to own such a rich and beautiful leather-bound edition.[33]

Mary was one of about seventy girls between the ages of 9 and 18 at Bloomfield. According to one source, applicants had to be able to read and spell satisfactorily. Since Mary presumably passed the entrance examination, her success was probably attributable to Bertie's diligent tutoring. The school, about thirty-five miles southeast of Emet, was located just north of the Red River. Initially, the

Thompsons took Mary in a surrey pulled by two of the horses Bertie had brought to the marriage, Blaze and Ginger. In Mary's last year or two at Bloomfield, they made the trip in an Overland automobile, which Thompson rarely drove on the road. He got stuck so often tearing across fields that a shovel became a permanent implement in the car.[34] The school was impressive both by design and in size; it was a long, two-story building with large gabled dormers jutting out from the roof. Each floor featured a wide veranda lined with white pillars. Mary thought it was the most beautiful building she had ever seen, and she was excited to be starting this adventure. But like many of her classmates, Mary soon was homesick and chafing under the school's rigid discipline. By Mary's time the school already had had several destructive fires; it was rumored that some had been set intentionally by girls acting out their unhappiness.[35] It clearly was a difficult, confusing environment for girls who had been raised in the Indian culture: Bloomfield and its curriculum were essentially a refutation of that culture.

If it seems incongruous that the tribal language would be outlawed in tribal schools, it should be remembered that after removal the leaders of the Chickasaw Nation turned to religious missionaries to establish schools for the tribe. The price was costly to the tribe in terms of cultural identity. For the missionaries correctly believed that language was inseparable from traditional tribal religion, beliefs, and customs, which were impediments to establishing Christianity. Moreover, these young teachers went to parochial schools in the East and wanted to transplant all aspects of their rigorous yet genteel education to Indian Territory. Although missionaries were no longer running the schools in 1905, their legacy lived on. Administrators and teachers had to be of the "highest Christian standing."[36] Although Mary had been raised in a home that was cross-cultural, there was so much love, support, and security that she probably could have adjusted to almost any setting that was not outright antagonistic.

She attended Bloomfield for three or four years. What she did not disclose about her time there was more intriguing and perhaps revealing than what she did say. For example, she summarized her studies by saying she was not much interested in schoolwork but described how creepy it was to look at a centipede floating in formaldehyde in the library. She also told about how she would do Indian beadwork at night under her bed by candlelight to avoid detection. She made headbands and belts, working with patterns intended to resemble the footprints of dancers, insects, or animals.[37]

Mary longed for letters and visits from her parents. She missed her family immensely, and that partially accounted for her unhappiness at Bloomfield. When they did visit, it was usually for a special event, and they joined other families for a picnic of fry bread and pashofa. Her family and relatives loved being entertained by her and were a constant source of positive reinforcement. At Bloomfield she was an ordinary student. She excelled only at running, jumping, and games, skills that did nothing to advance her class standing or status.

Still, the Bloomfield years probably had a substantial, maybe even pivotal effect on her development. For one thing, she learned that she was not happy always being lost in the middle of the bell-shaped curve. She had a strong need to be recognized and for that, she knew she had to excel at something important. For another thing, she was exposed to a classical curriculum that at least provided her with the basis for later academic success. The curriculum included logic, chemistry, astronomy, botany, typing, art, elocution, and music. She would come to have more than a passing interest in all of these disciplines, especially after she met Clyde Fisher.[38]

But Bloomfield probably had minimal impact in other important ways. Mary was apparently never motivated to perform academically, even though this was one of the school's main missions and she had large measures of curiosity and intelligence. More significantly, despite the school's attempts to prepare its students to compete in American society, Mary still identified primarily as a Chickasaw and cherished the little she knew about the tribe's past. Her early childhood years had corresponded to the last years of an active tribal government, and she was very proud of Uncle Doug (Governor Johnston) and her father, the tribe's last treasurer, though she probably had little notion of their duties. Congress had decreed that the Indian domains were to be carved up and parceled out to individual tribal members and that the Indian governments in Indian Territory were to be extinguished in 1906. At that point, Indians would work their "new" land and their children would be mainstreamed into American society.

This was the federal government's newest solution to its long-standing "Indian problem."[39] But Thomas Thompson had never been much of a farmer or rancher, and because his mercantile business was doing well, he decided to branch out in 1907, the year Indian Territory and Oklahoma Territory became the new state of Oklahoma. Thompson traded his store in Emet for a twelve-room, two-story house in Tishomingo and opened stores there and in Milburn and Byrds Mill. For capital, he sold all of the farm implements and almost all of the livestock.[40] That September the children entered the public schools in Tishomingo. For the first time most of Mary's classmates were white children, and although she was initially uncomfortable around them, at least she was living at home.

CHAPTER 2

Oklahoma College for Women

The Thompsons' move to Tishomingo corresponded with Oklahoma statehood. Although Tishomingo had been the capital of the Chickasaw Nation before statehood, the town had been growing and filling up with white people for several years and was clearly the place for an entrepreneur like Thompson. His employment with the tribe over, Thompson was able to devote his full attention to his stores. But as a businessman, he had some flaws: he had an unwitting tendency to hire embezzlers, and since his bookkeeping system apparently left a lot to be desired, the embezzlers could become increasingly greedy without running the risk of getting caught.

According to Bertie, Thomas hired a young man he had known all his life to work in his store. Bertie became suspicious and told her husband that he should watch the young man closely. Thomas must have been suspicious too, but he avoided confrontations. Finally the thievery became obvious and Thomas asked the clerk for his key to the store. The man was irate, claiming he had not been given notice. A month or so later the man's four-month-old son became critically ill. After an examination, the doctor said the baby would die soon and departed. The man's wife begged Bertie for help. Bertie walked nearly three miles to the man's house and found the baby looking purple, with thick and dry skin. He had not nursed in two days. Bertie bathed the child in warm cod liver oil, and after a time the baby nursed. That pattern was repeated throughout most of the night. By morning the baby was completely broken out with smallpox, but the crisis was over and the baby survived. The father never set foot in the same room with Bertie or thanked her for tending to his son. People told Bertie she was crazy, but she said the baby could not help the sins of his father. Furthermore, she told them she would have helped the man himself if he had been sick. "If you read the Bible, Christ says return good for evil," she said.[1]

In time Thompson had to close his branch stores but apparently still did not learn from these business failures. In operating his Tishomingo general store, he not only continued to trust his clerks, but that his customers would eventually pay their bills. Thompson had grown up in tight-knit tribal communities, where a person's word was all that was needed. Those few who were not honest were ostracized—a severe penalty, thought by some to be the ultimate penalty. By the time Thompson was in business in Tishomingo, he certainly knew that all people could not be trusted, but old habits apparently died hard, and he continued extending credit to people whose word was not good. In a sense, he was subsidizing some of his customers at the expense of his family.

Like her parents, Te Ata was an honest person who loved to do thoughtful things for people. Furthermore, she married a man who was scrupulously honest and liked to do unrequited favors for friends, but Clyde Fisher was also open and trusting like her father. Te Ata grew to be more suspicious of people, probably because of racism in Tishomingo and her mother's accounts of how Thomas' trusting nature had led to his business failures and the family's impoverishment. A key difference in mother and daughter was Te Ata's unwillingness to forgive such transgressions. Te Ata would not have tended the baby of the man who was stealing from her father.

In 1910 the family was completed with the birth of Thomas Benjamin Thompson, Jr. Counting Bertie's parents, the twelve-room house in Tishomingo now housed ten people. When Mary entered Tishomingo High School in about 1910, she found that most of her classmates and all of her teachers were white. Although she was predominantly white by blood, as was her mother, she apparently did not give that any thought. She had been raised a Chickasaw, and her mother was an intermarried Chickasaw. Nominally, if not so much in practice day to day, the Thompsons identified as Chickasaws. So did many

Though Mary was painfully shy (and the lone Indian student) during her years at the Oklahoma College for Women, her mentor, Frances Dinsmore Davis, shown here with Mary, played the pivotal role in helping Mary to develop as a performance artist.

impact on her career than Frances Davis. Without Davis, Te Ata, one of the greatest Indian performing artists of the twentieth century, probably would not have existed.

As it was in 1915, teacher and student were mutually impressed. Toward the end of the year, Davis was considering Mary for the lead in the college's big production of "The Pied Piper of Hamelin." Having already shown her remarkable ability to memorize long passages, Mary was asked to demonstrate her physical agility. Davis placed two chairs side by side and asked Mary to jump over them. She did, with ease; then she bounded over three chairs. Davis smiled and told her that the part was hers. She also told Mary that she wanted to begin giving her private lessons to improve her speaking voice.[18] This also was about the time that Mary started working for Davis, typing business letters to such faraway and alluring places as New York City. She knew that Davis had been to these places. Was it possible that someday, with her teacher's help, she would see them too? Mary's world was already opening up, probably before she was even aware of it.

Davis may have had "a laughing face," but she was completely dedicated to her work and career. At age 27, her long-term goal was to build a first-rate fine arts program. In 1916 she launched a visiting artist series by arranging to have May Peterson, a soprano with the Metropolitan Opera Company of New York, perform in concert in Chickasha. To get President Austin's approval, Davis had to personally guarantee Peterson's expenses. As it turned out, the receipts matched her expenses precisely.[19] Davis had little interest in developing relationships other than with her students and colleagues. Although she had to work within the narrow constraints imposed by inadequate funding, she was still a perfectionist, fueled by fervent pride and a large ego to wring the best out of those with the greatest potential. Mary was among them and soon topped the list.[20]

In effect, Davis conducted a continuous workshop in showing Mary the value of hard work, good organization, and meticulous preparation. She was a willing student in part because she was drawn to Davis's charismatic personality. But Mary also needed to focus her interest somewhere. She remained somewhat socially isolated throughout her four years at OCW. She had been raised in a culture and family that tended to hold things in rather than express them. Even when Mary was part of the group, she did not join in the discussions: "The bedtime chatter sessions in the dormitory, . . . all the talk was about things I didn't know anything of, things like dancing classes and parties and dating boys. I felt left out and odd."[21]

Still, Mary wanted to belong to an extent. She was in drama club and in 1917 was a cofounder of a YWCA-sponsored group called Em Hi's. It was created by the YWCA secretary, Annie Kate Gilbert, who had been to Randolph Macon College and was experienced in organizing clubs and sororities. The Em Hi's met regularly to perform campus or community service and to have fun, and so the fourteen girls would have a permanent vehicle for communication after graduation.

In that way it worked probably beyond any of its members' expectations. Starting in about 1920, the girls began to send letters, called "round robins" because a member's letter would be shared with everyone. Periodically, they would have reunions in Chickasha; in 1963 eleven members from all over the country attended.[22] Mary also attended parties in the home of a Maxie Woodring, a professor of foreign languages. Although they knew each other only casually, they developed a warm, abiding friendship when they were both living in New York.[23]

∽

Mary did well scholastically. Her transcript from 1915 through 1919 reveals about 60 percent As and forty percent Bs. It also shows that from the beginning of her coursework she was strongly influenced by Davis. The preponderance of her studies was in expression (probably a catchall term for courses in the drama department), English, history, and French.[24] Sometime during Mary's first or second year, Davis told her that she "should go on stage."[25] This was Te Ata's typically understated way of saying that Davis had told her she had star potential in the legitimate theater and that all of her actions and decisions should be oriented toward achieving that goal. Shy and lacking self-confidence as a self-promoter, Mary was happy to put herself in her teacher's hands.

After starring as "the Pied Piper," Mary often was relegated to men's roles because she was taller and had a lower voice than most of the other girls. At some point she also became known for her Indian stories.[26] This started one evening after some of her classmates had been teasing her about her clamlike silence during their gabfest. They began insisting that she tell them something about her people. She had no idea what to say, not having categorized aspects of her life consciously as Indian and non-Indian. When a classmate asked her to tell an Indian story, however, she was on firmer ground. She said that when she was young her father used to tell the children stories, especially on winter nights after supper and chores. She said her father explained that these Indian stories had been passed down over generations. One was the story about why the rabbit and owl do not get along. Te Ata waited for silence and everyone's attention, then began.

> Old Earthmaker had made everything just the way he wanted it. But one day he looked down from the sky and saw rabbit shivering in the cold. Rabbit did not want to be that way, so he began

making a song and dance, trying to tell Earthmaker how he wanted to be. Old Earthmaker looked down and he watched very careful and liked that song and dance. Rabbit told him that he wanted to have long hair to keep him warm on cold days. He wanted long ears, too, and he think he might as well have long legs like deer, to carry him fast and light over the cold ground. Earthmaker liked that song and dance, he did, so he said to himself: "I make magic for rabbit."

He told the animals: "While I make magic for rabbit, you keep eyes shut." Then Earthmaker pull rabbit's hair, make it long like rabbit wanted. Then he pull rabbit's ears way-ay-ay up, make them long, too. He start to pull legs and make them long when he see owl have his eyes open, peeking to watch the magic. Earthmaker got so mad, he grab owl and push his head down into shoulders and say, "You stay that way. And you stay up in tree all day long, not even come out to see sun shine." And owl have to stay that way. When Earthmaker returned to finish rabbit, he had hopped away, his legs just half way down. So he have to hop 'bout like this. Rabbit never come back to have legs fixed right, so he have to stay that way. So rabbit don't like owl. Owl don't like rabbit. That's the way it is.

The girls laughed and applauded, amazed that the diffident Mary had enlivened the story with drama and gestures. Suddenly Mary "really felt like somebody." Despite this triumph, when Davis was told about her impromptu performance and asked her to perform some of her Indian stories in a club in Chickasha for experience, she declined. But she could not refuse to do a one-woman performance during her senior year. It was required of all drama majors. Davis suggested that Mary develop her senior performance on Indian folklore. Although she knew several stories, she did not know enough for a full program. She remembered that Muriel Wright had told her she could learn more Indian stories by writing to the Smithsonian Institution in Washington, D.C. She had not written then, but she did now, and after a few weeks she received a sizable mailing from the ethnology division.[27]

It was an epiphany: "As I read, I became aware of how the patterns of those basic tales branched out like ragweed, as my father had put it when we were small, with a different twig for each tribe, adapted to the crops it raised, animals it hunted, the climate in which it lived." Mary read with strong but mixed emotions. She felt pride in the heritage of her people. But she also felt more acutely than ever sadness

During Mary's last year at OCW, Frances Davis began transforming Mary Thompson into "Princess" Te Ata. This picture was made about the time she auditioned for chautauqua manager, Thurlow Lieurance.

over the subjugation of the Indian nations and the accompanying loss of tribal ethos. By that time the federal government's policy of dividing up the land of the great Indian nations into individual allotments, on which the Indians would farm for a living, had proven a disastrous failure.[28] The allotment program was suppose to produce farmers who assimilated gradually into American society. Instead, by the time America entered World War I, most of the allottees were living in destitution, having had no money to begin or maintain a successful farm or having been swindled out of their allotments by white speculators who had descended like a plague on the tribes. Mary had seen some of both kinds firsthand and heard the stories of others from the Indian side of her family. A few years later, when she started traveling about America, she would witness the results of similar depredations suffered by other tribes.

But rather than dwell on past wrongs and sufferings, she felt intuitively that her role should be to recapture Indian heritage and share with others its "sense of richness, wisdom and wonder."[29] The spirit of Te Ata materialized at that moment. Later she decided to use her childhood Indian name for her program; "Mary Thompson" looked wrong. Actually, she was billed as "Princess Te Ata." This bit of theatricality was probably suggested by Frances Davis.[30] The senior performance was a collaboration between pupil and teacher, because both realized it was more than just an exercise for a grade. It was to be Te Ata's debut as an artist. She poured over the source material, selecting possible stories, songs, and dances and ruling out some of the ceremonials, such as the Hako ceremony of the Pawnee, as too sacred to be used on stage. With Davis's help, she adapted and modified the folklore into dramatic form. Davis had the artistic judgment and experience to help the young Chickasaw woman craft each piece and the ability to nuture her raw dramatic talent. Davis also selected from works by white men, such as Charles Wakefield Cadman, who had spent part of their musical careers blending authentic Indian melodies and themes into their own compositions. Te Ata was worried about what to wear for her debut. Chickasaw women had been wearing calico dresses for generations; she could wear one for the storytelling but not for the entire program. Again she turned to her teacher. From an acquaintance, Davis borrowed a Kiowa doeskin dress, pale yellow, richly beaded, and edged with wide fringe. It would be perfect for the dances.[31]

When the curtains parted, Te Ata, wearing the Kiowa dress, entered the stage, doing an interpretive dance to the well-known song "From the Land of the Sky Blue Water." She spoke rather than sang the words:

> From the Land of the Sky Blue Water
> They brought a captive maid,
> And her eyes they are lit with lightnings,
> And her heart is unafraid.
> But I steal to her lodge at dawning,
> I woo her with my flute,
> She is sick for the Sky Blue Water—
> The captive maid is mute!

Te Ata: Chickasaw Storyteller, American Treasure

After she changed into her Chickasaw calico dress, she told four short legends dealing with the creation of the world, romance, war, and death. She introduced the legends with lines from Longfellow's "Hiawatha":

Should you ask me when these stories,
When these legends and tradition
With the odor of the forest
With the dew and damp of meadows,
With the rushing of great rivers . . .
I should answer, I should tell you
In the birds' nests of the forest
In the lodges of the beaver
In the hoofprints of the bison
In the aerie of the eagle!
Listen to these Indian legends.

Later she dramatized four native songs, the kind she was prohibited from singing in Chickasaw or Choctaw when she was at Bloomfield. She did not sing the songs because she did not like her singing voice; her singing, she believed, detracted from the words and drama, but her increasingly powerful speaking voice heightened the drama and enhanced the words. She performed other short legends before closing with "The Moon Drops Low," by Cadman. It tells of the Indians' desperate attempts to avoid the forces that were destroying their way of life. Her backdrop was a sky blue screen with a painted sun setting over the trees. In front of the screen was a large spider web made of heavy twine, suspended from above and anchored snugly on both sides. As she neared the end of this last piece, the climax looming, she recited:

The moon drops low
That once soared high
As an eagle soars
In the morning sky
And the deep dark lies
Like a death-web spun
'Twixt the setting moon
And the rising sun.
Our glory sinks
Like the sinking moon
The Red Man's race

Shall Perish soon.
Our feet shall trip
Where the web is spun
For no dawn shall be ours
And no rising sun—
No dawn for us and no rising sun!

The music crescendoed as Te Ata danced ever more frantically about the stage, seeking to escape the forces of destruction. But she became enmeshed in the spider's web, the white man's way of life, and as the curtain rang down Te Ata was still trying piteously to claw free.

The program was an enormous success. The audience stood and cheered for several minutes, during which Davis kept pushing Te Ata back onto the stage for more bows. Lacking the grace with which she had performed, Te Ata acknowledged the ovation with stiff, awkward bows, and because she could not see faces beyond the glaring foot-lights, she squinted instead of smiling.[32] Still, hearts must have been melting in the audience. Although no photographs of the occasion are known to exist, her likeness from the time was preserved in a beautiful oil painting done by a young Oklahoma City artist, Nellie Shepherd. Tragically, the artist died less than a year later. The painting, for some reason not quite finished, now hangs over a fireplace in an Oklahoma City nursing home.[33]

Anticipating that Mary's performance would be successful artisti-cally, Davis had invited colleagues to attend. As a result, Mary was offered $50 to perform at a teacher's college in Edmond. She was also invited to perform at the University of Oklahoma and at a YWCA meet-ing in Dallas for $50 plus expenses. Although she loved performing and was happy to be recognized for her hard work and be well paid for it too, she was uncomfortable with the small talk and socializing that accompanied these occasions. In agreeing to perform for the students of Oscar Jacobson at the University of Oklahoma, she wrote that she would not be able to attend the party afterward. When Davis learned of this, she told Mary to write Jacobson immediately to say that she could stay for the party after all. Mary objected, but Davis told her that since this was "an important part of her training," she must do it. She did.[34]

As her college graduation approached, Mary fretted about a possi-ble confrontation with her father over her future. She knew that he expected her to be a teacher—a good profession for a woman. During the first two or three years of college, she probably assumed she would follow in her beloved teacher's footsteps. But whatever Davis might have thought about Mary's teaching potential, she made it clear that she believed Mary had the makings of an exceptional performing artist. Moreover, Mary's yen to teach (if she ever had one) had vanished after she visited a Catholic-run Indian school in Ardmore, where her younger siblings were enrolled. She had heard good things about the school and was thinking she might teach there following her graduation. But she was mightily put off while observing what she considered the white faculty's paternalistic and patronizing attitude toward the students.[35]

What she wanted to do was travel that summer on a chautauqua circuit. Traveling chautauquas sprang from a Methodist-Episcopal movement in the 1870s that provided secular and religious education. Eight-week institutes were held at Lake Chautauqua, New York; they featured lectures by eminent artists, authors, politicians, and scientists, as well as entertainment. Soon after the turn of the century, traveling chautauquas—tent shows that moved from town to town—were organized by commercial lecture bureaus.[36]

During the summer before her senior year, Mary had met Thurlow Lieurance, chairman of the music department at the University of Nebraska. He was in charge of the chautauqua that was traveling through Oklahoma. When the troupe was in Sulphur, Davis's mother, affectionately called Mother McClure, paid a visit to Lieurance to tell him about "this marvelously talented" Indian girl named Mary Thompson. When Lieurance was in Tishomingo, he auditioned Mary between the afternoon and evening performances. Lieurance was impressed; he said he had been wanting "an Indian act" for the next summer and thought he could build one around her. He said he would be in touch. Mary ran home and broke the good news to her parents, who were not pleased. Her father said, "This going on stage is no life for you," a sentiment echoed by her mother. Mary let the matter drop.[37]

But in March 1919 Lieurance wrote to Mary, offering her a part in the chautauqua company at $35 per week plus transportation expenses on the circuit. She would need to be in Lincoln, Nebraska, for ten days of rehearsal before setting out with the other Indians in the company. The date she was expected fell immediately after her college graduation.

She would not even have time to return to Tishomingo. Mary responded with several questions regarding length of employment, location of the circuit, expenses to and from Lincoln, and what was expected of her.[38] Apparently, everything got worked out; she accepted the offer at least provisionally before seeking her parents' permission.

Thompson showed up for his daughter's graduation wearing a suit coat and necktie, the first time Mary had seen him dressed so formally. Initially, he looked solemn and uncomfortable. But he loosened up when he met Frances Davis and Mother McClure. They bubbled on about Mary's impending chautauqua tour, and to her immense relief, Thompson told the women that his daughter "had to make up her own mind and live her own life." Bertie must have prepared him. He added that he took comfort in his daughter's shyness, as it meant she would not talk to strangers. At the end of the day, the Thompsons returned to Tishomingo without Mary, who stayed on until it was time to leave for Lincoln. She was seen off by Davis, who reminded her again that she was to be her teaching assistant in the fall.[39] At that moment, fall must have seemed like a lifetime away.

Te Ata: Chickasaw Storyteller, American Treasure

CHAPTER 3

Chautauqua Experiences

While Mary was growing up, the federal government was no longer rigorously pursuing its policy of stamping out Indian arts and culture. Articles describing the work of several Indian and white artists and writers dedicated to preserving and promoting Native American culture appeared in publications favored primarily by intellectuals.[1] As a distinguished and indefatigable professor of drama and an intellectual, Frances Davis was certainly aware of this movement. Moreover, she must have known that her gifted protégé could help to advance the movement while simultaneously benefiting from it.

A variety of gifted individuals had played important roles in the first two decades of the twentieth century. One of the earliest was Emily Pauline Johnson, a Mohawk writer and orator who toured the United States, Canada, and Europe conveying the richness of Indian culture through her stories and poetry. Taking the name Tekahionwake, she usually performed in a buckskin dress and leggings of her own design. Johnson, billed as a Mohawk "princess," often created romanticized stereotypes and idealized heroines to counteract the general public's notion of the bloodthirsty savage. Because she was only part Indian and had been educated in white schools, some members of her audiences, perhaps seeking to pay her the highest accolade, told her she performed just like a white woman. "But I am Indian," she said. "And my aim and joy and pride is to sing the glories of my own people." Though she died in 1913, her reputation was such that her name was included in listings of distinguished Native American women of the twentieth century.[2]

Gertrude Bonnin, half white and half Yankton Sioux, was born in 1876 on the Yankton Reservation in South Dakota. Raised on the reservation but schooled in white society, she endured the bewilderment and pain so often associated with cross-cultural conflicts. Still, without white schooling, particularly at Earlham College, she could not have contributed to the written literature—based on oral traditions—that was emerging in the first years of the twentieth century. She produced two seminal works, *Old Indian Legends* (1901) and *American Indian Stories* (1921). Christening herself Zitkala-Sa (Red Bird), she set her sights on becoming the literary counterpart of the oral storytellers of her tribe. If that ambition was not lofty enough, she felt compelled to live up to the critical expectations of her white audience. For a time she did. Several of her essays and stories were published in *Harper's Bazaar* and the *Atlantic Monthly*. Also an accomplished violinist, having studied at a Boston conservatory, she performed as soloist and orator with the touring Carlisle Indian Band. Her recitation of "Hiawatha" was reviewed in glowing terms by New York critics. Zitkala-Sa's literary and musical career virtually ended in 1902, however, when she married another educated Sioux, Raymond Bonnin, an official of the Bureau of Indian Affairs. Both were interested in Indian reform. In 1916 she joined an organized Indian reform movement, the Society of the American Indian, and was the editor of the society's magazine at the time of Mary's college graduation.[3]

Angel De Cora-Dietz of the Winnebago tribe graduated from the Hampton Institute and was pronounced an artistic "genius" by one of the world's great illustrators, Howard Pyle. But despite the avenue to commercial success opened to her by Pyle and others, De Cora-Dietz chose to produce only Indian art. She said, "The Indian woman from prehistoric times has been an artist. The work of her hand, the product of her thought, has been enshrined in the white man's museums throughout the world. The only difference between me and the women on the reservations is that I have chosen to apply my native Indian gift in the white man's world. We are a race of designers. And I look for the day when America will be proud to have her Indians make beautiful things for all the world." As the head of the art department at the Carlisle Indian School, she dispatched the notion that pupils must copy the white man, or any man; they must express themselves. She and her husband, William Dietz, also a Sioux artist, did their best to nurture native talent and then help the young artists to sell their work, whether oil paintings, watercolors, rugs, blankets, or silver jewelry. After such an auspicious start during the second decade of the twentieth century, it was hoped that De Cora-Dietz's example would influence the teaching of Indian peoples nationally. In 1920 Natalie Curtis wrote that De Cora-Dietz was "the first Indian artist to express in the white man's world what her people might become." Curtis hoped that the Winnebago woman's death would bring attention to her desire that the artistic power and scope of her people would flourish in America.[4]

The musician John Koon, known professionally as Red Cloud, was born on the Fort Peck Sioux Reservation in Montana. As a young child, he recalled his mother had taken him up on a butte to see his tribe battle federal troops: "It seems a kind of dream now. I saw the braves go forth on horseback with their brilliant costumes and their warpaint and I saw in the far distance the Government troops come out in their dark blue uniforms. Then the firing commenced and I saw the braves topple off their horses." Within a few years, Red Cloud was sent to white-run schools, including Carlisle, where he excelled at football and music. Like many Indians, he was hired by Buffalo Bill to tour Europe with his Wild West show. "Col. Cody understood Indians and treated them right," he said. Later Red Cloud joined the John Philip Sousa band. In 1920, the year after Mary's college graduation, Red Cloud said he was not surprised by the new interest in Indian music: "Many composers have caught the Indian idea in modern music by the utilization of real Indian themes. When I hear such music and know that it is real and not a parody, all of the old fire comes back in me. When we play such a piece as the *American Indian Rhapsody* by Preston Ware Orem, founded on real Indian themes given him by Thurlow Lieurance, I feel as though I could jump right up and 'holler.' I heard some of those same themes when I was a little papoose and they are in my blood and always will be in the blood of my children as long as the race lasts."[5]

In 1914 Charles Eastman (Indian name, Ohiyesa) wrote that there had only recently been a serious effort to collect Indian folk songs, "the very soul of the Indian." A few talented and devoted persons had been spending lengthy periods living with tribes, winning their trust and recording their songs before they were lost to history. The songs, Eastman noted, were often "simple, expressive and haunting in quality, voicing [the singer's] inmost feelings, grave or gay, in every emotion and situation in life."[6] Major collectors of Indian songs include the ethnologists Alice Fletcher and Frances Densmore. Fletcher collected hundreds of songs of the Omaha, Winnebago, and Nez Perce tribes. By 1920, Densmore had collected and recorded more than nine hundred melodies of the Teton Sioux, the Chippewas, the Northern Utes, the Pawnees, and the desert tribes of Arizona. Natalie Curtis, who was trained in music in Germany and France, made exhaustive investigations into the sources of Native American music.[7] She claimed to have gotten the government interested after she sent an Indian song to then President Theodore Roosevelt, "knowing that his literary taste would be instantly struck by the unusual imagery." In a subsequent meeting with the president, Curtis discussed her own efforts and that of her colleagues in "working to save from extinction the native arts of basketry, pottery and weaving." She recalled the gleam in Roosevelt's eyes when he said, "How many Congressmen do you suppose there are who would understand that there could be such a thing as Indian art?" Subsequently, Roosevelt appointed an enlightened secretary of the interior, Francis Leupp, who appointed a supervisor of Indian music. "The petty tyranny of the old oppressive educational system," Curtis wrote, "was at least nominally revoked at Washington. But on the reservations, where alone an appreciation of native arts and crafts might directly benefit the Indians, the old prejudice still prevails; it will take some time to banish the deep-rooted conviction that they are there to make the Indian over into a white man as speedily as possible."[8]

Whatever the uniqueness and artistry of Native Americans working and performing in the first two decades of the twentieth century, they were as unknown to the overwhelming majority of white Americans as their counterparts in China. Furthermore, many of the popular stereotypes of Indians were perpetuated by the major employers of Indian performers, the Wild West shows. Red Cloud's comments notwithstanding, Colonel Cody made his fortune through his Wild West show by giving the public what it wanted. An excerpt from a review of a 1910 Buffalo Bill production reads: "A horde of demoniac, yelling savages, their faces and bodies grotesquely painted, their long black scalplocks waving defiance, suddenly dash toward us from the distant plain, their cayuses at full gallop, the rider flourishing deadly spears, bows and rifles. These copper colored aborigines always suggest battle, murder and sudden death to those of us who recall the early history of this country." But at least the "warriors" were flamboyant, skillful, and entertaining. According to the same reviewer, native women were "most often seen in melodramatic capture scenes as the torturers of white captives."[9]

Highly successful for many years, Buffalo Bill's Wild West show was bankrupt by 1912. Others, such as the Miller Brothers show at their 101 Ranch in Oklahoma Territory, continued their performances for a few more years. In one 1905 show, a procession of cavalry-clad actors was led by the old Apache war chief, Geronimo, a government prisoner who was brought under guard from Fort Sill to appear in full regalia. Other Indian performances featured Indian ball games, a powwow, and a war dance. The closing feature was a wagon train attacked by Indian raiders. "In the gathering dusk the burning wagons with howling Indians riding fiercely about them, caused a feeling of awe to settle over the entire assembly."[10] However, by 1918, with the United States embroiled in World War I, no Wild West shows were touring. Other diversions, such as silent movies and radio, were capturing the public's fancy.[11]

Te Ata's first public performance included two works by Cadman, undoubtedly at the suggestion of Frances Davis. Though Cadman was a white composer, he lived much of his life in the West and often visited western tribes. He recorded several tribal melodies and incorporated them into his compositions in a highly artistic way. In his opera, *Shanewis* (The Robin Woman), he used at least twenty original Indian themes. He obtained some of the themes from Fletcher and Densmore and obtained others himself in 1909 on the Omaha reservation.[12] The opera was based on the life of the Creek-Cherokee Tsianina Blackstone. Before and after World War I, Tsianina, a mezzo-soprano, toured with Cadman, interpreting his Indian works in performances in many major American cities. By 1920 *Shanewis* was one of the most successful operas ever written by an American, having been performed at New York's Metropolitan Opera House over two consecutive seasons. Even more popular nationally was his song, "From the Land of the Sky Blue

Water," which was based on Omaha tribal themes.[13] Some critics complained that Cadman and others diluted the creative aspects of Indian musical themes; some Indians complained that after the white man had taken their land, he was now taking their music. Cadman responded in 1920 that neither criticism nor prejudice had stopped him and other composers such as Lieurance from their mission of popularizing Native American music. In fact, Cadman wrote, this American movement "seems to be growing."

❧

Thurlow Lieurance met Te Ata's train in Lincoln. Although she had only met him once in Tishomingo, he was easily recognizable because he always used a crutch or a cane to get about. Sensing her nervousness, he broke the ice by telling her about his disability. In her memoir, she wrote that Lieurance had been "out west" in Indian country on what he called a "music gathering expedition" when the wagon he was riding in plunged into a deep ravine. One of his legs was severely injured. Because a blizzard was raging at the time, he could not be moved from the Indian reservation to a hospital. A local doctor cared for him as best he could, but in this preantibiotic era, the infection grew worse. Finally, to save Lieurance's life, the doctor did what virtually all doctors did in those days: he amputated. After the surgery, Lieurance drifted in and out of consciousness, so he could not be sure if the incessant drumbeats he had been hearing were real or a hallucination. As his head cleared, he realized that the drumbeats were real, and he detected the sounds of rattles and gongs as well. Despite his condition, he became absorbed in the rhythms and subtle patterns of the music. He had been studying Indian music exclusively ever since. He told Te Ata that he had blended some Indian themes into his own compositions and played some for her. She liked them and him.[14]

That ultraromantic version does not square with printed accounts of Lieurance's disability. The sketch of his life used by Wichita State University, where he was later dean of the school of music, attributes his disability to polio or an accident in Montana, but there is no mention of his leg being amputated. According to an article in the magazine, Etude, "His legs became crippled for life" following an accident in the Yellowstone in subfreezing weather. A picture shows him leaning on crutches. It is likely that more than a half century after they met,

Te Ata had embellished the tale, probably unintentionally.[15] Further-more, in her account she gives the impression that Lieurance was little more than a musician and an entrepreneur, making extra money by supervising one of the chautauqua companies. As her memoir was not developed from source material but based mainly on her memory, she omitted some important details about the man. Lieurance combined extensive musical training with personal enthusiasm and ambition and the "mission to make the art and music of Indians understood by white Americans." By the time he met Te Ata, he had arranged for several of his Indian protégés to perform on the chautauqua circuit and on con-cert stages. The most renowned up to that time was Watahwasso, a mezzo-soprano who had toured with Lieurance performing his com-positions, such as his signature piece, *By the Waters of Minnetonka*, which was inspired by a Sioux love song he recorded in 1911 on the Crow Reservation in Montana. Since 1895, the year Te Ata was born, Lieurance had been recording and collecting Indian melodies. He had a talent for gaining the confidence and trust of his Indian informants. In 1920 he wrote that he had enough melodies to furnish hundreds of themes to interested composers and musicians.[16]

Even before they left the train station, Lieurance surprised Te Ata with the news that as she had more experience than the others in the company, she would be the leader. (Since Lieurance provided no job description and Te Ata, as usual, would not be so forward as to ask for details face-to-face, the responsibilities were somewhat fluid.) Then they were off to meet the other two members of the Indian per-formers of the chautauqua company. The singer was a contralto, Dowanwin, a Dakota Sioux who was studying nursing in Omaha. The pianist was an Oneida girl, Godje, a name she translated as "Hanging Flower." Apparently, the three women got along well and Te Ata's "leadership" role was accepted. An older lecturer who toured with them helped the inexperienced trio handle tickets and luggage. Lieurance, who did not accompany the group, purchased their train fare in advance and handed each of them a very long strip of tickets, one for each stop that summer.[17]

Te Ata thought that Dowanwin had a beautiful voice but that every song was delivered with the same "gentle, spiritual air." One aria she performed was from Cadman's opera, *Shanewis*. "For half a thousand years your race has cheated mine!" she sang sweetly. Te Ata's natural

Te Ata, right, and her two chautauqua partners, Hanging Flower, left, and Dowanwin. On the road, they made a pact to look after one another. Though they were occasionally the targets of racist remarks and actions, Te Ata turned the other cheek, as her mother had taught her to do.

reticence gave way to a desire to show Dowanwin how to inject "fire" into her performances.[18] Te Ata's own performances were enhanced by the exquisite buckskin dress she wore. She had acquired it from a trader named Reese Kincaide, who had come west as a missionary determined to save Indian souls but became more interested in learning about their traditional skills and wisdom. Kincaide found a niche for himself as a supporter and marketer of Indian arts and crafts. When he met Te Ata he was living among the Cheyenne and Arapaho in the small western Oklahoma community of Colony. Kincaide and Te Ata respected one another and continued to do business and remained friends for years afterward.[19]

As part of her program, Te Ata performed a hunting dance. Armed with a real bow and arrow, she pretended to track a deer in the forest. Spotting it, she followed very carefully, listening, peering out from tall grass and behind trees. Following the deer's trail to the river, she

remembering where they were or where they were headed. At the end of her first chautauqua summer, Te Ata was happy to be back in Tishomingo. But the 24-year-old woman had changed in a fundamental way. When she was in college, she had been content to spend her summers at home, helping her parents and playing with her younger sisters and brother. Once she had spent a summer living independently, sampling the beauty and diversity of the American landscape, getting acquainted with Native Americans who were simultaneously so different and so alike, and hearing the applause and experiencing the power of captivating an audience, she would never again be satisfied with staying home, marking time. People told her she had a remarkable talent, and as summer 1919 wound down, she thought maybe this was so.

When Te Ata had visited Indian country that summer, she saw Indians living in squalor both on reservations and on little plots of land. These people, particularly the full-bloods, would continue to suffer throughout the decade that white society called the Roaring Twenties. The Office of Indian Affairs, which the noted Indian historian Francis P. Prucha called "a bloated bureaucracy of rudderless, underfunded programs," was essentially incapable of addressing the needs of the nation's Native Americans for two reasons. The administration continued to implement the failed assimilationist policies that originated with the Dawes Act of 1887. And to deal with post–World War I inflation, the government was obliged to cut spending. As a result, when "Indian health and education programs needed massive increases in funding, the Indian Office was expected to economize."[28] Te Ata saw the bitter fruits of the government's failures, particularly in the Southwest, where so many Indians were concentrated on reservations. She learned that the Pueblo Indians of New Mexico had an annual per capita income of $23.

When she returned home, she saw things from a new or at least an expanded perspective. She saw pockets of Indian poverty that rivaled what she had witnessed in other areas of the country. Although poverty had always been pervasive among her people in her lifetime, one difference now was the perception that a disproportionate percentage of white people were doing much better economically. Another difference that had emerged in recent years was a creeping sense of hopelessness on the part of many Chickasaws and Choctaws. This ebbing faith in the future had to do in part with the government's unwillingness or inability to make good on its promise to sell the remainder of the tribe's wealth—all the unallotted and surplus tribal lands—and distribute the proceeds on a per capita basis to tribal members.

Periodically between 1904 and 1920, the government had sold parcels of the tribes' unallotted land, mainly timber land, the surface rights to coal land, and land for town sites. As a result, enrollees of both tribes had received per capita payments totaling about $1,000. These payments were made to each member of the Thompson family except for the youngest child, Tom, who was born in 1913, too late to qualify. Although these per capita payments over a sixteen-year period would not keep the Thompson family's heads above water, they must have helped. Te Ata knew that her father's business was not doing well. Moreover, the Thompsons were raising a grandson, Hiawatha Estes, Gladys's son, who had been born in 1918. Soon after the baby's birth, his father, Lawrence Estes, got on a train with the money from the sale of Gladys's allotment, ostensibly to provide the inventory for a proposed furniture store, and was never heard from again.[29]

This was a devastating blow to Gladys's already fragile self-esteem. Part of the family lore is the notion that after Gladys contracted a serious disease as a child, her personality was deleteriously and permanently affected. If Gladys was sensitive to sibling rivalry, she had a lot to live up to. Snake, four years her senior, was a college graduate, and Te Ata was following in his footsteps. What was also galling to Gladys, and probably the original source of her jealousy of Te Ata, was Te Ata's performing talent. Because Te Ata was only seventeen months older than Gladys, they were raised together and inevitably compared. When they were children, Te Ata was always dramatizing and dancing and getting the attention and praise that Gladys so badly wanted. By her teenage years, Gladys probably had a love-hate relationship with her older sister. On one level, she knew that Te Ata loved her and was bending over backward to maintain a good sisterly relationship. But at times, consumed with jealousy and self-loathing, Gladys would say hateful things about her sister; occasionally, she would lose control and attack her sister to her face.[30]

Te Ata: Chickasaw Storyteller, American Treasure

Perhaps to escape what she perceived as unfavorable comparisons to Te Ata, Gladys, at 19, married the first man who showed interest in her. Unfortunately, Lawrence Estes was only interested in her land allotment. This may have been the point when Gladys's jealousy and her rage over her husband's treachery combined to result in occasional paranoid behavior that she continued to exhibit, especially when under stress, for the rest of her life.[31]

❦

Te Ata returned to OCW as Frances Davis's teaching assistant for the 1919–20 school year. The summer of success on the chautauqua circuit had not turned Te Ata's head. As in previous years, Te Ata trusted her teacher to know what was best for her. The capable and strong-willed Miss Davis did not shrink from this responsibility. This was the time when she or they decided that Te Ata would prepare in earnest for a career on the Broadway stage.[32] During that year at OCW, Te Ata would continue to learn the business from the ground up while helping Davis with administrative duties and as a teaching assistant. Then she would take graduate-level training in drama at Davis's alma mater, the Carnegie Institute of Technology in Pittsburgh, Pennsylvania. With Te Ata's talent and experience and Davis's recommendation, she was sure to be admitted. In spring 1920, Te Ata applied for admission for that fall. Davis wrote a letter of recommendation, with some embellishments: "Miss M. Te Ata Thompson . . . acted as Student Professor for two years, and as a full assistant for two in that department [dramatic arts]." She listed Te Ata's roles in some of the plays and mentioned that she had skillfully directed plays. She wrote that her former student had "an unusual histrionic gift, possessing grace, fire and emotional response." She was "eager and teachable" and would "apply herself faithfully, for she is ambitious to do great things."[33]

At the end of the school year, Te Ata left immediately for her second summer on the chautauqua circuit. Near the end of the circuit, a letter from Carnegie Tech caught up to her: "We are interested in your application, but wish to point out that acceptance for graduate study in our theater department is based strictly on tryouts. If you are interested in trying out for admission, please appear, prepared to present a twenty-minute program." A deadline was given. She had time to beat the deadline but was longing to return home to see her family and so informed the admission's office. When she arrived home in

Tishomingo, a letter was there informing her that enrollment in the graduate school in theater for the coming academic year was closed. Te Ata informed her parents that she would not take no for an answer. She was well prepared—Miss Davis said she was good!—and she was ready. She had saved $800, and her mind was made up. She packed her bags and set off on the train to Pittsburgh.[34]

Te Ata's response was audacious, but she was confident that she had made the right decision. In contrast, she was still shy and reserved around strangers. On the train, despite the September heat, she wrapped a shawl that her mother had knitted for her around her shoulders. Adding to her nervousness, she was carrying her expense money for the year in her purse. When she arrived in Pittsburgh, she could not bring herself to ask anyone for directions to the Carnegie Tech campus. She watched many streetcars pass but hesitated until she saw one marked "Bloomfield" and took it only because it was the name of her old Chickasaw school. As luck would have it, "Bloomfield" was the right one.[35]

Te Ata found the drama building and took a seat by herself on a bench in a waiting area outside a number of offices. In a scene reminiscent of a Buster Keaton movie, people emerged from one door or another and noticed Te Ata sitting there, but because she did not make eye contact with them or look like she needed help, they passed by without speaking. Finally, a woman who had walked past her twice, paused to ask Te Ata, in an English accent, if she needed help. In the halting, parsimonious speech that she employed with strangers, Te Ata said she had come from the Oklahoma College for Women to be a student there. The woman said she had been to Chickasha once when she was touring with a Shakespearean company. "I stayed at the Geronimo Hotel," she said. Te Ata must have thought she was dreaming: here she was, a thousand miles from home, facing the first Englishwoman she had ever met and the first person she had spoken to in Pittsburgh, and the woman knew Chickasha. The woman introduced herself as Mrs. Gilmore; her stage name was Cecelia Radcliffe. She asked if Te Ata had seen Mr. Stevens, the school's director. No, she had not. "What is your name, dear?" asked Mrs. Gilmore. "Te Ata Thompson," she replied. "Lovely," said Mrs. Gilmore, who then marched off to tell Stevens that Te Ata was there to see him.[36]

Te Ata: Chickasaw Storyteller, American Treasure

Margaret Malowney (later Ball) and Te Ata are pictured at the outset of their lifelong friendship. Margaret accompanied Te Ata on the piano and tom-tom during Te Ata's last summer on the chautauqua circuit. Here they flank a lecturer named Dr. Curtain.

for the group's third member, violinist Fred Cardin, a Miami-Quapaw from Oklahoma, when they were both at the University of Nebraska. Cardin, also known as Pejawah, was one of Lieurance's protégés. After serving in World War I, Cardin joined the Kansas City Symphony Orchestra and began composing works for violin, chorus, and orchestra and for historical pageants. Still, living essentially hand-to-mouth, like most musicians and composers, he was obliged to perform in both chautauqua and lyceum circuits.[25]

The tour began less than satisfactorily for Te Ata. She wanted her ensemble to be all-Indian and was disappointed when none of her former Indian accompanists could go. Lieurance vouched for Margaret because she was such a fine musician and person. She and Cardin played beautifully together. He did not tell Te Ata that they were also dating. This situation, of course, had the potential to create dissension in a group that would be traveling, living and working together quite closely for the summer.[26] According to Margaret, her relationship with Te Ata was a bit strained and formal for a while. "She was an artist and I thought basically a serious, no-nonsense person," Margaret recalled. But Te Ata broke the ice one night when Margaret had returned from a date with Fred, teasing her by singing a song called "I'm a Kiss-Me Doll." (Seventy years later Margaret could still sing the song.) The trio got to be good friends, and the relationship between Margaret and Te Ata became extraordinarily close and stayed that way for the rest of Te Ata's life. Not only was Margaret her accompanist—on the tom-tom, not the piano—but she was also a sounding board and critic when Te Ata tried out new material. Te Ata recalled, "I'd try something and if Margaret didn't like it or understand it, I figured a general audience wouldn't either. I was learning that my stories had to relate in some way to the experiences of my audiences. I had to discard certain stories that I loved because they required too much explanation."[27]

One traditionally long story that Te Ata successfully adapted for performances was an account of how day and night came to be. If she performed at night, she usually told the stories standing in a soft spotlight. In daylight she favored a sitting position near the front of the stage, as storytellers traditionally invite their listeners to draw near and be comfortable. She never told this story exactly the same way twice. But her performances—even early in her career—were improvisational to some extent. Her word choice varied some, particularly the verbs, as did rhythms, inflections, and mood. This is her typed version of the narrative:

> The animals called a great council, presided over by Bear, who was chief. They would decide how to divide day from night. Everyone was allowed to express his opinion. Some wanted day all the time. Some wanted night all the time. They talked and talked and talked, like people will do. Finally the little ground Squirrel spoke up. "I've been lookin' at the Raccoon's tail. He has rings on his tail, divided evenly, a dark one, a light one, all up and down his beautiful tail. I think it would be good to have day and night divided just like the rings on Raccoon's tail."

Though this photo is undated, it was probably taken during Te Ata's early years in New York City. It may have been about the time Te Ata decided to craft a career as an American Indian folklorist and performance artist.

The animals were surprised that little ground Squirrel had so much vision. So they voted to adopt his plan, thinking this ought to satisfy all the animals. But old Bear wasn't satisfied. He was envious that the little Squirrel had thought of such a fine solution. So when the little ground Squirrel dashed by him, Bear reached out with his great claws and scratched little Squirrel down his back. Now, all the little Squirrels have stripes on their back, even to this day, and it makes them so handsome.

The trio toured throughout the Midwest and at one point visited Margaret's parents for a weekend. By then Te Ata had talked her into studying piano in New York rather than return to teach music in the Lincoln public schools. "I had a contract to teach music in the fall, but Te Ata said that since we were ending the tour in Philadelphia, I should come with her to New York and study at Julliard," Margaret recalled. "Te Ata said she could get me in the Three Arts Club. I said, 'What about my contract?' She said they would just get somebody else. It seemed crazy in a way and I was sure my father, a banker, would tell me I had to honor my contract. But he didn't. He and my mother supported my decision in no small part because they took to Te Ata right away."[28]

The years 1923–27 were a transition period for Te Ata. Her commitment to the theater was weakening while her desire to do more Indian programs was intensifying. She hated having to grub for theater parts, being interviewed and, talking about herself: "I was much too diffident; things had to be pulled out of me. I could not brag about myself, even when I felt sure I could do a good job. A casting director once told me that I was about the most silent little thing that had ever appeared in his office." Another time, after an extended wait in line for her interview, she was greeted by a man with his feet up on his desk and a big cigar clenched between his teeth. "What is it?" he barked, not even bothering to look up from his newspaper. She was so galled by the man's lack of civility that she answered, "Nothing," and turned and left the room. She was offered the lead in a summer play about a South Seas islander but turned it down because she would have been too scantily clad, "wearing mostly a hibiscus behind her ear." One of her old Carnegie Tech classmates who was in the play told her, "You don't love the stage enough."[29]

In 1924 Te Ata's picture appeared on the cover of the June issue of *McCall's*. She had been selected by the magazine's artist-in-residence, Neysa McMein (who illustrated all the covers between 1923 and 1937) to appear in her Types of American Beauty series. It was said

beautifully illustrated with the images of the renowned photographer Laura Gilpin.[6]

The artist most closely linked with the works of Charles Cadman in the early and mid-1920s was Tsianina Blackstock, of Creek-Cherokee ancestry, from Oklahoma. Together, they toured major American cities, including New York, where in her debut appearance Tsianina was interviewed by twenty-one newspaper reporters. Although Te Ata did not mention Tsianina in her existing correspondence during this period, she must have been following her career. For Tsianina, though a singer, was in other ways a paradigm for the career on which Te Ata was embarking. A critic who heard her perform in Pittsburgh at the Conswongo Club wrote, "[She] thrilled me, made me fairly breathe the spirit of the great West." Tsianina impressed both her audiences and the critics. However, one critic, J. Walter Kramer, who lauded the performance, evinced a patronizing and provincial attitude and a mind-set fixed on Indian stereotypes: "Until we heard Tsianina, our idea of the Indians' artistic aptitude was that it was limited to that revealed as performers in a Buffalo Bill Wild West or a Kickapoo Medicine Show." With such prejudicial thinking coming from a supposedly sophisticated New York City newspaper critic, what could she expect from her audiences? Tsianina steeled herself for Boston, which, a friend told her, "will freeze you out. They sit with their hands in their laps, fingers clasped, critically surveying the artists with preconceived ideas and gloved-fingered applause." As she waited in the wings of Jordan Hall, she ruminated on that phrase, "freeze you out," and grew fearful. But she and Cadman were greeted enthusiastically, and their program was a resounding popular and critical success.[7] While Te Ata must have been buoyed by Tsianina's success in many of the venues she herself hoped to play, she realized that for every Tsianina, there were hundreds of other Indian artists toiling in obscurity. Alexander may have hated it, but his contemporaries in the performing arts were basically correct when they said, "Indian stuff doesn't go."

Beginning in the mid-1920s, Te Ata had become acquainted with faculty members at the Columbia University Teacher's College. The introductions had come through Maxie Woodring, one of her former instructors at OCW before Woodring had moved on to Columbia in

1923 or 1924. They developed a warm friendship in New York, particularly after Woodring took her to Loon Island.[8] Although Woodring had grown up in Nashville, she had lived for years in Chickasha and missed its small-town charm and tranquillity after she moved to New York. When she began looking for a retreat from the city, a colleague at Columbia told her about a house that was for rent in rural New Hampshire. It was a three-story house and accompanying cottage on an island in a large lake named Winnipesaukee, near the center of the state. According to a postcard sold in the area, the name Winnipesaukee meant "smile of the Great Spirit."[9] The island got its name from the bird with the beautiful, haunting call that is native to the area. Woodring, or Mona, as she was best known, first rented Loon Island and then gradually acquired it through lease-purchase in about 1924. Te Ata's first visit apparently occurred about then. She loved it immediately for its scenic beauty and isolation, which provided her with periods of solitude that she craved throughout her life. Time spent at Loon Island became essential to her, and she soon began to think of it as her true home in the East.

Unfortunately, Mona's network of friends also wanted to spend getaway time at Loon Island. Occasionally in the summers, both the big house and the cottage were filled with guests. One of the guests whom Te Ata had met at Columbia was Ernest Fretwell. He and Te Ata became friends, and he happened to become the conduit for an important change in her life. He introduced Te Ata to the Bear Mountain region of New York.[10] Fretwell and his wife were both active in the Boy Scout movement, and after he saw Te Ata perform, he introduced her to Ruby Jolliffe who was director of camps in the Bear Mountain and Harriman State Parks, located in the Hudson River valley about eighty miles north of New York City. These summer camps were for poor inner-city children who otherwise would not have had the opportunity to go camping. A conscientious administrator, Jolliffe was always on the lookout for ways to improve or vary the camping experience, and when she observed Te Ata's interpretation of Indian folklore at Columbia, it was like an answered prayer. Te Ata and "Jolly" struck up an immediate friendship, and Te Ata began spending occasional weekends at Jolly's rustic cabin at Bear Mountain.[11] The camps were set in and around the palisades overlooking the Hudson River; most of the landmarks had Indian names, many dating from

Te Ata: Chickasaw Storyteller, American Treasure

This photo of a dancing Te Ata may have been taken during one of the camp sessions for inner-city children at the Bear Mountain State Park. For many summers of campers, she exemplified the beauty, wit, and wisdom inherent in tribal values and stories.

the time when the Iroquois and affiliated tribes lived in the area. The names were there but not the Indians. Te Ata could represent these tribes in educating the city kids in Indian culture.

Te Ata's first performance at Bear Mountain was in 1929. Afterward all of the directors wanted her to perform for their camps, but she hesitated, not wanting to make a summertime commitment that might mushroom out of control. She longed to have at least a few weeks in the summer for Loon Island. One of the directors, however, would not be dissuaded. "Our children are selected by settlement houses [which provided community services for the underprivileged]. This is their one week to get out of the heat and dirt of the city, their one chance to learn about the world of nature." Thinking she was behaving selfishly, Te Ata agreed to perform a second time, then for another camp and another. "I was soon hooked," she recalled. Each camp paid her a small fee, but she said she "would have performed for nothing."[12] She probably meant it, but she was not saving any money and could scarcely have afforded to forgo so many paychecks.

Sometimes camps would join together at a central site at Bear Mountain amid the pines overlooking the Hudson River far below. A campfire was built, and more than two hundred squirming kids would sit cross-legged in a big semicircle around Te Ata. She would begin as the sun was setting. Sometimes she recruited Jolly to provide the opening drumbeat. She liked the power of the Navajo chant:

> You see, I am alive.
> You see, I stand in good relation to the earth.
> You see, I stand in good relation to the gods.
> You see, I stand in good relation to all that is beautiful.
> You see, I stand in good relation to you.
> You see, I am alive. I am alive!

Te Ata liked to finish at sunset with something quiet and nostalgic: "As my voice and the drumbeat died away and I sank down with lowered head before the flickering fire, there was a moment of almost reverent hush." Then the children swarmed around her, wanting to pull her braids to see if they were real and touch her buckskin dress and comment or ask questions about her stories and about her own people in Oklahoma, the Chickasaws.[13] Clearly, she could captivate children too.

The person who most resembled Te Ata as a performing artist was Mary Stone McClendon, known professionally as Ataloa. Also a Chickasaw from Oklahoma, Ataloa was about Te Ata's age, size, and build but was not as beautiful or charismatic. On the other hand, Ataloa had a good singing voice, was more scholarly, and was given to writing and delivering lectures on socioeconomic and political issues of interest to Native Americans. Occasionally, Te Ata and Ataloa performed together at Columbia University and other locations in

New York, but it seemed that they were headed in different career directions.

They began sharing a Manhattan apartment after Margaret Malowney's 1928 wedding to John Ball. The two Chickasaw women may have been distantly related but in any event had always referred to each other as cousin.[14] When and where they met is not known; presumably, there must have been some childhood contact in Oklahoma. Te Ata's autobiography does not introduce Ataloa until they are both living in New York in the mid-1920s. Mary Stone was one of four siblings born to a white man, William Stone, supposedly a descendant of the Randolphs of Virginia, and Josephine McLish Smith, who is identified on the Chickasaw roll as one-fourth Indian.[15] They lived in Duncan, Oklahoma.

According to a biographical sketch, Ataloa's childhood is strikingly similar to Te Ata's. Like her brothers, she "rode, fished, hunted and learned volumes of nature lore. To her, the haunts and habits of animals were a constant source of delight. She knew the calls of birds and the ways of other wild creatures. She knew about clouds, trees, plants, rocks and streams, not from books but from actual experience." She learned tribal lore from her grandmother Nancy Love McLish Smith, who also shared her memories from as far back as the Trail of Tears and gave young Mary her Indian name, Ataloa, meaning "Little Song."[16] At age 17, Mary married Ralph McLendon, who was then or would soon be in the U.S. military. He died in the army within a year of their wedding. Widowed at 18, Mary never remarried. After her husband's death, Ataloa moved to Redlands, California, to be with her mother and brother. She graduated from the University of Redlands in 1925 and moved to New York where she was doing graduate work at Columbia University and living as the "resident Indian on display" at the university's International House when she and Te Ata decided to look for an apartment.

Because Ataloa had an aversion to the "overstuffed, moldy furniture" that seemed to come with furnished apartments in their price range, they selected an unfurnished unit west of Central Park near the American Museum of Natural History. Since neither "cousin" had any furniture to speak of, they bought the bare necessities and whatever inexpensive houseware items struck their fancy. On one weekend they took the subway to a neighborhood of junk shops called Brass

Town on the Lower East Side. Te Ata found a blackened and battered but handsome brass jug that she filled with dried grass. Ataloa bargained with a shopkeeper for a well-worn gateleg table, and to accompany it they used wooden crates. When a guest asked why they had no chairs in their apartment, Te Ata said only half in jest that they had returned to the "floor culture of our people."[17]

Their friends donated more furnishings, including a delicate rose velvet hassock, a beat-up rolltop desk, and a Louis XV love seat, which Te Ata "domesticated" by covering it with a Navajo blanket. Their Amish rocker reminded Te Ata of her mother sitting beside the fireplace in Emet. One of the friends who helped them to get settled was Sylvester Long, known professionally as Chief Buffalo Child Long Lance. He was one of the best-known American Indians of the time. Not yet 40 years of age, Long Lance had just published his autobiography. He told of his heritage with and later leadership of the Blackfoot tribe, honors at the Carlisle Indian School in Pennsylvania, appointment to West Point by President Woodrow Wilson, military service during World War I with the Canadian army, and success in New York City as a writer, aviator, and actor.[18] In 1930 he would star in a Hollywood film titled *The Silent Enemy*.

According to his biographer, Donald B. Smith, Long Lance was exceptionally handsome, with high cheekbones, copper skin, and a trim, athletic physique. He was "charming, engaging, eloquent and, somehow, self-effacing." In New York in 1930, he was "the new sensation in a city of sensations." He attended the "best parties and courted actresses," including Te Ata, whom Smith described in his book as a "striking beauty with long, black braids." They dated for a time but the always discreet Te Ata only told Smith "[Long Lance was a] very handsome man and I liked going out with him." There is no way to know if romance blossomed between this striking, engaging couple, but if it did, it must have been brief. Another quote in Smith's book that is attributed to her, "All the ladies, married or not, loved him," suggests that she was quite aware that Long Lance was not looking to get tied down. Neither was she. Furthermore, it was not his looks, charisma, sex appeal, or sexual prowess that she chose to comment about; she was mainly attracted to his "inquiring mind" and the interests they had in common, such as their enthusiasm for new books and movies.

Te Ata might also have been on to Long Lance. In her memoir, she contradicted his claim that he was a full-blood Blackfoot, saying she thought he was really a North Carolina Cherokee (which he was in part). There were many inaccuracies and inconsistencies in Long Lance's autobiography, such as his claim that the Blackfeet (he included) were hunting the last of the buffalo and sending out war parties in the 1880s. Smith found that much of Long Lance's autobiography was pure fiction, and while a few people recognized this at the time, in 1930 Long Lance apparently was still fooling most of the people most of the time.[19]

Among them was the membership of the Explorers Club, who voted to admit him in October 1929 as a "full-blooded Chief of Blackfeet [sic] Indian Tribe," honored in "Canada and the western states not only as an explorer, but also as a writer and lecturer on Indian experience and affairs." At the same meeting, Charles Lindbergh was elected an honorary member. After his admission, Long Lance moved into the Explorers Club and was the first and only nonwhite member living there. Two other members in particular had championed his application for membership. One was the artist E. W. Deming, who had studied and sketched Indians of the West in the 1880s and 1890s.[20] The other was Clyde Fisher, an eclectic scientist and a curator at the American Museum of Natural History.

Long Lance probably appealed to Fisher for the same reasons he appealed to the public. In addition, Fisher had an abiding interest in American Indians. He had traveled to the West in 1927 to film cere- monial dances of about a dozen tribes in the Dakotas, New Mexico, and Arizona. He also spent several days with the Sioux on the Standing Rock Reservation and, among other things, made the first films of sign- talking with translations. At a ceremony Fisher self-consciously and rather clumsily shuffled his way through the Kahomni dance and then found to his delight and amazement that he was to be adopted into the tribe. He was given the name Mato-Kokipapi, after a warrior who had been killed in a battle led by Sitting Bull. Mato-Kokipapi's Indian brother, Philip Bull Head, was at the ceremony and gave Fisher a pipestone ceremonial pipe and a decorated buckskin pouch. His new name meant "Afraid-of-Bear," which never failed to amuse whomever he was talking to.[21] But Fisher felt deeply honored by the gesture and was very proud of his adopted name, sometimes using it to sign letters to family members.

Ataloa and Clyde Fisher, pictured with Te Ata in 1932. Ataloa, also a Chickasaw performance artist and a distant cousin, shared a New York apartment with her that had so little furniture they referred to living in the Manhattan "floor culture." Fisher was trying to help Te Ata with her career, but he was also beginning to court her.

It may have been his interest in American Indians that led Clyde Fisher to attend an evening program at Columbia University, probably in late 1929. Or it may have been that Fisher knew that Te Ata would be performing and wanted to meet her. He and Long Lance may have gone together, but Te Ata recalled that her friend, Ernest Fretwell of Columbia Teacher's College, introduced her to Fisher after the program. She remembered him mainly because of his thatch of snow white hair. Although there is no record of Fisher's first impressions of Te Ata, it is not difficult to imagine that he was simply swept off his feet; this beautiful, enchanting Indian artist was the materialization of a

Te Ata: Chickasaw Storyteller, American Treasure

romantic vision. A few weeks after that program Ataloa and Te Ata decided to give a housewarming party in honor of their newly furnished apartment. According to Te Ata, it was Ataloa who suggested inviting "that nice man," Clyde Fisher.[22] At this time, Fisher was 51 years old, married since 1905 to Bessie Fisher, and the father of their three daughters. He also had graduated in 1905 from Miami University in Ohio and received his Ph.D. in botany from Johns Hopkins University in 1913. That same year he was hired by the American Museum of Natural History and, as curator of visual instruction, was in charge of the museum's educational offerings. He came well prepared and developed his knowledge and skills still further. At Miami University he had won honors in public speaking, been editor in chief of the college magazine, and studied zoology, botany, invertebrate paleontology, and geology. He did scientific research at the biological laboratory at Cold Spring Harbor on Long Island. He also taught college courses in natural history and ornithology and edited two volumes titled *Nature's Secrets*. He was an expert nature photographer, both still and movie. In 1925 Fisher received an additional title, curator of astronomy, and a challenging set of responsibilities: he would be doing the research and development for a proposed great hall of astronomy at the museum. He traveled to Germany to study the Zeiss Planetarium and visited American astronomical museums and observatories. In 1930 he was spending at least half of his time on the planetarium development project. [23]

Fisher arrived at the housewarming party with Long Lance, who said that Fisher also lived at the Explorers Club. If so, then Fisher already had separated from his wife. Although little is known about the Fishers' marriage, friends believed that the couple had grown apart. "When they met in high school, they were a country boy and girl [from rural Ohio]," said Dorothy Bennett, one of Clyde's staff members. "After they got married, she was a house-bound housewife, raising three daughters, and probably that suited her. She was nice enough but probably quite boring to a man with such a lively intellect and such eagerness to learn. They probably had been unhappy together for a long time and the separation [and later divorce] were probably long put off and late in coming."[24]

At the party Te Ata treated Fisher deferentially, as befit an older gentleman and scholar. Despite the white hair and academic background, however, Clyde—as he asked everyone to call him—was not stuffy and remote but lively and full of fun.[25] He seemed to know something about everything; yet this impression did not come across in the overbearing manner of boorish people but in a delightful, almost boyish way that made Te Ata feel she was fortunate to be in his company.

❧

During the Christmas season following the stock market crash of 1929, Te Ata was invited to a party in the Manhattan apartment of the wealthy industrialist Samuel Tucker and his wife, Anne. As a housemother at the Three Arts Club, Mrs. Tucker had been an early benefactor of Te Ata. At this party, however, Te Ata was invited as a guest. As was their Christmas custom, the Tuckers had invited many of their friends, and at the end of the evening, gathered by the Christmas tree, they distributed gifts to everyone. These included silver pen and pencil sets, ascots, and lacy scarves. Te Ata received an evening bag. Later, as she was preparing to leave, Anne Tucker told her to wait until the other guests had left; they had one last gift for her. Returning to the Christmas tree with the Tuckers, she saw perched on a branch an envelope with her name on it. Inside was a note and a round-trip ticket to London in the spring on the SS *Olympia*. Te Ata was speechless. The note said, "The English people should see you. . . . We give you the ticket and you will do the rest."[26]

In giving this wonderful gift to Te Ata, the Tuckers had acted astutely. They could have given her the ticket and the cash necessary to pay her expenses, but they probably realized that such largesse might exceed what Te Ata would be willing to accept. Knowing that the trip would be very expensive, they decided to help her by passing the word among their friends that Te Ata would be touring England in the spring and it would be helpful in the meantime to invite her into their homes for after-dinner entertainment. They got the message, particularly Mr. and Mrs. Arthur Curtis James, who hosted no fewer than six dinner parties. Te Ata entertained the guests of the Morgan sisters in their homes several times. Eleanor Roosevelt also engaged her for an appearance at her Greenwich Village apartment.[27]

As her departure time neared, Mrs. James told Te Ata, "[We] know you will have a marvelous trip. The English people will love you as we do here. And we want you to be able to accept their hospitality without concern as to what you should wear." That prelude led to an offer to choose "two evening gowns, slippers and a wrap" at the Designer Salon at Saks Fifth Avenue. Te Ata declined the offer. Nevertheless, Mrs. James told her she could charge clothes in a certain London shop if the need should arise and Mr. James wrote on a card the name of a London bank where she could obtain cash. "Please don't stint," he said. "I don't like to think of a nice girl running around in a strange country without plenty of money." Te Ata assured them she had enough money but took the card and told them she would use the bank if an emergency should arise. Though she had no intention of charging clothes or spending someone else's money, she was very pleased by the offer, which also may have bolstered her sense of security.[28]

One of these sponsors must have contacted Charles P. Curtis, vice president of the United States, to ask him to write letters of introduction for Te Ata. Curtis, an enrolled Kaw Indian, wrote to several American diplomats in Great Britain and Europe, that Te Ata was "visiting Europe with the desire to give a program in native dress so she may help as far as possible to offset the unfavorable impression of the American Indians created in foreign countries. She is a college graduate and it is her desire to preserve and popularize the aboriginal American Indian arts, legends and music."[29] In referring to the "unfavorable impression" in Europe of Indians, the vice president may have been thinking specifically of the British, French, Dutch, and Spanish, colonial powers that had tried to exterminate American Indians from their own lands and in the process had seen many of their fine young soldiers and traders tortured and killed.

The *Olympia* sailed on March 28, 1930. Te Ata was accompanied by Margaret Ball. She had asked her to come along, and Margaret's parents agreed to finance her trip. Te Ata was deeply touched that so many of her friends, including some of her patrons, had come to the pier to wish her and Margaret bon voyage. It is not known if Clyde Fisher was among them, but she was increasingly in his thoughts. For her part, Te Ata considered Fisher only one of several new acquaintances whom she found intellectually stimulating and who, through his network of friends and colleagues, might be helpful in booking programs.

The trip to Great Britain was a present and an opportunity. However, Te Ata's clippings and letters on the trip do not reveal if she had an itinerary or bookings before her departure.[30] A program or two probably had been arranged, and then it must have been expected, as the Tuckers had told her, that she must do the rest. A month before she sailed Te Ata had paid $5 to join the English-Speaking Union of the United States, which had a counterpart in Great Britain and provided her with housing in London and letters of introduction. Furthermore, the Tuckers, who were longtime Anglophiles, asked their English friends to arrange for Te Ata to get some paid performances.[31]

One friend was Sir Archibald Flower, the mayor of Stratford-on-Avon. Te Ata had written him before she sailed, and he responded with an invitation to stay with him and Lady Flower and see Shakespeare performed on the home grounds. Once in London, she met a British Broadcasting Corporation (BBC) staffer who arranged a test for her with the BBC on June 4. The first radio broadcast of her career, a ten-minute program on the BBC, for which she was paid "a nominal sum," occurred on July 7. Later she did another program and was asked to do others but could not fit them in before sailing home.[32]

Te Ata accepted Mayor Flower's invitation and spent a few days in Stratford-on-Avon, where she gave a brief impromptu performance. She was received so well that she was permitted to do a special matinee there in July. It turned out to be a benefit performance for the new Shakespeare Theatre, which was under construction. Perhaps the fact that it was a Monday matinee accounted for the low attendance, which was reported in a review by Bladen Peake. Peake was a windy though discerning observer: "Her quaint idiom, the weird half-chant of her singing, occasionally breaking into a momentary yodel, and ever seeking a minor note in preference to the natural key, is both inspiring and impressive, and aided by a memory of the grace of her movements and the even more graceful pose she assumes when immobile echoes in my ears as I write, so that I am indeed grateful for having made a brief acquaintance with her art."[33]

The program was in two parts, with an intermission.[34] Peake spent half of the lengthy review praising Hartley Alexander's "The Scalp" and Te Ata's interpretation of it. It is the story of the pursuit by an Indian woman, Broken Wing, of the brave who had killed her husband in combat and scalped him. So that her husband could reach the Happy Hunting Ground, Broken Wing had to retrieve his scalp and place it with his bones. Accompanied by the quickening beat of the tom-tom, Broken Wing avenges her husband by scalping the brave and returning her husband's scalp to his grave.

> I gave him my kisses; Oh! my Singer,
> So that you should find peace.
> I bury thy hair beside thy bones; Oh! my Singer
> In the place where I have left my heart.

"Is that not beautiful," asked Peake, "even in the coldness of the print used in the columns of an English newspaper?" Then he noted that in playing Broken Wing, Te Ata's "expressively inexpressive face was the mask worn by a nation living so near to Nature that the slightest emotion dare not be shown thereon" and reflecting the "saga of a whole race, the glories of which we of the East can merely guess." The denouement came after Broken Wing herself was scalped by an avenging brave. Her indomitable spirit "returned to the place where her heart lies buried." Peake ended his review by writing that Te Ata triumphed despite the sterile setting of the lecture room. Although the setting was not ideal, it was located in Stratford-on-Avon, one of the great seats of drama in the world; though the audience may have been small, Te Ata knew they were probably an unusually tough crowd to please.

As in the United States, word of Te Ata's unique performances circulated in certain gentrified circles and she was invited to perform in private residences. She performed at a party for the American actress Peggy Wood, who was starring in *Bittersweet* and was the darling of London at the time. According to the *Daily Mirror*, Miss Woods's party at Claridge's was "a huge success, owing to the presence and performance of a unique artist—"Te Ata, a Cherokee [sic] Indian Princess, who made the best negro [sic] spirituals seem commonplace after her rendering of Red Indian love songs. She can talk with the hands and arms in a way that anyone can understand."[35]

In London Princess Marie Louise, King George's cousin and King Edward's niece, hosted "a command performance" for Te Ata at the Forum Club, a club for literary and artistic women. One guest who wrote an account of the occasion was none other than Anne Tucker, who made Te Ata's trip (and perhaps this performance) possible. Te Ata was Princess Marie Louise's special guest, and the Tuckers were seated at dinner across the table from them. During dinner (the menu was

One of Te Ata's wealthy benefactors made her trip to England possible in 1930, the date of this photograph. Armed with a letter of introduction from the U.S. vice president, Te Ata took it from there, obtaining a booking at Stratford-on-Avon and another one, dubbed a "command performance," for British Royalty in London. Photo by Dorothy Wilding Studio, England.

printed in French), the princess talked about her recent trip to South America. Te Ata, wearing a pale pink satin dress, "looked lovely." Her performance "thrilled" the princess, wrote Mrs. Tucker. For the record, Her Highness thanked Te Ata through a note written by one of her ladies-in-waiting, saying "how much the Princess enjoyed your delightful and artistic entertainment." Anne Tucker seemed to think that

Te Ata: Chickasaw Storyteller, American Treasure

Her Highness enjoyed Te Ata almost too much. Toward the end of the evening, Mrs. Tucker was exhausted, but protocol prevented any-one from leaving before Marie Louise, who kept up her conversation with Te Ata. She would not let her go. Nevertheless, Mrs. Tucker said, "I was very proud of our American Princess standing in her lovely Indian beaded dress beside the granddaughter of Queen Victoria."[36]

☙

While Te Ata was abroad, the reverberations of the great stock market crash of late October 1929 were felt in virtually every part of American society. By the time she returned to New York in July 1930, the Great Depression was settling in in what would be astounding proportions and duration. By mid-1932 American industry was oper-ating at less than half its maximum volume for 1929. Stock prices had plunged. Sixty percent less in wages were paid out in 1932 than in 1929. Twelve million Americans were out of work. Breadlines and soup kitchens appeared in cities, as did many more vacant shops and "Hoovervilles," the tarpaper shacks of the homeless.[37] The increasingly desperate situation was especially apparent in New York, the finan-cial capital of the nation. Te Ata probably did not fret much about the possible impact of the country's economic depression on her bur-geoning career; she had lived hand to mouth for so long that she just plunged ahead.

One option now open was for Te Ata to base her career in Europe. There were people in London and Paris who were quite willing to manage her career or arrange bookings for her.[38] She could be promoted as an expatriate artist, an American Indian Princess, estranged from her homeland by the U.S. government's pernicious and genocidal Indian policies. Of course, this status would only be implied. She was an artist, not a lecturer; her emphasis would be on entertaining as well as teaching the European societies about the beauty and simpli-city of her people's precolonial culture.

Te Ata never really considered the expatriate role. As she made clear in her letters and by her frequent trips home, she sorely missed her family, and for that reason alone she would not have considered living abroad. Furthermore, she did not fit the image of an expatriate because she did not feel alienated from America. To the contrary, her role in American society was not only viable, it was also appealing—as her enthusiastic American audiences and the critics attested. If her

Indian folklore performances were well accepted in London or Edinburgh, they were no less so in most American settings.

When she returned, she considered hiring a manager but decided she would have to make more money to afford one. For the time being, she wrote all her own business letters and press releases, made her own telephone calls, negotiated her fees, and arranged her schedule. If she did not have enough problems meeting her own needs in a depressed economy, Te Ata also was supporting her parents and her nephew Hiawatha Estes, now 12 years old.[39] She had been sending her parents money since the late 1920s when the last of her father's stores failed and her father, then in his sixties, lacked either the assets or the will to try again. Te Ata had moved the family to Sulphur, and from then on Thompson was retired—with income from only a small amount of lease money from their allotments.

The Chickasaw and Choctaw tribal governments still had millions of dollars in assets in mineral lands and potentially millions more in pending court claims, but no resolutions were in sight. Since the end of World War I, the federal government had not been interested in acquiring vast amounts of coal, and now, with the onset of the depression, Congress was of no mind to pay two Indian tribes millions of dollars.[40] When Te Ata returned home for visits, she saw many destitute Indian families and knew that her mother and father would join them if she stopped paying their rent and sending them $25 to $35 a month. This was a motivator at least as powerful as her ambition to succeed. Her brother and sisters helped when they could, but Te Ata was more often able to bear the load.

Still, there were times after she came home in triumph from England in summer 1930 when she was broke, bills were overdue, her bank balance was overdrawn, and she did not have a booking in the immediate future. She often said that the Great Spirit was looking after her. But she was also working hard looking out for herself. She had to spend much more time getting jobs than doing them. To make business contacts and connections, she attended a large number of social functions and public events such as lectures. She called on friends and colleagues to learn if they might have any leads or knew anyone in Philadelphia. It was dismaying and sometimes galling to realize how much of her time was spent drumming up business. She sometimes wondered if her life would always be so out of kilter.

Te Ata: Chickasaw Storyteller, American Treasure

CHAPTER 6

Clyde Fisher

Te Ata's papers covering the early 1930s reflect a remarkable range of professional activities but not much bill-paying work.[1] The *New York Times* ran a photo of her on an auditorium stage with about fifty Bronx Camp Fire girls, all wearing Indian headbands. She performed for children attending Camp Hiawatha in Maine; later some of them collaborated to write a poem in her honor and a remembrance of her visit: "When the princess left us on the following day, we felt enriched by the wonderful old legends and songs we had heard and many of us had learned to say, 'I love you' in sign language." At Manhattan's St. Mark's-in-the-Bouwerie Church, she starred in a program that was given on the Sunday before Thanksgiving. She played two roles in one of Alexander's masks, "Carved Woman." Another role was played by Te Ata's friend and sometime accompanist, Kuruks Pahetu, a full-blood Pawnee musician and tenor. Also from Oklahoma, Kuruks, whose English name was Ralph Allen, had attended Muskogee's Bacone College and had had a fellowship at the Julliard School of Music.

Te Ata and Kuruks also teamed up on a radio broadcast on New York City's WOR on December 10. Called "Spirit Trails," their presentation consisted of Te Ata narrating and dramatizing legends interspersed with Kuruks singing "spirit songs." Te Ata concluded the program with Alexander's "God's Drum." She wrote a piece for *The Forward*, the periodical of the Three Arts Club, titled "A Lone Bird-Call Is Part of Me!"

A lone bird-call is part of me. For I sing with the meadowlark—the song he always sings—when he sits for a breath's moment in a golden field of new mown hay.

I am inside the oriole, when he sits on a branch of the catalpa tree, tuning his golden harp. . . . I am a ray of the Sun. Its great and varied colors make my heart leap, when unexpectedly my eyes see the handiwork of our mighty "Keetchie Manido" to the West.

I sink to rest with the sun—and the colors so vivid in the western sky are the colors in my blanket that I wrap me in. A lone bird-call is part of me. I am a part of Spring and growing things.

As Te Ata looked toward 1932, she carried a substantial and ongoing financial burden. She knew she needed a breakthrough in her career. She was almost 37 years old and sensitive about her age. She replied to the commissioner of Indian affairs, who wanted biographical information about her, asking that he not reveal her age if inquiries were made.[2] Though she looked younger than she was, Te Ata was no longer an ingenue; she had been out on her own for almost a decade and wanted at least a measure of stability and security, especially as the Great Depression deepened. Unfortunately, her memoir does not deal with her insecurities; her life story is virtually free of introspection. It was as if Te Ata had skipped through her professional career from one success to another.

Some people were in a position to help her, either directly or indirectly. One was Clyde Fisher. He had missed seeing her during her three-month absence and soon was crafting ways to renew their acquaintance, including a business proposition. As curator of public education at the American Museum of Natural History (AMNH), he lectured to groups of adults and children and occasionally brought in guest lecturers. Would she consider presenting one of her programs for children at the museum? She performed her first of many appearances at the AMNH in October 1930.[3]

After Te Ata's first performance there, Fisher wrote a formal, stiff, thank-you note, addressed to Princess Te Ata: "The program which you gave for our children of members was most excellent and satisfactory. I would like to congratulate you on your dramatic ability and dignified Indian bearing. You held our children spellbound. We hope to have you again in the near future. Sincerely, Clyde Fisher."[4] Meanwhile, he could and did sing her praises to his friends and associates,

Te Ata: Chickasaw Storyteller, American Treasure

among whom were other scientists, artists, educators, entertainers, writers, explorers, and sports figures.

In fall 1930 Dorothy Bennett, a recent graduate of the University of Minnesota, traveled to New York to look for a job. With a rather thin background in science but a lively intelligence and much determination, Dorothy was hired to work for Fisher in the AMNH's visual education department. Although she worked for him for a decade, she got to know him as well as she ever would in a relatively short time because he was "absolutely natural and sincere" and because he never discussed personal matters, either past or present. By her account, he was both a "perfect gentleman" and a "country boy." He had wonderful personal qualities: "[He] radiated warmth, was kind, honorable, trusting and interested in people. He was utterly without guile or pomposity. Everybody liked him." Though Fisher was an excellent educator, he was not a very good administrator. He was lenient to the point of neglectful as a supervisor, and he could not stand museum politics, controversies, and confrontations. And, according to Bennett, "[h]is friends and colleagues were legion and many of them took advantage of him and his time. Worse, Dr. Fisher had a hard time drawing a conversation to a timely conclusion so that he could get on to the tasks at hand."[5]

Dorothy had not been working at the museum very long before she noticed that Te Ata had joined the ranks of Fisher's friends. Te Ata would attend a lecture periodically and then join Fisher and others for lunch or dinner. It was not until after Dorothy had seen Te Ata give one of her programs at the museum, however, that she really took note of the Chickasaw Indian.

> I can't remember that first performance, per se, but do recall how dignified and beautiful and affecting her programs were. The audience response was always very warm. In one of those first performances, I was particularly struck by Te Ata, as a frail old woman who had been left behind on the trail by the tribe because she could no longer keep up. She was sitting on a rock under a tree with a shawl drawn up around her shoulders, reviewing her life, lamenting some regrets but accepting the fact that she had grown old and infirm. Every elderly person could relate. In small, barely perceptible ways, Te Ata was a master of transforming herself. She was a fine

actress and as an Indian raised in Indian culture, she was performing in her ideal medium."[6]

Despite her commanding presence onstage, Te Ata was "very reserved" otherwise, Dorothy recalled. "I was seeing her fairly often at the museum, but she was a very private person and I didn't get to know her better for a few years. I think she was inwardly self-conscious of the fact that she was moving with people who had very different backgrounds [from hers] and she was at heart still a little Indian girl." Dorothy knew that Te Ata and Fisher were friends, but "Dr. Fisher had a lot of friends."[7] She also knew that Fisher was separated from his wife and was living at the Explorers Club, but she saw Mrs. Fisher and the three Fisher daughters every so often at the museum and probably figured that the family that was still in touch may also be still intact.[8]

To keep herself in the public's eye literally throughout 1932, Te Ata sent out a number of wall calendars featuring a large captivating photo of her beautiful face nicely framed by long braids pulled forward in front of her shoulders. Glued into place at the bottom center were tear-off slips of paper representing the months of the year. The photo was obviously done by a skilled portrait photographer. Not only was it excellent technically, but it captured her intelligence, sensitivity, and strength. She inscribed the calendars, "Greetings from Te Ata."[9] She rang in 1933 with John and Margaret Ball and other friends first at a nightclub that featured nude dancers and later at the opera *La Notte di Gocaima*. She also noted in a journal that her bank account on January 2 "shows $46.50 and I owe about 5 times that much." Nevertheless, she wrote that the Great Spirit was providing for her because she had "secured (3) paying programs" for January. How much she was charging is not known; she was not including amounts in her papers as she would periodically later in her career. It is likely that her fee varied, depending on the client's ability to pay, how advantageous the booking might be to her, or how badly she needed the money. In one January 1932 note, she wrote that the Friends School near Philadelphia "could not even pay $50," so she had settled for $35 because her family needed the money.[10]

Throughout January and half of February, Te Ata kept a journal that recorded her jobs, busy social life, and personal thoughts that she presumably would not share with many if any other people.[11] There is not much detail or depth, however, because she selected a journal that provided space for only a few lines per day. According to the notes, she was battling to make ends meet. But compared to most Americans toiling through the front end of the Great Depression, Te Ata was living a privileged life. She was getting by financially, had an array of interesting and stimulating friends, was a habitué of New York City cultural activities, and got instant gratification, often adulation, from her audiences.

Still, Te Ata did not take success for granted. According to her journal entries, she believed her preparation on Hartley Alexander's "How Death Came into the World" was not adequate for her to be a "big hit" later that month at the prestigious Folk Festival of the Homelands at the Guild Theater in New York. She rehearsed the mask repeatedly, alone and with Kuruks, her accompanist on the tom-tom.[12] The festival was presented by the Folk Festival Council of New York, and groups representing eleven nations performed traditional songs and dances. It was a major cultural event in the city and received wide publicity; of all the performers, Te Ata's picture was chosen by the sponsor to appear in newspapers. Representing American Indians, Te Ata performed the mask and provided the evening's prologue, reciting the long-ago vision of the Cheyenne chief Hiamovi, a prophecy of racial and ethnic harmony, which was so attuned to her belief and mission that it became a permanent part of her repertoire.

> It was meant by the Great Mystery that the Indian should give to all peoples. But the white man has never known the Indian. It is thus: there are two roads, the white man's road and the Indian's road. Neither traveler knows the road of the other. Thus ever has it been, from the long ago, even unto today. . . . But I know that it is the mind of the Great Mystery that the white men and the Indians who fought together should now be one people.
>
> There are birds of many colors . . . yet it is all one bird. There are horses of many colors . . . yet it is all one horse. So all living things— animals, flowers, trees. So men: white, black, yellow, red, yet all one people. That this should come to pass was in the heart of the Great Mystery. It is right thus. And everywhere there shall be peace.[13]

In her journal Te Ata wrote that the festival had gone very well and that the newspaper accounts had singled her out for praise. Earlier that month she had revealed to the public another side of herself, an opinionated side. In a newspaper interview, Te Ata noted a gulf between actual Indian life and the way white people perceive it. This misconception had serious ramifications. Indians need the type of education "which will give them the knowledge to live more richly and more sensibly, an education to make them proud of the old, beautiful things they have, and at the same time, show them how to build on those old things for a wider future." What is happening now, she said, is destructive. In a misguided effort to produce leaders, the government puts Indian students "into schools that are strange to them, with insensitive, inferior teachers and incomprehensible books." The Indian student is "so overwhelmed with his own sense of inferiority that it is hardly to be expected he will go back to his tribe as a leader."[14] If she mailed a copy of that news clipping to her parents, they might have remarked to one another about the autobiographical tinge to her remarks. Though they had tried to ignore her complaints and pleadings from Bloomfield, they could not have forgotten them.

❧

In the journal, covering just six weeks, her feelings for Clyde Fisher took an interesting course. On January 3 she wrote that she spent the afternoon reading a book loaned to her by "Dr. Clyde Fisher." Two days later "Dr. Clyde Fisher" took her to dinner at the Hearthstone, and they met the Balls and went to a party where "Dr. F gave us a delightful and informal talk on Lapland, using colored slides. He is a nice person—our relations so far has [sic] been purely platonic and I bet last evening that it was up to me to keep it so. I like him—but he's married though separated for long time and I am still the very old fashioned one—in spite of N.Y.C."

On January 10 they again had dinner, as part of a group that included a poet, a theatrical critic, the concert pianist Leo Godowsky, and others "of lesser fame." They wound up the evening stargazing at the Columbia Observatory. On January 23 she went to the museum to see Fisher's film of penguins in some unidentified Arctic region. On January 27 they dined at the Maple Grove and dropped by an art exhibit before attending a lecture and slide show on the Tower of London at Carnegie Hall. "D.F. [Dr. Fisher] is perhaps beginning to like me too well—and I do not know what to do about it. He is a very sweet and nice human being."

On January 30 they dined at the "Russian Bear," served by Russians in costume while listening to Russian folk music played on Russian instruments. Later they dropped by the Balls' apartment, where they played gin rummy and entertained each other with a 1930s version of "read and discuss," reading aloud selected passages from a couple of books and then discussing the passages. Two evenings later Fisher took Te Ata to an East Indian restaurant called The Rajah. Then they saw the movie *Mata Hari* with Greta Garbo and Lionel Barrymore. On the bottom line of the journal page for February 1, she wrote, "My feelings for D.F. are altogether mixed?" They went with the Balls on February 7 to the Tenth Street studio of the artist and mystic poet Kahlil Gibran, who had died only a few months before. Of his classic, *The Prophet*, Te Ata wrote, "[It touched me] very deeply. It binds me to him." Four days later they had lunch at a vegetarian restaurant and then enjoyed a walk through Central Park. "D.F. told me he was something of a tree expert," but then, she said, he was embarrassed in an amusing way after he could not identify the first tree she asked him about.

On Abraham Lincoln's birthday, Te Ata and some Oklahoma friends went to a Lincoln reading at the St. George Hotel in Brooklyn. "We were meeting another young man there . . . and we really took to each other—at least he seemed to like me and I was intrigued with him." While taking her home in his "Chevy Roadster," he told her his hobby was boats. "He seems a nice person and I feel I shall like him and I truly hope he calls me." Not the type to stay home waiting for the telephone to ring, Te Ata went the next day to the Three Arts Club to meet the famous Mexican artist Diego Rivera and his wife. "He drew a sketch of me and signed it—for the club." (Some lucky person probably owns that sketch today, but my attempts to find it have been futile.) In her final entry, February 15, she wrote that Fisher and a half dozen others called: "I am dreadfully tired. Too much going for this Injun and too many people. I am going to bed early tonight regardless of who calls me!"

The driver of the Chevy Roadster was never identified or mentioned again, but then her journal ended three days after they met. Perhaps he never called; perhaps they dated for a time. What is most significant, however, is not how she felt about him but that while Clyde Fisher was obviously pursuing her, she was still interested in

In Ruby Jolliffe's cabin at Bear Mountain, Te Ata describes her "Clyde Fisher dilemma" to her friend, known as Jolly. Fisher had been trying to woo Te Ata, and though she liked and respected him, he was seventeen years older than her and a married man, though he and his wife were separated.

this other man. In light of what happened in the next few months, Te Ata's interest in this mystery man probably represented her acting out doubts about the wisdom of deepening a relationship with a married man who was seventeen years her senior. Intuitively, she knew she soon would have to decide whether to keep seeing Clyde Fisher. She went to Bear Mountain in late February, perhaps to think or talk things out. Possibly reflecting this dilemma is a February 20, 1932, photo of Te Ata and her friend Jolly, sitting facing one another on either side of the stone fireplace in Jolly's cabin. Te Ata is talking and gesturing with

Te Ata: Chickasaw Storyteller, American Treasure

Max Big Man, a Crow from Montana, was clearly smitten with Te Ata. Here they pose in front of the American Museum of Natural History for the photographer, Clyde Fisher.

the long tapered fingers of her left hand; Jolly seems to be listening intently, her chin resting in the crook of her left thumb and forefinger.[15]

Of course, Clyde Fisher was not the only man interested in Te Ata. Presumably most of them did not write her letters, showering her with praise. But one who did at about this time was a full-blood Crow, Max Big Man, who was visiting New York from his home on the Crow reservation in Montana. He was probably in town to participate in a Columbia Broadcasting System series on Indians for children or to appear at selected city schools. He was also active in tribal affairs, representing the Crows in Washington, D.C., and a painter;[16] he drew several small sketches in the margins of the letter he wrote to Te Ata. How they met is not known, but it may have been after one of her performances. The Crow was clearly smitten. He wrote "It [the performance] brought back . . . the picture of the plains, which was one time full of buffalo and other game. You place a picture in my mind . . . of the beautiful mountains, the father hills, the worshiping grounds of my father['s] fathers. I was sure proud of you today, thinking what an Indian could do."

They had lunch at Te Ata's apartment, and later Max Big Man wondered if it had really happened or if he had been dreaming. Later, alone in his room, he wrote, "it seems I could see you standing in front of me. When you said goodby to me the sound of your voice is still in my ear. Sitting here among the many high stone teepes [sic] of the white race, I took the picture that you give me, place it in front of me." He wrote that when he returned to Montana, he would remember her first, then New York.[17] It seems their friendship endured, for several photos of Te Ata and Max Big Man are housed in the photo collection of the American Museum of Natural History. The photographer was Clyde Fisher.

It is possible that a tragedy played out on the night of March 19, 1932, may have brought Fisher and Te Ata closer together. Their mutual friend Long Lance was found dead in a Los Angeles house while on a tour to promote his movie, *The Enemy Within*. Shockingly, the cause of death was said to be a self-inflicted gunshot wound. There was compelling physical evidence as reflected in the sheriff's report, and, as many of his friends and acquaintances were aware, he had a motive. For some time rumors had been circulating that Long Lance had never been a heroic Blackfoot warrior, that his 1929 autobiography was largely a work of fiction, and, most damaging, that he was actually part African-American. As the rumors persisted and spread, Long Lance felt increasingly uncomfortable at the Explorers Club. He began drinking

Te Ata: Chickasaw Storyteller, American Treasure

Long Lance at Roosevelt Field. Though Long Lance was a bona fide adventurer, athlete, writer, and film star, he was in other ways an imposter. He dated Te Ata for a time and introduced her to Clyde Fisher. Long Lance's suicide in 1932 brought Clyde and Te Ata closer together. Courtesy Dept. of Library Services, American Museum of Natural History, neg. no. 281393.

heavily. By the end of summer 1930, he moved to the Roosevelt Field Hotel to escape the scrutiny of the members of the Explorers Club and to begin taking flying lessons. With only a few hours of flying time, he began executing preposterous and unscheduled stunts, nosedives at full throttle, tailspins, and loops and rolls. Without training, he parachuted out of an airplane, having volunteered to try out a new automatic parachute .[18]

Over the next months only a few people stuck by him, but two of the most loyal were Clyde Fisher and Te Ata. Te Ata and Long Lance continued to correspond into 1931. She invited him to a program she was giving at Town Hall. He replied he would be there if he could but provided an excuse in advance that he was preparing for a flying test.[19] Fisher had reviewed Long Lance's autobiography favorably in the *Explorers Club Journal*, with no hint of skepticism. When he asked his AMNH colleague, the anthropologist Clark Wissler, for his opinion of the book, Wissler did not know what to say. According to Donald Smith's 1982 book on Long Lance, Wissler, who had done fieldwork twenty years before on the Peigan tribe of the Blackfoot Confederacy, knew "without question . . . that the autobiography was fiction." When pressed by Fisher, Wissler said, "If you begin it, I think you will finish it." So blindly loyal and trusting was Fisher that he ended his review of the book with Wissler's quote, unaware that it was an evasion. In a 1933 letter to Canon S. H. Middleton, Long Lance's executor, Fisher wrote that he did not believe that Long Lance took his own life. "[N]one of his close friends, that I know, believe it either," he added.[20]

While it is not possible to know if Fisher and Te Ata really believed Long Lance's story, they did believe in him. Te Ata probably admired and respected Clyde all the more for standing by Long Lance in life and honoring his memory in death. Smith noted that it is possible that those who stood by Long Lance did so out of admiration for what he had accomplished: "In an age when the Indians were viciously treated, as much by the slanderous stereotype pushed by Hollywood as by the ruthless bullying by whites on the plains, Long Lance succeeded at least in capturing something of the essence of the Indians' heroic and noble history. If it was fiction disguised as fact, then it was fiction done well, and in its own peculiar way, done accurately."[21]

Te Ata's mixed feelings about developing a deeper relationship with Clyde Fisher appear to have been resolved—in favor of proceeding. In April she wrote him the kind of short, sweet note, laced with private terms of endearment, that is characteristic of romantics in love:

I like
    Love letters from old halfi![22]
    Penguins
    Mexican sweets
    Watches that keep time
    Walking on ice (not kneeling)
    Animals up Bronx way
    Dinners with Ikhana

Te Ata: Chickasaw Storyteller, American Treasure

Bird walks and tree talks
And Dawn in the country![23]

Writing from Loon Island, Te Ata invited Fisher to come for a weekend in June—if he would not be too busy preparing for his two-month lecture tour of several midwestern and western states. After Fisher replied that he would be there, she wrote back with suggestions of what to bring and fretted about how far he was coming for such a short stay: "[I hope] you will not be disappointed in the place and us, but—I am glad you are coming!" She wrote that the island "is only about a block long and narrow but is wooded. You will like it." And she closed with a mock warning: "Don't back out!"[24]

He did not. After the weekend rendezvous, she wrote, "There is an emptiness here where you have been. I miss you greatly and in many ways." She wrote to thank him for sending her some knickers but implied they were a bit large. "How you would have laughed could you have seen me all dressed up in the knickers. I might be right good size woman but I'm not much of a man, I reckon." She returned them to him, saying he would look better in them than she would. Knowing that they would not see each other again for two months, they wrote often. After acknowledging that she knew he would leave on his trip in ten days, Te Ata added, "I am coming (under separate cover) to go with you!" Knowing that Oklahoma was on Fisher's itinerary, she gave him the addresses of her family and Frances Davis's mother, Mother McClure. In the middle of one rather chatty letter, Te Ata inserted a sentence that came abruptly and straight from the heart: "I can hardly go to the woods anymore without you—you have made yourself indispensable to me."[25]

By then she loved him, and despite the substantial differences in their ethnic, cultural, and educational backgrounds, she thought they would make a good match. Previously she had refrained from asking him personal questions about his background. Now she was totally absorbed in his story. Normally very reticent, Fisher felt that with Te Ata his life was an open book.

George Clyde Fisher was born on his family's fifteen-hundred-acre farm near Sidney, Ohio, on May 22, 1878. He was the second of eight siblings born to Amanda and Harrison Jay Fisher (the first one died at birth). Although Clyde (he never went by George) spent every spare moment of his childhood outdoors, he was always much more attracted to natural history than agriculture. In reflecting on his childhood, he wrote that the "life of a dandelion or a daisy was more interesting than the development of a corn crop." Like most children, Clyde was naturally curious, but what distinguished him was the lengths he would go to satisfy his curiosity. When he learned that the family farm was located on the glacial drift, he began collecting the evidence: scratched cobblestones and polished and grooved bedrock. By the time he had collected more than one hundred varieties of rocks from among the glacial boulders, he had learned so much about geology that he thought he should become a geologist.[26]

He switched from geology during the day to astronomy at night, after having learned to his astonishment in school one day that the earth rotated on its axis and revolved around the sun. Having assumed that the earth was flat and stationary and that the sun simply moved across the sky every day, Clyde was so excited by this revolutionary news that he raced home from school to tell his father, who was milking a cow. When his father nodded and went on milking, Clyde was irritated at his nonchalance and at the fact, he subsequently learned, that his father had been aware of this astounding news and never told him. Fortunately for Clyde, two uncles had taken up astronomy as a hobby. Clyde later told an AMNH colleague that he set such store by his uncles that he feared all knowledge of the sky would die with them. Accordingly, he began teaching astronomy to anyone who would listen.[27]

Clyde started school in an archetypal little red schoolhouse but apparently dropped out to work on the farm. One article says he never went to high school but at age 17 began teaching in a country school for $30 a month.[28] (This was 1895, the year Te Ata was born.) He started teaching probably as a natural extension of his "lectures" on astronomy and geology. His father had made it plain to his children that if they wanted to attend college, they would have to work their way through. Clyde taught for six years in country schools in western Ohio and in the summers attended Ohio Normal University at Ada. There he got his first formal introduction to the physical sciences and for the first time looked through a telescope at the mountains of the moon.[29] (Almost fifty years later he wrote a book titled *The Story of the Moon*, which was distributed to the U.S. Armed Forces in 1945 and translated into several languages.)

At 24, Clyde enrolled at Miami University in Oxford, where he mastered a variety of science courses, was a student assistant in astronomy, and became a skilled orator, debater, writer, and editor. As groundwork for geology, he did so well in zoology, invertebrate paleontology, and botany that he was awarded a summer scholarship in 1903 and 1904 for advanced study at the Marine Biological Laboratories in Cold Spring Harbor, Long Island.[30]

Clyde graduated from Miami University with honors in geology in 1905. That summer he married Bessie Wiley, his high school sweetheart and neighbor in Sidney. He intended to pursue an advanced degree, but first he needed a bankroll. He taught high school science at Troy, Ohio, until 1907. Then the Fishers moved to DeFuniak Springs, in the Florida panhandle, where Clyde was principal of the Palmer College Academy and in 1909–10, at age 31, acting president of Palmer College.[31] A newspaper reporter there once described him in print as "plain as cotton stockings and as comfortable as old shoes."[32]

During those three years in Florida, his exposure to the state's remarkably diverse and exotic flora and fauna may have been a factor in his decision to do graduate work in botany. Also, an AMNH colleague of Fisher's remembered that his work at Cold Spring Harbor "opened new vistas" to Clyde. He became just as fascinated "investigating sea weed, fungi and flowering plants" as he had been studying rocks and fossils.[33]

Having saved enough money by 1910 to finally begin his graduate studies, he resigned from Palmer College and entered one of the nation's premier science institutions, Johns Hopkins University in Baltimore. Although he was studying botany, he became a recognized expert in ornithology as well as an exceptionally well rounded student of natural history. In time he came to the attention of George Sherwood, curator of education at the AMNH. So anxious was Sherwood to secure Fisher's services as assistant curator of education that he offered him the job six months before he received his Ph.D. in botany.[34] The offer to begin a new program in visual education—combining his catholic knowledge of science with excellent photographic and public-speaking skills—at one of the nation's foremost natural science research centers and museums was too tempting to pass up.

The museum was founded by New York's great financiers and industrialists—J. Pierpont Morgan, Morris K. Jessup, Theodore Roosevelt, Sr., and various Whitneys, Rockefellers, and Dodges. These wealthy board members subsidized the museum, paid for its many international expeditions, and donated or helped to secure vast collections of animal bones, stuffed birds, and gems. Under the leadership of Henry Fairfield Osborn, who became president in 1908, the museum in the second decade of the twentieth century was moving toward increased exploration and research.[35] To keep pace, the education department was likewise expanding, and Fisher knew he would have the freedom to organize all the diverse products of museum research into a course of study suitable for students and the general public. Within a few years, Fisher, with his tremendous versatility, became "the moving spirit" of the department—as curator of visual instruction.[36] In 1924 Fisher had spoken at the National Geographic Society in Washington, D.C., and its president, Gilbert Grosvenor, had enjoyed the presentation so much that he had written a note praising his speaking ability and excellent color slides and motion pictures. In attaching a copy of Grosvenor's note, President Osborn wrote, "I feel confident that your future is bright."[37]

The lecture Grosvenor referred to dealt with Fisher's three-month stay with the Lapps in Arctic Lapland, living in their primitive huts and subsisting on reindeer meat and milk. He shot ten thousand feet of film with his Akeley camera and took more than five hundred slides showing the Lapps' summertime activities.[38] The high point of his trip, literally and figuratively, occurred on July 4, 1924, when he struggled through knee-high snow to the top of Mount Akka, a six-thousand-foot Swedish mountain, and patriotically unfurled a small American flag, along with the standard of the Explorers Club, which he had joined in 1923.

Fisher also gave lectures on a variety of subjects to educational institutions, primarily in the East. He was an especially popular speaker because his lectures normally were accompanied by color slides and film. By the 1920s he had extended his reach to include more lay audiences, and by 1924 the Emmerich Lecture Bureau was handling his bookings and had developed an expensive and lengthy publicity brochure, featuring about a dozen of his photographs. According to the publication, Fisher offered seven lectures, including wildflowers, birds, small animals, one with the provocative title "How Life Begins," and probably his favorite, the life of the renowned naturalist and writer John Burroughs.[39]

Fisher had visited his hero at his Riverby home in November 1915 when Burroughs was 78. He took several photos of Burroughs and had long conversations on farming (both men were reared on farms) and rare plants that grew in the area. Burroughs took Fisher to Slab-sides, the isolated cabin he had built in 1895 to escape civilization and where he subsequently wrote most of his essays on natural history.[40] Thereafter Clyde visited Burroughs periodically at Slabsides or at his farm in the western Catskills. One day Burroughs told Fisher that he would rather be the author of Thoreau's *Walden* "than of all the books [he had] ever written." Fisher countered, "I would rather be the author of *Wake-Robin* [by Burroughs] than all I have ever read of Thoreau's works." In *Wake-Robin* Burroughs wrote, "Take the first step in ornithology, . . . and you are ticketed for the whole voyage." Fisher once paraphrased that line: "Take the first step in John Burroughs' books, and you are ticketed for the whole long shelf full." (Burroughs wrote about fifty books).[41] Fisher was hooked not only because Burroughs's observations on flora and fauna always brought new knowledge and fresh insights but also because the author put so much of himself in his essays. In fact, Burroughs once told Fisher that literature is observation plus the man. That is why he replied to a friend who was urging him to write his autobiography, "My books are my autobiography."[42]

Fisher's last visit with Burroughs was on November 6–8, 1920. He cooked Fisher what he called a "brigand steak," steak, bacon, and onion skewered on a sharpened stick held over a camp fire. Burroughs died in the spring, at eighty-three. In a tribute to his late mentor, Fisher wrote that Burroughs "did perhaps more than anyone to open our eyes to the beauty of nature, and he has left us a priceless legacy in his books."[43] Clyde always kept Old John alive in his heart. He admired Burroughs more than any person he had met or ever would meet. Early in their courtship, Fisher introduced Te Ata to the works of Burroughs and took her on day trips to Burroughs's "favorite haunts," as he called his homes and stomping grounds, and to meet Burroughs's family. Though she had not heard of Burroughs, she immediately recognized that his writings spoke to some of her deepest feelings;

Burroughs's elegant prose about the sanctity of earth complemented her own elegant programs of Indian folklore. In her own way, Te Ata became almost as devoted to Old John's memory as was Fisher.

In 1924 Osborn entrusted to Fisher the responsibility of developing a new department, astronomy. Although not a university-trained astronomer, Fisher had sound judgment and his knowledge of the science was encyclopedic. Appointed temporary curator, Fisher showed such enthusiasm for his additional duties that he was dispatched the next year to Europe, chiefly to investigate the new planetariums recently introduced in Germany. Fisher had heard that the Carl Zeiss Optical Works had perfected an instrument that could project on a dome the thousands of celestial bodies visible to the naked eye. After witnessing a demonstration in Jena, Germany, Fisher said he was "astonished, overwhelmed." The Zeiss projector was the "greatest invention ever devised as a visual aid in teaching." The rising and setting of the sun, moon, and stars were represented just as they occurred in nature, due to the rotation of the earth on its axis. The moon went through its phases, and the planets were shown traveling their natural courses among some forty-five hundred stars visible to the unaided eye.[44]

Returning to New York with missionary zeal, Fisher wanted the AMNH to be the first in America to acquire a Zeiss projector and advanced an ambitious plan to establish a $3 million astronomical palace centering on a planetarium. To his dismay, he was informed that the museum could not even consider such a plan until other projects had been completed, including a bird hall, an African hall, an education hall, and a power plant.[45] Meanwhile, Fisher created the Amateur Astronomers Association in 1927 and served as its first president and the editor of the association's quarterly magazine.[46] Fisher's plans for a planetarium were still on hold as the 1920s gave way to the new decade, but he had established a palpable and irreversible momentum.

CHAPTER 7

From Lake Te Ata to the White House

On June 29, 1932, Clyde Fisher left New York by train on what would be a two-month, eleven-thousand-mile lecture tour.[1] During two segments of the trip, he was joined by his three daughters and his estranged wife, Bessie, who were traveling by car. As a family reunited for this special but limited occasion, there were undoubtedly awkward and stressful times, but Fisher kept everybody busy with a full schedule of sight-seeing and educational activities. One of the main objectives of the trip was to visit the Sioux at the Standing Rock Reservation, who had adopted him into the tribe in 1927, especially his Indian brother, Philip Bull Head, who had given Fisher the name of his late blood brother, Mato-Kokipapi (Afraid-of-Bear). Bull-head's wife gave Bessie and the girls some beaded Indian moccasins, and Bull Head presented his brother with a red pipestone ceremonial pipe.

Fisher left his family at Standing Rock and caught the train bound for Oklahoma. After arriving in Oklahoma City, he called on Te Ata's youngest brother, Tom Jr., who resembled his sister. Fisher said of him, "[He had] the sweetest smile I ever saw in a man." He also visited with Mother McClure, the mother of Frances Davis and a poet whose work, Fisher noted, had been included in some recent anthologies. They talked about Te Ata, agreeing that she was a wonderful artist and person, but given Fisher's reserve it is unlikely that he confided his feelings about Te Ata to Mother McClure or anyone else.[2]

117

After lecturing at the University of Oklahoma, Fisher left Oklahoma City on July 10 on the Santa Fe Railroad bound for Lamy, New Mexico, eight miles southeast of Santa Fe. He visited his old friend, Ernest Thompson Seton, who along with Fisher had been adopted into the Sioux tribe in 1927.[3] Naturalist, artist, writer, storyteller, explorer, and educator, Seton, at 71, had moved from Greenwich, Connecticut, to New Mexico in 1931 to found the Seton Institute of Indian Wisdom on a campus known as Seton Village. When Fisher arrived on July 11, Seton and his assistant and lover, Julie Buttree, had just launched the first six-week summer session. They taught classes and acquired a staff of qualified teachers and local Indians known for their artistry and craftwork. The curriculum offered Indian arts and crafts, outdoor activities such as Indian dance, nature study and camping, and leadership skills, including Indian philosophy and history. Students had access to Seton's eleven-thousand-volume library and museum of Indian artifacts and mounted mammal and bird specimens.[4]

On the day Fisher arrived at Seton Village, July 11, Te Ata was at Bear Mountain, two thousand miles to the east, canoeing across a small lake that the campers called the Triplet. She was not alone. Flanking her canoe were two others paddled by city boys dressed up in Indian costumes. As they rowed, thousands of campers came into view, lining the banks of the lake. Although the sun was getting low, they could see Te Ata, standing in the middle canoe, wearing a doeskin dress. Her canoe was paddled by the Oklahoma Pawnee Kuruks Pahetu. The canoes headed for a clearing, where most of the campers were gathered. Te Ata could see her good friend Jolly Jolliffe and several other familiar employees of the Bear Mountain and Harriman State Parks. They were gathered around Eleanor Roosevelt, whose husband, New York governor Franklin Roosevelt, had captured the Democratic presidential nomination in Chicago only ten days before—as Clyde Fisher was passing through town on his trip West.

Mrs. Roosevelt was holding a beribboned champagne bottle that had been filled with water from all the other lakes in the parks. As New York's first lady, Mrs. Roosevelt had supported the efforts of state park officials to provide camping opportunities for underprivileged inner-city children.[5] She knew that Te Ata had given her time and talent to these endeavors and had made a positive and lasting impression on the children. That was the official reason she had suggested to the park commissioners that one of the lakes be named in Te Ata's honor. Furthermore, she let it be known that she would be happy to take part in the christening ceremony. Not surprisingly, the commissioners voted to approve Mrs. Roosevelt's suggestion.

Mrs. Roosevelt kept other possible reasons for honoring Te Ata to herself. But it is known that she admired and perhaps envied (at that point in her life) talented and independent women like Te Ata who were recognized and acclaimed for their own achievements. Mrs. Roosevelt had known and admired Te Ata since the mid-1920s when she was working to get her career started by entertaining in the homes of well-to-do New Yorkers, such as herself. Furthermore, Mrs. Roosevelt felt it was appropriate that a lake in a region of New York that used to be Indian hunting grounds should be named after the Native American who was dedicating her life to educating the public on the beauty of her ancestors' way of life.

Mrs. Roosevelt broke the champagne bottle on a rock, and at that instant, as the water from the other lakes mixed into this body of water, Lake Te Ata was born. In writing to Clyde about the christening, Te Ata said that from afar "the people who were gathered at the lower end and up on the hills looked like a great mountainside of daisies." She said the christening was "killingly elegant" and thanked him for sending a telegram of congratulations.[6] After the christening, as the sun set on Lake Te Ata, the Chickasaw woman from Oklahoma stood by the flames from a campfire and chanted, sang, and recited stories about respecting Mother Earth.

Te Ata accepted the honor in the spirit it was given. She knew that such honors usually were bestowed on the wealthy and powerful as political tokens and that Mrs. Roosevelt could have used the occasion to reward one of her husband's New York supporters. Te Ata mentioned the honor in her promotional materials from that day forward and usually squired visitors from Oklahoma up the Hudson to see the lake. She did this not to impress her visitors but because they wanted and expected to see Lake Te Ata. She kept the honor in perspective. She did not cherish things; she cherished people.

Fisher was joined by his family in the Southwest (though Bessie is not mentioned again in his journal). Everywhere they went, Fisher

Te Ata shows her older sister, Selena, the spot where Eleanor Roosevelt christened the Bear Mountain lake after her in 1932. A year later Te Ata performed for the Roosevelt's first State Dinner in the White House. (Photo by Clyde Fisher.)

recorded the moments with his still camera and often his movie camera and then noted the subjects in his journal. He took pictures of objects, scenes, and people and carefully labeled them. He knew a story or bit of information about them all. Fisher seldom if ever took a picture spontaneously. Photography was not his hobby; it was part of his work. He also sent copies of photographs to the people pictured with a line or two reminding them where and when the photos were taken. Although this practice may have seemed like good public relations for the museum and for him, it is more likely that Fisher did this throughout his life as a gesture of thanks or kindness.

Te Ata: Chickasaw Storyteller, American Treasure

The Fishers ended their trip in California. In Los Angeles he visited the Olympic Village housing the athletes of the Tenth Olympiad, which began that day, July 30. Later he took the hero of the 1912 Olympics, Jim Thorpe, and his wife for lunch at Hollywood's famed Brown Derby; then they made a pilgrimage to the grave of Long Lance in the Inglewood Park Cemetery.[7] In New Mexico, at San Ildefonso Pueblo with his AMNH colleague Clark Wissler, Fisher shot movie and still film of Maria and Julian Martinez crafting their famous black-on-black pottery.[8] When he arrived in New York on August 26, he received a telegram from Te Ata, who was at Loon Island, asking if he could come for a visit the next weekend. After an eleven-thousand-mile trip, what was three hundred more?

๛

In the autumn, Te Ata spent a few weeks in Pittsburgh. With the help of some of her old Carnegie Tech professors, friends, and contacts, she strung together several paying engagements. She wrote to Fisher about one in particular: a large auditorium filled with about six hundred multiethnic schoolchildren, mainly from the city's slums. The stage was dark except for a spot illuminated by a shaft of amber light. When Te Ata, unannounced and unexpected, wearing her white doeskin dress, suddenly stepped into that spot, the children cried out in amazement and then burst into wild, joyful applause.

During her stay in Pittsburgh, the lovers wrote each other affectionate, newsy letters they always called "talking leaves." In closing one talking leaf in which she had encouraged Clyde to visit her in Pittsburgh, she drew a stick figure of a man carrying a suitcase and walking among skyscrapers on a path leading to an Indian woman sitting with legs crossed as the sun breaches the horizon behind her. Clyde called her his "Dawn Girl" and "Bearer of the Morning" and told her how much he missed his "glorious Indian" and how he longed for her to be with him to share the moment. No matter how tender his sentiments, however, he always signed the letters "Clyde Fisher." At some point that autumn, the esteemed scientist and educator noted a correlation between his eating pie and receiving talking leaves from Te Ata. He mentioned that on some days he was eating pie twice hoping to receive more letters from her. She teased him, writing that while they were apart she was "skeered" that he might adopt "a handsome blonde." She also reciprocated his feelings: "I can't begin to make you know how truly I appreciate the hundreds of nice things you've done for me. And I miss you dreadfully."[9]

Included in some of Te Ata's letters were checks that she asked Fisher to deposit in her account. The check amounts were substantial for the time. One was for $600 and others were for $400 and $340. Fisher congratulated her on the size of one, adding, "I almost decided to go to Sweden on it." Te Ata previously must have expressed anxiety about owing Fisher favors or a small amount of money. He wrote her, "Listen, Bearer of the Morning, you are not getting yourself in debt to me. You are as free as the air. You don't owe me anything. I do like to do things for you and with you." He called them "sacred privileges," and wrote, "May they never grow less!" In Pittsburgh she bought him a suitcase that was on sale and mailed it to him. Perhaps that gesture had given him the idea to suggest they take a cruise together in January. In early December she left Pittsburgh for Cleveland and Chicago en route to Oklahoma for the holidays. She replied that she would like to take a cruise: "But darling, I can't manage one in January—I *must* have *some* time with my Dad & Mother—besides I have two or three bookings there in January. I *want* to go in March or April— Doesn't anybody have cruises then?"[10]

She would not have the opportunity then either. Just before leaving Pittsburgh, she appended to one letter this P.S.: "I had a letter from Mrs. Franklin Roosevelt and she said she hoped to have me at the White House when she was there." Actually, Mrs. Roosevelt's note implied that an invitation would be issued: she said, "[I hope] that it will be possible for you to come to the White House."[11] Mrs. Roosevelt's note was a response to Te Ata's letter of congratulations on her husband's election to the presidency in November 1932. Of course, the Roosevelts had gotten thousands of congratulatory letters and telegrams, but very few received such a personal reply.

When Mrs. Roosevelt's invitation came, it was for an occasion that exceeded anything Te Ata could have imagined. She was invited to entertain at President Roosevelt's first official State Dinner, honoring British Prime Minister Ramsey MacDonald, on April 22. The invitation came in a roundabout way. It appears that while Te Ata was visiting her family in Oklahoma, she received a telegram from Anne Tucker, her benefactor from Three Arts Club days, asking if she would be interested in appearing at the White House. Mrs. Tucker was involved probably because it was felt that she could locate Te Ata. There was momentary excitement in the Thompson household, but because it was unseemly to demonstrate too much emotion and because Bertie was ill, everyone turned in early. Te Ata had just fallen asleep when a reporter tapped on her window, wanting an interview about her White House invitation. Apparently there had been a leak at Western Union.[12]

⤜⤚

Te Ata took the noon train to Washington. Her suitcase contained her Indian attire, an evening gown, and some overnight things. She planned to stay in a hotel and return to New York early the next morning.[13] It was an exciting trip on a beautiful spring day, which she described for Fisher in terms she knew he would appreciate: "The maple trees are uncurling their tender red leaves and the elms are a vivid yellow," and the brilliantly colored redbud "brought Oklahoma, my own stamping grounds, very close to me!" Although the train arrived late, pulling into Union Station at 5:30 P.M., a White House car, chauffeur, and footman were waiting. The car must have been recognizable because Te Ata noted how much fun the short ride was, what with people twisting their necks and staring, trying to recognize the passenger or catch a glimpse of "Mrs. Roosevelt."[14]

Te Ata was shown to the Lincoln bedroom, on the second floor near the entrance facing Pennsylvania Avenue. She wrote Fisher, "[The room] is very large. Your living room is about a fourth the size—so I have plenty of room to soar and float." Instinctively, Te Ata walked over to the great windows, and as she was marveling that she was inside looking out at the passersby, Mrs. Roosevelt arrived, extending both hands in greeting. They had tea while chatting and discussing the evening's State Dinner and program.

Unfortunately, Te Ata did not record their conversation in detail. Her description is perfunctory, giving the impression that these two great women only had a brief, business-oriented visit. But that was not Eleanor Roosevelt's style. It is more likely that in addition to the evening's details, they reminisced about the Three Arts Club, Mrs. Roosevelt's Greenwich Village apartment, and the beautiful ceremony at Lake Te Ata. As a solicitous person and a skilled interviewer, Mrs. Roosevelt would have asked Te Ata about her career. Te Ata might have asked her about her first weeks in the White House.

Te Ata noted that Mrs. Roosevelt asked her if she preferred to wear a gown or her Indian costume to the dinner. To that point, Te Ata had not known if she would be invited to attend the dinner. She had brought an evening gown just in case. Then Mrs. Roosevelt told Te Ata that if she did not have to return to New York that evening, she would be delighted to have her stay overnight. Thrilled, Te Ata said she would love to but she would have to leave early the next morning. She later told a friend that Mrs. Roosevelt's eyes twinkled in response. "Then, you must stay," said the First Lady, who excused herself to permit her guest to rest before the eight o'clock dinner.[15]

Rest? It is inconceivable that Te Ata—so energetic and imaginative and about to face the high point of her career, performing before the Roosevelts and the prime minister of Great Britain—would be able to rest in the White House bedroom of Abraham Lincoln! Perhaps to harness her thoughts or make this incredible experience more tangible, Te Ata wrote some letters on White House stationery. One was to her parents. In another, to Frances Davis, she wrote, "You made me what I am today." Regrettably, those letters have been lost. But a third letter, which she wrote to Fisher after the evening's festivities, still exists: "I wore my cream colored evening gown with the turquoise beads on the shoulders. You saw me fitted."[16]

Some sixty-three guests assembled in the Blue Room for the dinner honoring Prime Minister MacDonald and his daughter, Ishbel.[17] Among them were the president's mother, Sara Roosevelt, his son James and daughter Mrs. Anna Dall, cabinet members, Vice President John Nance Garner, selected members of Congress and the State Department, spouses, and the British ambassador to the U.S. and his wife heading several members of the official British party. Te Ata was escorted into the room by Raymond Moley, assistant secretary of state, who was one of the president's small group of advisers known as "the brain trust." Toasts to MacDonald and the president were made with glasses of water, as Prohibition was still the law of the land.

Te Ata sat between Moley and A. E. Overton, one of the prime minister's staff members, and opposite the president's mother and daughter. Soups, salads, green beans, and turkey were served on the formal White House gold service. The tables were decorated with Columbia roses and maidenhair ferns.[18] After dinner Te Ata excused herself to dress for her program. She wore her Sioux dress, white buckskin with a broad-beaded band circling the neck and shoulders, a long fringe, and little bells on the hem that tinkled delicately as she walked and danced. While she was dressing, two dancers began the evening's entertainment. Characteristically, Te Ata did not mention them; if she was not the solo performer on a program one would never know it from her correspondence. She entered the East Room, where a small, low stage had been erected. She wrote, "[It was] entirely masked on three sides by thick wood ferns. I felt as if I were seated in a sylvan dell."

Eleanor Roosevelt introduced her as "a friend of long standing." Te Ata's thirty-minute program, she later wrote, "consisted of old translations from various tribes, native legends and songs—numbers that I hoped would leave with the audience a true impression of the native people of this land." She had performed all of these numbers numerous times; this was no time to break in new material. She rendered the Chickasaw love song about the first two birds of spring, the legend of the green grass, the dance of the corn ceremony, "How Death Came into the World," and the "Song of the Old Woman Abandoned by the Tribe."

The audience presumably applauded her performance enthusiastically. But Te Ata's own accounts of the evening omit such detail. In her view, it was immodest and distasteful for her to characterize or describe an audience's appreciation of her performance. The newspaper accounts of the prime minister's visit and the State Dinner mentioned that she had performed, but nothing more.[19] After Te Ata's performance, Mrs. Roosevelt asked her to join her table for the dancers' second number. She was seated just behind the president, who turned to compliment her and thank her for her program. Later she spent fifteen minutes talking with the prime minister, who asked several questions about the history and current status of the Chickasaw people. She also talked with other members of the British party and some of Roosevelt's new cabinet officers, including Secretary of the Interior Harold Ickes, who just the day before had persuaded the president to appoint the knowledgeable and capable John Collier the new commissioner of Indian affairs.

Though Collier would soon fashion new federal Indian policy—one that would help tribes to strengthen tribal life and government—there is no evidence that Te Ata's White House appearance was intended to officially mark a new era in federal-Indian relations. If she had been invited to symbolize the government's new Indian policy, President Roosevelt would have said so and Collier would have been present. Eleanor Roosevelt invited Te Ata to entertain because she had done so before in other settings—always with excellent results. Moreover, she undoubtedly had been told of the prime minister's interest in American Indians.

At 11:30 the president and Mrs. Roosevelt went over to the door, signaling that the party was at an end. The First Lady came to Te Ata's room to thank her again and to tell her about the arrangements for her early-morning departure. Alone, Te Ata contemplated Lincoln's bed. She was sure it must have been President Lincoln's bed because it was so huge. She found she could easily lie crosswise on it. Then she spread-eagled herself on the bed trying to touch its four corners simultaneously. She could not. Unable to sleep, she wrote Fisher that the Roosevelts had been "most cordial and kind." She added, "I think I shall be invited again."[20] Her forecast was correct, but six years would pass before the second invitation came.

᭪

That Te Ata wrote to Clyde Fisher from the White House signified how important he had become to her. She had written to the people she cared for most. Fisher probably would not have made that cut through most of 1932. But sometime later that year her feelings for him—as reflected in her letters—had deepened. They had been spending much more time together in early 1933. After her White House performance, Te Ata stayed mainly in the city, with the notable exception that in June she appeared before a thousand "fashionable friends" of Ellis Gimbel at the Philmont Country Club in Philadelphia. The local newspapers mentioned that "Princess Te Ata" had performed recently at the White House, where she had been "summoned" by Mrs. Roosevelt, and in 1930 had given a "command" performance before Princess Marie Louise. She was introduced at the Gimbel party by J. Henry Scattergood, former commissioner of Indian affairs under President Herbert Hoover.[21]

It may have been at about this time that Te Ata made up her mind to marry Clyde Fisher. He had paved the way earlier in 1933 by obtaining a divorce from Bessie. It is unlikely that Fisher would have taken this step if marriage to Te Ata were not in the offing. Did Te Ata

Best friends. After their chautauqua days, Te Ata enticed Margaret Malowney to move to New York City, where they roomed together until Margaret became the wife of John Ball, left. When Te Ata asked Margaret which of three men she should marry, Margaret emphatically endorsed Clyde Fisher, second from right.

break up the marriage? Not in the sense that her friendship with Fisher disrupted the marriage; he and Bessie had been unhappy together for some time. But it is likely that as his friendship with Te Ata deepened in 1932–33 and he dared to believe that marriage to Te Ata was possible, he moved into the Explorers Club to demonstrate that he was prepared to go all the way. That summer Te Ata took the train to Bronxville, New York, to visit the Balls and ask Margaret's advice on which of three suitors she should marry. Besides Fisher, two New York lawyers were in the running, although they are not even alluded to in her papers.

More than sixty years later Margaret could not remember the lawyers' names or much about them. But she recalled Te Ata saying: "Now, Margaret, you know all three. Which one of them do you think is the best for me?" And she replied, "Tata [her pet name for Te Ata], I would rather spend a few years with Clyde than twenty years or more with either of the other two." Margaret continued: "She smiled and said she agreed with me. Those lawyers were just looking for a beautiful wife. I think either one of them would have discouraged her from continuing her career. Clyde, on the other hand, loved the fact that she was Indian and an artist. He actively promoted her career. Of course, Clyde was much older [seventeen years] than Te Ata, but that's why I answered her question the way I did."[22] A few days later Te Ata wrote that she and Clyde would be married on September 26 in Oklahoma. Margaret and John wrote individual letters on September 16 saying how thrilled they were and regretting that they could not attend. Margaret wrote: "I expected it of course but somehow it seems a great surprise anyway." And John: "You folks are the last word in surprise artistry."[23]

In her memoir Te Ata skipped the details of how and when the decision to get married was made. Instead, she wrote: "Gradually I realized that I enjoyed everything more when I was with Dr. Fisher, even simple everyday things back in the city. So we were married in the autumn of 1933." More precisely, they were married on September 28 at Bacone College in Muskogee, Oklahoma. Te Ata wanted to be married among her own people, but it was probably Ataloa's idea that the wedding should be held at Bacone. Ataloa had returned from her Columbia University studies the year before to develop at Bacone a first-class traditional Indian art department. Her ambition was large, but she had the energy, talent, and shrewdness to succeed. Having the ingenuity to realize that fund-raising and recruitment would be enhanced by a symbol that was tangible and alluring, she designed and supervised the building of a log and stone lodge where Indian students would create art and a collection of diverse Indian arts and crafts would

Te Ata: Chickasaw Storyteller, American Treasure

be on display. The fireplace and chimney, symbolizing the history and tradition of Indians, were constructed from more than five hundred types of stone gathered from tribal lands from Maine to Alaska.[24]

The lodge was mentioned prominently in every news clipping resulting from Ataloa's fund-raising trips around America. Having the wedding of Clyde Fisher and Te Ata in the lodge was also good publicity, which appeared not only in Oklahoma but also in and around New York City, where the newlyweds would be making their home. While the wedding at the lodge might have aided Ataloa's cause, Te Ata would not have agreed if she had not thought it was an appropriate site. As it was, they were married in a structure built by and for Indians amid a collection of Indian art, a few pieces of which had been donated by Te Ata. Curiously, the ceremony itself was devoid of symbols of Indian culture. Just before the ceremony began, the director of the Bacone Glee Club, Gordon Berger, sang "Beloved It Is Morn." He also led the men's glee club in "Believe Me If All Those Endearing Young Charms." Then, without attendants, Te Ata and Fisher entered to the strains of Mendelssohn's "Wedding March." Te Ata wore a "suit of dark brown crepe with fur, harmonizing accessories and a corsage of tea roses." The ceremony, held near the large stone fireplace, began as the setting sun's soft rays illuminated the hearth. The wedding vows were read by Dr. B. D. Weeks, president of the college. Te Ata became Mrs. Clyde Fisher legally, but professionally and socially she was still Te Ata.[25]

It was a relatively small wedding party, consisting mainly of Bacone faculty, including the artist Acee Blue Eagle, and Te Ata's parents.[26] Apparently none of Te Ata's siblings were present. They were not listed as guests in the newspaper accounts or included in any of the pictures taken that day by Clyde Fisher. According to Te Ata's niece and Avis's daughter, Helen Cole, the family members surely were invited but were probably unable to attend. "This was the depression and everybody was struggling," Cole said. "I imagine Te Ata hoped they could come but didn't expect them."[27] The other noteworthy absence was Frances Davis. Undoubtedly, she must have been ill or far away. Te Ata was a bit anxious about how her father would handle this new and unexpected development in her life. He, who had repeatedly preached to his children that white people cannot be trusted, had gotten dolled

Wedding day at the Ataloa Lodge, Bacone (Indian) College, Muskogee, Oklahoma. After the wedding, Clyde returned to New York while Te Ata stayed in Oklahoma to fulfill professional engagements. It was a preview of the next sixteen years of their married life.

up in his best clothes to witness his daughter marrying a white man, one old enough to be her father.

After the wedding Ataloa hosted a buffet supper. At one point Te Ata noticed Fisher and her father sitting together "in intense silence."

Te Ata: Chickasaw Storyteller, American Treasure

Although Fisher was a sterling conversationalist, he apparently could not pry loose Thompson, who had no knack or liking for small talk. After she chided them about their "sparkling conversation," they both smiled. The ice cracked a bit, especially after Thompson realized that he "was not being properly hospitable."[28] Fisher took several photographs of Te Ata and her parents on that day and Thompson appears to be both pleased and proud.

A newspaper article had the newlyweds leaving town the next day for a short trip through the Ozarks on their way back home. But according to correspondence, it seems that Fisher returned to New York and Te Ata stayed in Oklahoma to help her parents move and to fulfill other program commitments. Their wedding had been sandwiched into their busy schedules. When Te Ata finally left Oklahoma City, she was heading to Pittsburgh, where she would be performing for several days. A proper honeymoon would have to wait.

While apart, they usually wrote each other several times a week.[29] In his first letter to his new wife, Fisher referred to her as his "Scarlet Tanager" (a bird with brilliant plumage) and said that he had mistakenly called a friend "Te Ata twice this evening" to show "how far gone" he was. The contents alternated between news, comments, and outpourings of affection and passion. "I loved the last paragraph of the last letter you wrote me before our wedding day. Dearest person! Intense One! Lovely Indian! How fortunate I am! Yesterday I sent you a little poem by Christina Rosetti, to tell you so." Showing that old habits are indeed hard to break, Fisher was still signing his talking leaves to his new wife, "Clyde Fisher." Occasionally, he signed "C.F." or used his Sioux name, Mato-Kokipapi.[30]

In his second letter, Fisher wrote, "I don't want to give anyone reason to say,—after observing us in the coming years,—'They're married. I can pick out a great many of them, and so can you,'—but let us fool them! Can we?" [31] Te Ata agreed, noting that she wanted "desperately to make a grand success of it [the marriage]." She reminded (the recently divorced) Fisher that they should not forget that marriage is a business and must be worked at—very hard. "Can we remember to always be nice to each other? Will we remember all the things that so pleased us in the other? Yes, let's try."[32]

Te Ata stayed longer in Oklahoma than she had intended because her mother had become quite ill. Bertie had eaten "practically nothing" for a week and was very weak. At 64, having lived the hard life of a frontier woman, Bertie was breaking down physically. Fortunately for her parents, Te Ata was almost totally supporting them, although Bertie still did occasional odd jobs for neighbors to supplement Te Ata's checks. Fisher's mother, still living in the family's farmhouse in Sidney, Ohio, was also not well, suffering from dementia.

Under the sponsorship of the Henry Clay Frick Foundation, Te Ata presented programs at several Pittsburgh high schools. During that week, a newspaper article emphasized the radical or at least unpopular idea of a married woman having a career traveling about the nation. "Surely, I'm going to keep up my work. I wouldn't think of dropping it, and settling down to keeping house," she said from her room at the Fort Pitt Hotel. "My husband is intensely interested in my work and wouldn't dream of having me give it up just because I happen to have 'Mrs.' engraved on my calling card. I'm keeping my Indian name, too, for my professional work." As she talked, she tidied up the room, "folding a white buckskin dress covered with colored beads and gathered up two quills for her hair, a pair of beaded leggings and moccasins." Her "tidying up" probably was done for effect, preceding this comment: "You see, I have some housewifey instincts."[33]

Of her career, she said she wanted to entertain and educate. She explained that the majority of Americans are "vastly ignorant" about Indians and that through her carefully crafted programs she was "trying to show white people something of Indian womanhood and traditions." She said people often told her that they had met Indians before, but not like her—an observation that was at once obtuse and true. She said that she particularly enjoyed performing in England. "The English are more like Indians. They take their time in trying to know you. They have a dignified reticence that is characteristic of my own people. In New York, the people are more inclined to make a big fuss over you—and then drop you."

Te Ata was clothed, as she often was for such occasions, in a fashion that she had modified to signify her Indian heritage. The Eton jacket of her Spanish tile wool suit was bordered with Indian embroidery. "The princess looks much like any other successful young business woman—prettier and much more vivid than many," the reporter wrote. "Her eyes are black and her skin has a deep olive hue."[34] Vain about her age, Te Ata either said or gave the impression that she was in her early thirties. She looked younger than her nearly 38 years, but the publicity photo she was using was taken when she was in her midtwenties.

⋙

There is no record of when Te Ata and Clyde moved into their apartment at 41 W. 72d Street. Logically, Clyde would have moved out of the Explorers Club and into the apartment before their wedding, with Te Ata joining him on her return. They may have lived together before the wedding, but it is doubtful because they both had been traveling (especially Te Ata) a lot since they had decided to get married. Personal morality probably would not have precluded them from setting up housekeeping before the wedding. And it would scarcely have raised any eyebrows among their metropolitan circle of friends. But there is no evidence that this was the case.

Their three-room apartment was small. Its location, just a few blocks from the museum, and its size were selected for practical reasons. They needed to hold down their expenses because they were both supporting other family members. Moreover, a small place might discourage guests from staying too long, and one or both of them were often away from home. They had separate checking and savings accounts. In one 1934 letter, Te Ata asked Fisher if he could put $75 in her checking account; she would pay him back either from her savings or after she got paid for another program. She told him, "[Do not] embarrass yourself to do this for I understand that you are buying a car and will need available cash."[35]

No letters or records from this time mention long-range career plans for Te Ata. But it is likely that by then she planned to be on the road intermittently in different regions of America. Fisher also had a certain amount of traveling to do on museum business, and he could supplement his income with lectures arranged through his agent. Some of those elective trips to universities and other scholarly settings could be arranged in conjunction with Te Ata's schedule. Their extended transcontinental honeymoon planned for summer 1934 would include a few paying jobs along the way.

As soon as she returned to New York, Te Ata began furnishing and decorating their apartment in a Native American motif. The major drawback to their small apartment was lack of space for displaying and storing the Indian artifacts they liked to collect and Fisher's extensive and ever-multiplying collection of books. She was just starting on the project when she learned that her mother had suffered a heart attack while on a trip.[36] Although the doctor apparently did not think she would survive and said that her family should be notified, Bertie refused to let the telegrams be sent or to die. Later Thompson sent Te Ata a letter announcing that Bertie had had "an actack [*sic*] of the heart" but that she did not want any wires sent unless she died. She did not want anyone "paying two or 3 fares [to visit her] when one would do [to attend her funeral]. She looks ten years older than when she left." He teased about his last observation, saying he would be sure to avoid the same trip if it accelerates the aging process that much.[37] Whatever Bertie experienced, whether it was a mild heart attack or angina, she began taking digitalis, a heart stimulant. She lived another seven years, experiencing periodic spells and attacks of one kind or another. Despite Te Ata's entreaties to her mother to take things easy, Bertie continued quilting and working, telling her husband she was "not afraid of Te Ata," as "she is too far away."[38]

Attending a scientific meeting in Boston after Christmas, Fisher poured out his heart on paper, not just once but twice in one day. In one, addressed to "Toad of Toad Hall," he trumpeted again about his good fortune: "How I wish you were here! Te Ata, my Dawn Girl, you are a grand and gorgeous person. I am grateful from my heart for Te Ata. I can see you, living embodiment of grace, dancing around our Christmas tree. My tenderest love to you, my Indian!"[39]

CHAPTER 8

Coast-to-Coast Honeymoon

In January 1934 it was announced that a New York banker, Charles Hayden, had donated $150,000 toward the development of a planetarium at the American Museum of Natural History. The donation would pay for, among other things, the Zeiss projector.[1] Groundbreaking ceremonies were held in May. As curator of astronomy and education, Fisher was to work closely with the architects of the two-story structure and supervise the installation of the scientific equipment.[2]

Sandwiched in between, Fisher departed for a lecture tour of the Midwest. Feeling lonesome and sentimental, Te Ata wrote a poem for her husband and mailed it to him. (Unfortunately, the letter has been lost.) He, in turn, sent her a dozen Hollywood red roses. Then, because he had never sent flowers before, he worried that they might not make it, so he sent her a letter explaining step-by-step what he had done. His inscription was to "My Indian Poet."[3] Te Ata received the roses but told her friend Mildred Powell that she could not imagine who had sent them. Mildred guessed, "Your husband," but Te Ata said she doubted it. She was chastened to admit this to him later in a letter.[4] He said he did not blame her a bit for doubting that he had sent the flowers. "Just so you didn't have heart failure," he wrote. "I know it was a dangerous thing for a sober, serious, literal scientist to do. But it came out so well that I may do it again—sometime."

During his two-week absence, Te Ata's letters were full of descriptions of her gadding, as she called making the social rounds:

lunches, dinners, lectures, shows. Once she impulsively invited her wealthy benefactor and friend, Anne Tucker, for lunch. "Pray for me!" she wrote anxiously to Fisher. For added security, she asked Margaret Ball to come early to help out. She teased Fisher that since none of her old beaus had called her lately, she reckoned she would still be on hand when he returned.[5]

In Kansas City Fisher spoke to the Woman's City Club and mentioned Te Ata to the club's president, who asked to receive her publicity mailing. Fisher warned his wife, "[Don't] go for $50.00. My manager should never have sold me for that." After her lunch for Anne Tucker, which seemed to have gone well, Kuruks Pahetu called to say his father was in town and wanted to meet her. She asked them to stay to dinner, and though she was not much of a cook, she said she could always whip up bacon and eggs, which she knew "an old Injun would like." She said she could not pronounce the father's Pawnee name, but its delightful English translation was: "He Who Always Has a Good Day." A package arrived the next day for her from Stern's Department Store. It was a "very very red clock [with] faces on both sides and very modernistic and electric, and very nice." It was from Anne Tucker.[6] In another talking leaf, titled "Injun girl talks," Te Ata wrote a lyrical narrative of longing for her husband: "The tipi seems empty with no chief smoking by the fire; the pot of *pashofa* gets smaller and smaller; winter is still around us; and the wind sings a cold haunting song around my tipi. When will the warm days come and the geese come again to tell us it is Spring? I am waiting for the time of growing things and for the warmth of the Sun god and the call of my chief. Ugh! I have said it!"[7]

Throughout their marriage, their talking leaves were similar in tone and content. Interspersed among their comings and goings and the business matters of married couples were sweet sentiments, teasing, and pet names. They almost always enclosed clippings of interest or oddities in the news, such as the following from the *New York Times* that Te Ata sent in April 1934. A letter from Will Rogers, writing from his Santa Monica spread, noted that President Roosevelt invited his 1904 Harvard graduating class to the White House. "There was over 300 of 'em and all Republicans. I think he was just quietly rubbing it in on 'em, for the press couldn't name a one of 'em that anybody had ever heard of. I think F.D., with his usual sense of humor, was just in

Te Ata: Chickasaw Storyteller, American Treasure

a subtle way impressing on the boys, 'If there hadn't been a Democrat in the class, youse guys would never have got to even see the inside of the White House.'" A second clipping reported that Indians who lived near La Paz, Bolivia, had received a group of white Bolivian officers in a most unconventional way. To show their opposition to government war policies, the Indians killed and later ceremoniously consumed them.[8]

When possible, Te Ata continued to purchase Indian arts, crafts, and artifacts from Reese Kincaide, manager of the Mohonk Lodge in the tiny town of Colony, Oklahoma. In March 1934 he wrote to thank her for an order and to say that Commissioner of Indian Affairs Collier had appeared at a recent council of some two thousand Indians at Anadarko, Oklahoma. He wanted their support for the Wheeler-Howard Bill, which he had authored as a revolutionary change in the federal government's Indian policy. The bill, introduced in Congress in February 1934, would abolish the assimilationist allotment policy and reverse the ebbing of tribal authority by using government aid to strengthen tribal life and government. Because of significant opposition in Congress and within some tribes, Collier had been conducting a series of Indian congresses at which the bill was openly and thoroughly discussed.[9]

According to Kincaide, Collier received little support in Anadarko: "They [the Indians] said they did not want to live like old time Indians and be restricted on reservations, but that they wish to go forward and live like their white neighbors. It was a most interesting experience, and gave me great respect for them as I saw full bloods intelligently fighting for what they thought was better than the old tribal reservations. I know you would have enjoyed it immensely, and wish you could have been there."[10]

In spring and summer 1934 Te Ata and Clyde were working on their honeymoon itinerary in earnest, though their work kept them apart for most of that time. They both continued to solicit paying engagements in appropriate locations along their proposed trail. In June Te Ata typed Clyde a long letter and for once dealt almost exclusively with one topic: the business aspects of their honeymoon trip. From the number of typos and words inadvertently omitted from sentences, evidently her mind was racing faster than her fingers.[11] She suggested that he write to San Ildefonso Pueblo in New Mexico and offer to pay $10 to film the Eagle Dance. She also wanted Eagle Dance lessons and said it would cost $5. Reminding him that they would not have enough money to film everything they wanted, she thought they should hold some money back to pay for filming dances they might encounter on their trip. She apparently thought Clyde needed some coaxing on negotiating travel expenses with the museum. The museum's education department might pay for the films, she reminded him. As for buying a car, she wondered if the dealership would cut Fisher a better deal if they knew who he was and that it would be good advertising for them if he were driving their model while representing the AMNH on this cross-country car trip.

"Talk yourself up," Te Ata advised him. People like "Anne Morgan and many actors and actresses" use products free just to be seen using them. "Wish I were there to help you out." (One can imagine the scene: the dignified white-haired scientist standing slightly behind the doeskin-clad Indian maiden wheeling and dealing with the car salesman.) While Te Ata was at it, she advised that he should tell Wayne Faunce, AMNH executive secretary, that the museum "should pay [his] expenses to the coast to investigate the new planetarium there [Griffith Observatory in Los Angeles]." She continued: "tell him you cannot go further than Santa Fe [without additional expense money]. I rather believe that he will see the importance of it." She closed by saying how excited she was getting and thanking him for his many letters. "[They] bring me closer to you. For I must admit that some-times I feel like it [the marriage] is all a dream."[12]

Few newlyweds in 1934 had honeymoons comparable to Te Ata and Clyde's twelve-thousand-mile, ten-week transcontinental passage. From New York they traveled through the Midwest, the Dakota bad-lands, and the deserts of New Mexico and Arizona to California. From Los Angeles they retraced their steps, except for the badlands. Their trip got off to a much-publicized start. The museum had sent out press releases, playing up the intriguing contrast between the distin-guished scientist and his Indian artist bride. Photos in several New York papers showed them in front of the museum posing side-by-side: Fisher, looking every bit the scholar in wire-rim spectacles and a dark three-piece suit, set off by his corona of white hair; Te Ata, wearing a buckskin dress, a beaded headband and moccasins, her long raven hair parted in the middle and hanging in two braids pulled forward. In one photo, Te Ata had a striking Navajo rug draped over her shoulders while Fisher sported a canvas travel bag. In a *New York Times* photo, the museum's president, F. Trubee Davison, was bidding the couple good-bye. As soon as the photographers had departed, Fisher and Te Ata slipped back into the museum to change into more comfortable travel clothing and set off in their new car, a Pontiac. Te Ata named it Miko, Chickasaw for "leader" or "king."

The stories run by the New York press were replete with the racial and cultural errors, stereotypes, and crudeness of the time. The lead of the *New York Sun* is representative: "Sioux and Chickasaw Indian, burying the hatchet of past scalpings and the like, started out together on a 12,000-mile honeymoon trip from the Museum of Natural History today." The reporter explained that Clyde Fisher had been adopted by the Sioux tribe. The reporter went on to opine that Te Ata was "really a princess, that is, she has the same right to the title, and more, than most of the Indian Princesses that abound these days." However, the reporter noted that Te Ata did not like to use the title because "there are about as many Indian Princesses as beds that George Washington slept in."[13] Actually, Te Ata seemed ambivalent about the title. She used it in some promotional brochures and press releases and only rarely corrected reporters who addressed her as princess during interviews. But she never introduced herself as a princess and would sometimes mark out the title in newspaper clippings that she saved. It is unlikely that she initiated the title, although it may have been the idea of Frances Davis. Often "princess" was bestowed on her by the press in keeping with a widespread stereotype.

Fisher kept a daily diary of the honeymoon.[14] Like his other travel diaries, it was unfailingly prosaic, factual, and succinct. He faithfully recorded their locations, a summary or listing of some of their activities, who they met, and the number of miles driven every day even if zero. It is the diary of a well-disciplined mind with a need for order. Although Fisher referred to the trip as a honeymoon, his diary contains virtually no romantic sentiments. In marked contrast are the two surviving pages of Te Ata's diary, dated July 13 and July 14, that turned up inexplicably at the end of Fisher's diary. In contrast to Fisher's terse objective account, her version contains considerable information and opinion. Te Ata described the northern Illinois countryside, "rolling hills" and "great fields of red clover, corn, alfalfa," and the growing impression "of the natural world's freshness and cleanliness" as opposed to the "dirt and smelliness and ugliness of man's world." She also wrote that when they arrived at the Stevens Hotel in Chicago, a beautiful bouquet of flowers was in their room, compliments of the hotel's owner.

≈

After their big send-off at the museum, Fisher, the archetypal absent-minded academic, apparently had forgotten to gas up the Pontiac, and they sputtered to an unscheduled stop somewhere on the eighty-mile stretch to Bear Mountain. They had a late lunch at the Bear Mountain Inn, the management of which entrusted $500 to Te Ata to purchase Indian blankets for the inn on their trip. She and Jolly had been discussing this; Te Ata wanted to buy the rugs "to indirectly help the Indians, certain traders and to make the inn more beautiful." With her own money, she wanted to buy a rug for Jolly, one for Mona Woodring, and a few for herself that she could mark up and sell from time to time when money was tight.[15] They departed via Lake Te Ata and headed west toward the American mother of honeymoon havens: Niagara Falls. From there they drove to Detroit to visit Fisher's brother Otto, a surgeon. After they lunched at the Detroit Yacht Club, Clyde and Miko took a boat across Lake Michigan to deliver a lecture in Milwaukee. He then drove to Chicago to be reunited with Te Ata, who earlier had appeared at Buffalo State Teacher's College.

They spent the next two days in Wisconsin, visiting the Yerkes Observatory and the wild rice fields in and around Clam Lake. A foot above the water level in July, the rice would be harvested in September by Indians who would then commence the rice dancing celebrations. They visited a camp of Chippewas, living much as they had for ages in dome-shaped structures covered with birch bark and walled with mats of cattails. Mrs. Green Sky showed them how she prepared the splits from black ash for baskets and gave Te Ata a birch-bark jar. Later Te Ata presented programs at colleges in Duluth, Minnesota and Superior, Wisconsin.

On July 11 they drove back into Minnesota to visit the pipestone quarries, a source of Indian legends and the site where Indians laboriously and meticulously quarried the red and pink clay they used in making ceremonial pipes. According to a Sioux legend, the Great Spirit

Te Ata: Chickasaw Storyteller, American Treasure

created human beings out of the pipestone. In another legend, the Great Spirit, saddened by intertribal warfare, called all Indian nations together and they met on a battleground stained red with blood. From a red rock, the Great Spirit fashioned a sacred pipe; he told them to smoke the pipe only as a pledge of peace.[16] Fisher took several photos of Te Ata wearing a buckskin dress, striking various poses by the quarries.[17] He noted that the material was called Catlinite after the artist George Catlin, who in 1837 was the first white man to see the quarries. Fisher did not say what the Indians called the clay, but it probably was not Catlinite. Te Ata would have been more sensitive to such distinctions, making the absence of her presumed diary all the more regrettable. Also lost to history are her descriptions on the long honeymoon of her encounters with tribal people—at a time when she was especially active collecting and processing folklore and songs from living sources. Fisher cannot be faulted for not describing these meetings, nor can it be inferred that he was disinterested. On the contrary, for a white man who had never lived among Indians and who was neither a historian nor an anthropologist, he was very knowledgable about and interested in Native Americans. He recorded these visits in his own way, on film, which subsequently would activate his remarkable memory, so that he could virtually adlib what seemed like a polished lecture.

On July 17 they arrived at Te Ata's parents' home in Oklahoma City and traveled around the state until July 28.[18] Coming almost directly from the encampments of the Chippewas and other northern tribes, the contrast between them and Te Ata's more assimilated tribe, the Chickasaws, was stark. Simultaneously, as Collier's appearance in Anadarko had demonstrated, a great debate was sweeping through Indian country about the federal government's Indian policy.

In the 1930s, the Chickasaws who remained living within their former nation were widely dispersed. While many managed to eke out a meager existence on their allotments, others had sold their land or been swindled out of it and moved into larger towns such as Ada, Tishomingo, Sulphur, Pauls Valley, and Ardmore. If Clyde Fisher had asked Te Ata to take him to a place where tribal members congregate, she probably could not have done it. The closest approximation would have been an Indian church, where they could have heard the congregation sing in Chickasaw or Choctaw or some combination of both. But the melodies would have been familiar to Fisher, Christian hymns such as "The Old Rugged Cross" or "Amazing Grace." Traditional tribal songs and ways had almost died out. Stickball games and stomp dances, held only rarely, were mainly memories to the elders.[19]

At Tishomingo Clyde was introduced to Te Ata's relatives, friends, and former neighbors. While this experience enlivened and personalized the small town for him, what he observed there must have underscored the fact that it was the *former* capital of the *former* Chickasaw Nation. Except for the distinctive pink granite building on the hill, Tishomingo looked like any other depression-era town. That building with the tall, narrow cupola was the tribe's former capitol building. It was completed in late 1898, after the fate of the Chickasaw Nation had been sealed a few months earlier with the passage of the Curtis Act. A greatly emasculated tribal government functioned off and on in the capitol building until 1907; a year later, the building was sold to Johnston County (named after Douglas Johnston) to use as its courthouse for $7,500, about one-third of its original cost. In 1934 the building could symbolize the death of the Chickasaw Nation. But most Chickasaws seemed proud of it; from their perspective, it was a monument to a tribe that was once "unconquered and unconquerable," as many of them liked to say.[20]

Since statehood in 1907, the Chickasaw government had consisted of a single caretaker and an attorney, both paid from tribal funds generated by a small amount of royalties from coal leases owned jointly by the Chickasaws and Choctaws. The Chickasaw caretaker was still Governor Johnston (Te Ata's "Uncle Doug"), though the title was little more than a remnant from the era before land allotments. Johnston had been appointed and reappointed governor by the president ever since 1906 because the Chickasaw and Choctaw Nations could not be liquidated completely until their hundreds of thousands of acres of mineral land had been sold.[21]

Johnston and the Choctaw leadership had been working since 1902 to sell the mineral lands, but any sale had to be sanctioned by the federal government and ratified by both tribes. Despite the annual efforts of Oklahoma congressmen Charles Carter and Wilburn Cartwright—responding to numerous letters from Chickasaws and

The distinctive, stately building that the Chickasaw Nation built in Tishomingo in 1898 served as its capitol until 1907. The figure in the picture is Te
Ata's father, Thomas Thompson, who once had an office in the pink granite
building. (Photo by Clyde Fisher.)

Choctaws urging Congress to buy or sell the lands—only small tracts
had been sold.[22] The administration in power thought the appraised
value was too high, while most rank-and-file Chickasaws felt the
appraisal was too low. In the 1920s, the coal market was depressed;
in the 1930s, the entire nation was depressed. At a time when millions
of Americans were out of work, queuing up in breadlines and at soup
kitchens, the notion of Congress paying millions of dollars to two tribes
for their coal and asphalt lands was out of the question politically.[23]

Furthermore, in 1933–34 Collier was proposing his own New Deal for tribes via the Wheeler-Howard Act. Instead of continuing to assimilate Indians into American society, the government would assist tribes to revitalize politically and culturally. Instead of selling their remaining lands, willing tribes would be assisted to buy lands and establish businesses, control their own trust funds, and establish cooperatively conducted Indian communities.[24] Speaking to a group of Chickasaws at Seeley Chapel [25] in September 1934, Governor Johnston praised the bill: "The general plans and policies meet my complete approval."[26] Not so, the Oklahoma congressional delegation, and the bill was amended by Senator Elmer Thomas to exempt Oklahoma-based Indians from the act. Thomas was reacting to a fear that Oklahoma would lose significant tax revenue because Indian lands and businesses would be tax exempt.[27] Nevertheless, the Chickasaws at Seeley Chapel voted their approval of the legislation, which had been dubbed the Indian Recovery Act (IRA).[28]

Simultaneously, Governor Johnston was still receiving mail from Chickasaws imploring him to sell the mineral land. A few of these correspondents were relatively well off and educated, but many were completely destitute and in their desperation were susceptible to believing the wild, unfounded rumors that circulated thereabouts: the government was hoarding millions of dollars belonging to the tribes, and the tribes' mineral lands were worth at least $100 million.[29] These people wanted the immediate release of the funds to tribal members. Johnston replied to one and all that the tribes had only tens of thousands of dollars in their trust accounts. If they were liquidated, each tribal member would receive less than $10. Furthermore, the prospects were not good for selling the mineral lands at any price in the foreseeable future.

There is no record of Te Ata communicating with Johnston about per capita payments or political matters, such as the IRA. According to Fisher's diary, Te Ata discussed the IRA with the trader Reese Kincaide. Fisher did not record their conversation, but there is little doubt that Te Ata supported the federal government's new Indian policy. How could she not support the initiative to restore tribal sovereignty and pride? Not as important, but probably still a factor, was the fact that she was a Democrat, like her father, and admired Franklin and Eleanor Roosevelt. She was not, however, a political activist; she was temperamentally unsuited to participating in prolonged political discussions, which she said gave her headaches or made her gloomy, much less engaging in the rough and tumble of political action. She was an artist, and she felt that artists were obliged to practice their art.

≈

During their eleven-day stay in Oklahoma, Te Ata and Clyde helped to move her parents from Oklahoma City to Norman, where their grandson, Hiawatha, sixteen, would be enrolling at the University of Oklahoma.[30] Although Hi, clever and industrious, would be working his way through college, Te Ata would pay his tuition and fees—in addition to supporting her parents. It was the Indian way; whomever could help family members in need was obliged to do so. And of all the Thompson siblings, Te Ata apparently was the only one at this time who could afford it. Hi's mother, Gladys, was living in Omaha with her third husband, Thomas Rogers. In about 1928, after she had been married to Rogers for a few years, Gladys told her parents that she wanted Hiawatha to live with them. The boy refused. He was attached to his grandparents, who showered him with love and affection. And Gladys had always been physically detached and emotionally remote. Moreover, her paranoia was getting worse; she was writing letters home accusing various people in Omaha of stealing from her, when in fact she and Rogers had little or nothing of value to steal.[31]

Meanwhile, the good-natured Fisher photographed the family as the entourage drove around the old Chickasaw Nation. Though he, with his intellectual bent, professorial looks, and courtly ways, must have seemed exotic to some of Te Ata's relatives, they liked him. They saw how good he was to Te Ata, and the couple's mutual affection was evident. Furthermore, Fisher, with his warm personality and conversational skills, was able to put them at ease, even the reserved and skeptical Thomas Thompson. Hiawatha was "almost in awe" of Fisher after the scientist had explained to him on just the right level how volcanoes work. Fisher also displayed his love and understanding of nature, sometimes almost to a fault. Hi remembered once when Fisher was driving the family somewhere and became so absorbed trying to identify a bird from its whistle that he ran off the road.[32]

The couple resumed their honeymoon trip, heading west on U.S. 66, enjoying simple pleasures. Near Tucumcari, New Mexico, they stopped to have dinner by the side of the road, next to a prairie dog town; at twilight their picnic was accompanied by the hooting of a burrowing owl.[33] After he delivered two lectures at a university in Las Vegas, New Mexico, Fisher was abruptly called back to New York on "Planetarium matters." He left on the train at 1:35 A.M. and reached Grand Central Station two days later. After a day of meetings, he boarded a train to return to New Mexico. On the way he stopped in Chicago to visit his friends, Maria and Julian Martinez, the famous San Ildefonso Pueblo potters, who were at the World's Fair, making and selling their pottery. Such was their star power that they had free housing and the promise that they could keep all the money from their sales. Fisher also stopped by the fair's Hall of Science and learned that some of his own sound movies were being shown there daily. Learning that one of his films was about to be shown, Fisher delivered an impromptu introduction to the audience. On August 4 he left Chicago at 11:35 P.M. "for the Southwest and Te Ata."[34]

His train was met on August 6 by Te Ata and Ataloa, who had been shopping in the Santa Fe area for bargains on distinctive Indian arts and crafts. Ataloa's aim was to furnish the Bacone College art lodge with Indian artifacts from as many tribes as possible, and she had, at various times in recent years, enlisted the help of her "cousin," Te Ata.[35] The Chickasaw women whisked Fisher away to Seton Village, where at the College of Indian Wisdom he delivered a lecture titled "Earth and Neighbor Worlds." Reunited, he and Te Ata spent the next two days talking at length with their host, Ernest Thompson Seton, and Tony Luhan, a Taos Indian whose home near Taos with his wife, Mabel Dodge Luhan, was a mecca for artists and writers such as Georgia O'Keefe, Edward Weston, Ansel Adams, and D. H. Lawrence. The Luhan home also attracted intellectuals and activists in Indian affairs like John Collier, who during his first visit in 1921 decided to dedicate his life to preserving and strengthening the nation's Native American heritage. Following a long conversation with Seton, Fisher wrote that his friend "is a rare genius,—a combination of naturalist, artist and story-teller. His grasp of world history and especially the history of the American Indians is amazing."

On August 8 Fisher and Te Ata drove to the San Ildefonso Pueblo to photograph and film the Eagle Dance and Suzanne Aguilar grinding corn and then preparing and baking paper bread from blue-corn meal. Two days later they were driving through the Painted Desert

Te Ata: Chickasaw Storyteller, American Treasure

On Te Ata and Clyde's 1934 honeymoon, they visited friends from coast to coast, including one of the world's greatest athletes, Jim Thorpe, in Los Angeles. Their link had been Long Lance. Later they visited Long Lance's grave in Los Angeles. (Photo by Clyde Fisher.)

and the Petrified Forest. Fisher took a gorgeous black-and-white photo of Te Ata leaning against a giant petrified tree trunk; she was looking off into the distance against a backdrop of the desert floor dotted with plants and a deep, rich sky decorated with billowing cumulus clouds.[36]

They spent six days on the California coast, mainly in Los Angeles and Santa Barbara, where Fisher had more lectures scheduled. They were wined and dined by their hosts and visited the Franciscan mission that was first erected in 1786 and for a time was home to the Chumash Indians. In a visit to Jim Thorpe's home in Los Angeles, C.F. took photos of Thorpe's sons, Philip, 7, Billy, 6, and Dicky, 20 months. They also called at the Beverly Hills "palatial home" of movie tough guy Edward G. Robinson and found only his wife, Gladys, at home. How they had become acquainted is unknown, but Gladys invited them to return two nights later when "Eddie" could join them. On August 17 the two couples had a "fine visit." That was all Fisher recorded, except to note that he and Te Ata went later to see Robinson's latest movie, *The Man with Two Faces*.

A day and a half later they were standing on the rim of the Grand Canyon. Fisher took some dramatic photographs of Te Ata standing perilously close to the edge of the abyss, at Navajo Point. They spent two days at the canyon driving to the best vistas and descending by mule on the Bright Angel Trail to the Colorado River. Then they drove to Cameron, where Te Ata bought four Navajo rugs at the Little Colorado Trading Post, and from Flagstaff, they drove northeast to the Hopi Reservation. They spent three and a half days driving up and down the mesas both for the views and to witness Hopi dances. On Mishongovi Mesa they saw the Butterfly Dance, performed by fifty dancers, fifteen singers, and a drummer. A crier announced the Flute Ceremony would be held on Walpi Mesa the next day at sunrise. They attended that and witnessed a Snake Dance at Hotevilla.

Instead of descriptions, Fisher made lists, but what his journal lacked in detail he made up for by taking well-composed, well-lighted photographs. He took a photograph of Te Ata standing tall and statuesque in a Hopi cornfield with Walpi Mesa just visible in the distance. She was wearing a bandanna and a sleeveless white dress that accentuated her slenderness and dark skin. The cornfield was set off by a sky of immense cumulonimbus clouds, gray with white crests. Fisher also photographed Te Ata standing by a Hopi basket she had evidently bought (or hoped to buy) at Tom Pavatea's chocka-block stone trading post. Te Ata and the basket were framed by the proprietor's name in large letters across a ten-foot-long sign hung above the front door.[37]

Te Ata claims a beautiful basket in Hopi country. She probably spent too much of her money on such treasures, usually as performance accouterments and gifts for friends. Photo by Clyde Fisher. Courtesy Dept. of Library Services, American Museum of Natural History, neg. no. 282776.

They spent the last week of August at the annual Indian ceremonial dances at Gallup, New Mexico. Fisher shot movie film of the Navajo Fire Dance, the Apache Devil Dance, and the San Ildefonso Eagle Dance (again). On September 1 they headed east to visit Te Ata's

John V. Satterlee with Te Ata. Satterlee, eighty-two, was a Menominee who hosted Te Ata and Fisher during their visit in Wisconsin. While visiting tribes, Te Ata would seek out the keepers of the tribal folklore and adapt some of the stories for her repertoire. Photo by Clyde Fisher. Courtesy Dept. of Library Services, American Museum of Natural History, neg. no. 284212.

parents in Norman. They made two other stops in Oklahoma, to pay respects to Kuruks Pahetu's father, He Who Always Has a Good Day, and to the writer-historian Joseph Matthews, a Rhodes scholar and Osage tribal council member. On September 5 they arrived at Clyde's mother's house in Sidney. After visiting with her and two of Clyde's sisters, he and Te Ata drove to Circleville, Ohio, to see the immense Logan Elm, sixty-five feet high with a foliage spread of one hundred eighty feet. The tree was named for the Mingo tribe's Chief Logan, who delivered an eloquent and anguished address under its branches in 1774 about the relationship of Indians and whites. Earlier that year in an unprovoked massacre by British soldiers, his family had been wiped out. After a rampage of revenge, Logan accepted peace terms and made his famous address.

The trip had been part pleasure and part business, and sometimes the two blurred together. Along the way contacts were made and promotional material was left behind. Te Ata and Fisher visited several Indian reservations and settlements to observe, record, or participate in cultural activities of one kind or another. Some of these contacts had been made by Te Ata through tribal members, and some were made by C.F. through his fellow academics who had tribal friends. The evidence indicates that virtually all of these encounters were friendly and respectful despite the outward differences in the visitors and the visited. Many of the Pueblo and reservation Indians were living lives that were in many respects similar to their ancestors of the nineteenth century. Imagine the reaction by these Indians to the glamorous Chickasaw and her white, erudite husband arriving in their Pontiac. Did she perform for them? Undoubtedly she did to repay them for their hospitality and perhaps to prove herself worthy of their attention. Even if some of them did not understand her words, they responded to the magic in her voice and hands, her sublime poses and range of expressions—from unbridled joy to blanketing sorrow. Such was her emotional power that she could touch even those whose embers of tribal spirit were nearly extinguished. After she had won a measure of respect or at least sparked curiosity, she might ask to speak with some elders. If there was time and they were so inclined, they would share some stories with her. Thus was her knowledge and repertoire enhanced.

CHAPTER 9

Talking Leaves and Repertoire Building

Te Ata headed west again in the Pontiac, Miko, in January 1935. She spent a week in Chicago rehearsing, performing, and being squired around by her friends and sponsors. Beautiful, exotic, with excellent social skills, she was much in demand, and when she was on the road her appointment calendar was nearly always full. She either had a hard time declining invitations or thought that a lunch here and a dinner there might well lead to more bookings in the future. She also would not pass up time with the local press, a source of free publicity. On the road she often sacrificed her need for solitude, the source of emotional and spiritual refreshment. And she missed C.F. and told him so in almost every letter. She ended one long, chatty letter in a way that was as sexually explicit as she ever got: "Bad man. I wish you were here and I would be *real mean* to you—'cause I feel mighty mean, you know—do all the things that you like."[1]

After Chicago she may have been intending to return to New York. But at some point, she learned that her mother's health had taken another turn for the worse, and she set off in the dead of winter for Omaha. Some of the roads were so icy and treacherous that at times she slowed to less than ten miles per hour. She was forced to stop in Des Moines and boarded with a family until the weather improved.[2] She arrived in Omaha to visit her sister, Gladys, who insisted that she and her husband, Tom Rogers, accompany Te Ata to Oklahoma to visit the ailing Bertie.

When they arrived in Norman, the temperature was minus three degrees and the wind was howling. Even so, as she had during her childhood, Te Ata found beauty and delight in the way Jack Frost had painted all the windows. She may have been concentrating on the windows at odd moments to relieve her stress at seeing her mother suffering from severe, intractable pain. Bertie's ailment is not identified in the surviving letters, and it is possible that no definite diagnosis was made. Fisher's brother, Otto advised the family to take Bertie to a certain professor of urology at the University of Oklahoma.[3]

On January 30 Bertie experienced a crisis; Te Ata thought her mother was dying. She pulled through, though, and a doctor told Te Ata that he thought it would be safe for her to leave.[4] Te Ata and Tom Rogers left Norman for Omaha two days later. Gladys would stay another two or three weeks to care for Bertie, and Te Ata would pay her fare back to Omaha on the train. Still, Te Ata was worried; her mother seemed somewhat better, but the pain in her back and limbs remained. The osteopath who was treating Bertie thought the inflammation might have resulted from damage done years ago, from an accidental fall, for example. "I hated to leave her . . . even though I could do nothing much . . . but I had to take what programmes I could get," she wrote to C.F.[5]

On February 5 Te Ata performed for members of Chicago Woman's Aid. Very few of her printed programs survive from the mid-1930s, but this one is similar to programs from five years before. She performed three of Hartley Burr Alexander's pieces, "The Last Song," "God's Drum" and "When We Dance Altogether." She also did "The Blue Duck" by Lew Sarett and often-used legends, such as "How Pine Trees Came to Be."[6] Some of these were requested by the client, for Te Ata had come to be associated with many songs and legends; other clients wanted the same program that Te Ata had performed at the White House or at Stratford-upon-Avon. By this time Te Ata was modifying or experimenting with her presentation's staging or style. For example, she seemed increasingly to be using spotlights with colored filters to bathe her in soft, warm glows. On the stage she requested a platform, four to six feet square and about eighteen inches high. The background should be a velour, preferably in black, dark blue, or red. If acoustics were not good, she wanted microphones placed before the platform and near center stage.[7]

Te Ata
Program
of
American Indian Folk Lore

The Last Song
God's Drum
Cities of White Men
When We Dance All Together
Hartley Alexander

NATIVE LEGENDS

Iroquois Creation Legend
Seneca Romance Legend
Why Folks Die
Sign Story

NATIVE SONGS

Lullaby
Love Song
Sunset Song

The Grass on the Mountain	-	-	-	-	Paiute
Song of the New Born	-	-	-	-	Grande Pueblo
Song of a Woman Abandoned		-	-	-	Shoshone
Song of Greatness	-	-	-	-	Sioux

Translated by Mary Austin

The Blue Duck	-	-	-	-	Lew Sarett
Corn Planting Ceremony					

Music by Thurlow Lieurance

Tenney Management
Steinway Hall
113 West 57th Street
New York City

Though this program is undated, it was one of several used throughout the 1930s and 1940s. This photo was a particular favorite; she used it in publicity mailings and ads until she was about fifty.

She also worked new material into her programs if the forum seemed appropriate. For Woman's Aid, she included an informal talk, "The Indian's Contribution to America," a significant departure from her usual program. Perhaps it was her contribution to the widespread dialogue on relations between the federal government and Indian tribes. Although some of her talk involved Indian contributions to American culture, much of it was an elaboration on the beauty and wisdom of Indian culture. She began by saying that she realized the audience would process her words through a cultural prism. Or in the words of one chief she quoted: "I think one way, My way, but when I try to say it to you . . . it is like passing a flower over the fire to you, what I say wilts, and the flower has lost its perfume."[8]

She also quoted her friend Oscar Jacobson of the University of Oklahoma's art department, whom she had met while she was still at OCW: "The Anglo-Saxon smashed the culture of any primitive people that got in the way, and then with loving care picked up the pieces and placed them in a museum." Of course, she added, Indian culture is not dead and continues to influence America and Americans. "This country belongs to the Indian and it will always be so regardless of how little he may tangibly call his own. He was born here; his roots are deep; his songs, dance, legends, rituals have come from a deep understanding and a oneness with the things about him. His tales came from a direct acquaintance with animal and plant life and a desire to explain their peculiarities to himself and to his children, his music from opening his ears to the sounds of nature, his sense of color that he so richly and beautifully utilizes came from an awareness and close observation of nature."

She provided lists of contributions: foods, plants used for medicines, architecture, modes of transportation, inventions, and so on. She reminded the audience that the Indian had and has "a wonderful capacity to create, a poetic urge to express himself in beauty." Music was thought to have special power, she continued. "The Bible," she said, "tells of the world being called into being by the spoken word. In Indian myths, the Indian sings his world into being. They had songs for everything, for bringing the deer down from the mountain, curing the sick, making a bow and arrow, grinding corn. It has been said that nothing so disconcerted the Indian as to find out that the white American could grow perfectly good corn and not sing over it."[9]

On Lincoln's birthday Te Ata arrived at the executive mansion in Albany, New York. In a note on the governor's official stationery, she told Mato-Kokipapi that she was too excited to say or eat much before her performance. From the text, it seems likely that she wrote the note to help calm herself. She said the white man's ways were not entirely her ways. "I believe I am made rather to walk the trails of the wood and prairie." In a sense, she believed that she was. But it is also true that she had stopped walking those paths many years before when she left home for college. And since the late 1920s, her paths had been America's highways.

✍

To read her correspondence from this period, it would seem that Te Ata was about the only Indian traveling those highways or using art to interpret Native American culture. In fact, she was one of several who were active and received some degree of public recognition. Whether she was the preeminent Indian artist of the 1930s is a matter of conjecture. There were no fan polls or other means to gauge who among them was the most popular or influential. Furthermore, the artists themselves apparently seldom if ever mentioned their counterparts. That did not denote ignorance of the field but probably signaled a mistaken notion that sharing the spotlight was somehow detrimental. From references made at least in passing to the following Indian artists, surely Te Ata was as well aware of them as they were of her. Though most were born and raised in traditional culture, they, like Te Ata, left Indian country to receive an education in the dominant society. And like her, the impact of the experience, particularly in secondary schools and colleges, rubbed off to the extent that they spent much or all of their careers translating ancient folklore and stories into a medium that American audiences could applaud.

James Paytiamo, a full-blood Pueblo, incorporated the stories and ceremonies of his youth in Acoma, New Mexico, into a book, *Flaming Arrow's People*, that he wrote and illustrated. He also recorded Pueblo folktales for Columbia University, which were published in the *Journal of American Folk Lore*. Known by his Indian name, Flaming Arrow, he also led a Pueblo chautauqua company and performed at the Indian Hill Ceremonials at the Wisconsin Dells. Like Te Ata and Fisher, Paytiamo was a friend of Ernest Thompson Seton and taught for a time at his school of Indian wisdom near Santa Fe. In a 1936 book, *Indians of Today*, George Peake (Little Moose), a Chippewa, was said to be the only reservation Indian earning a living as a dramatic reader of Indian lore. A graduate of the Haskell Institute, like Paytiamo, and the McPhail School of Dramatic Art, Peake began his career in the early 1920s and for years was a featured attraction at the ceremonial at the Wisconsin Dells. Billed as the "Chickasaw Nightingale," Daisy Maude Underwood from Ardmore, Oklahoma, was an honor graduate of the New England Conservatory of Music where she studied piano, pipe organ, and voice. She was a featured performer at Indian Day ceremonies at the Chicago Century of Progress in 1934 and made numerous appearances singing on national radio. She not only performed opera, she also organized the Tulsa Civic Opera Company, the first in Oklahoma.[10]

Like the others, Christine Quintasket, a Salish Indian born in 1888 on the Colville Indian Reservation in Washington, was dedicated to preserving her tribe's oral histories and folklore. But her interpretation as a storyteller emerged first in a novel, *Cogewea, the Half-Blood*, in 1927 and then in a 1933 collection, *Coyote Stories*. Using her pen name, Mourning Dove, she was a self-made, self-directed woman who lived not only in two very different cultures but also two almost oppositional ways of life. One, to earn a living, working ten-hour days picking fruit, was unrelieved drudgery and destructive to her health. In the other, she sought to build a literary bridge between her Indian culture and the larger American world that she increasingly inhabited. She was at work on three other book-length manuscripts when she died in 1936. Another artist, Acee Blue Eagle, ascending while Mourning Dove was literally wearing down, grew up wanting to capture his people on canvas the way he remembered the tribal storytellers describing them when he was a child. A Pawnee and Creek from northeastern Oklahoma, Blue Eagle began using watercolors and oils to paint pictures and murals in the early 1930s. By that time Te Ata knew him mainly through his association with Ataloa at Bacone College. He served for a time as head of its art department. Praised by noted white artists such as Thomas Hart Benton, Blue Eagle parlayed his increasing notoriety into one-man shows in major American and European venues. When he was in Europe, he also searched museums and research centers for information on Indians provided by seventeenth- and eighteenth-century colonial explorers, soldiers, and traders. In

America, his relentless pursuit of authenticity took him into the major archives, to stomp dances, and to Indian festivals.[11]

While these artists were credible and at least accepted by well-intentioned critics, the same could not be said for Indian actors trying to get roles in silent movies. As in the Wild West shows of the previous generation, Indians were most often cast as extras, attacking, pillaging, torturing, and murdering. When the script called for an Indian in a prominent role, a made-up white star usually played the part. Scripts portraying Indians in the silent movie era up through 1930 almost invariably showed them either as savages or as noble but doomed, suggesting their inferiority to whites. In the 1925 film, *The Vanishing American*, white filmmakers using mainly white actors as Indians applied the concept of social evolution: in history as in nature, only the fittest survive.[12] Ten years and hundreds of such films later, one critic excoriated the movie industry for misrepresenting, falsifying and sensationalizing Indians. The critic was Walter Campbell, a friend of Te Ata's and Fisher's at the University of Oklahoma. Writing under his pen name, Stanley Vestal, in *Southwestern Review*, Campbell referred to "Hollywooden Indians." As a chronicler of Western history, Campbell wrote of Indian pictures that "all Westerners gag at them, finding the celluloid Indian completely indigestible." Even when real Indians are used, "the director commonly makes a frightful hash of their manners and customs." For example, the pipe is sent the wrong way around the circle; warriors leap to their feet and dash away at the command of a chief, as though he were a general; the representation of Indian camps is ridiculous, and the buckskins used are obviously cloth. Most directors, he wrote, turn intelligent, intuitive, talented Indians into "Red Devils, Noble Savages, Sentimental Hiawathas. There is not a human being in a carload."

Campbell noted that a vast potential exists for good Indian movies if Hollywood would "take the pains" to produce them. Moreover, he wrote that there are hundreds of thousands of American Indians proud of their ancestry and that it seems "stupid of producers to offer them nothing but caricatures of their race." He pointed out that Congress had recently enacted a law making it a crime to knowingly offer for sale Indian arts and crafts that are fake. "It seems time for similar legislation designed to prevent the sale of fake Indian drama."[13] Of course, Campbell's article in a scholarly journal was mere preaching to the choir

Te Ata: Chickasaw Storyteller, American Treasure

and brought about no change in the way Hollywood portrayed Indians. Not even a critically acclaimed model of how to do things right, *The Silent Enemy*, featuring an all-Indian cast and a meticulously researched script, had any more than an ephemeral impact on the industry. The *New Republic* said it was "the only significant film to be produced in this country for a long time." Despite stellar reviews, the film was a box-office dud, in part because it was released when audiences were becoming accustomed to talkies. The film's male and female leads, Long Lance and Molly Spotted Elk, apparently received no other firm film offers. Long Lance was by then enmeshed in personal problems. Molly, a beautiful, talented, intelligent, educated Penobscot, was proud of the film and hoped for more film offers. But at year's end she wrote in her diary: "Reviews—some publicity—then oblivion again."[14] Though she continued to get plenty of work in New York nightclubs, she did it only for the money. Her real love was writing, and she longed to produce a collection of Indian stories for the general market. Molly spent almost every free moment of 1930 on this task. She completed the collection, but no publisher was interested. Dancing remained her most bankable talent. She made her Indian dances as authentic as possible given the strictures of the Broadway clubs, but as she wrote: "The more I dance, the more I want to interpret my emotions without limitation, to create a freedom of primitiveness and abandon. If only I could dance solely for art! Maybe someday I will have that chance. If not in America, then in Europe." In 1931 Molly had moved to Paris.[15]

It would be interesting to know if Te Ata knew about the casting for *The Silent Enemy*, and if so, if she was interested in playing Neewa, the female lead. Did she audition? Molly, who won the role, took the screen test in New York. Te Ata was living in New York and by 1929 had developed a reputation in the city for her folklore performances. Because no mention of the movie appears in her papers from this period, it is unlikely that she showed an interest. Had the director, Douglas Burden, asked her to do a screen test, she might have done it. But she had made an irrevocable decision that she was through "grubbing for parts," even highly desirable ones. Movie acting was something that Te Ata could have done, and if not typecast as an Indian, she might have become a star. But if she had pursued Hollywood, it is very likely that her career would have been brief. Very few stars of the silent era were able to make the transition to talkies success-fully. In any event, the theater, not film, was her calling; that is why she headed to New York, not Hollywood. Part of the reason stemmed from Frances Davis's commitment to theater. Even if they did discuss a movie career, Te Ata and Davis knew there was no future in the movies for an Indian woman. She might have gotten by as a white actress, but there is no reason to believe that she would have devel-oped a passion for acting on the silver screen, not while Hollywood was depicting her people in such shameless and insulting ways. Besides, by the mid-1930s, Te Ata felt sure she was on the right career path as a dramatic folklorist. While she joined Molly Spotted Elk, Flaming Arrow, Mourning Dove, Acee Blue Eagle, and others as interpreters and preservers of the heritage of Indian people, Te Ata was alone at the top of her artistic medium.[16]

⌇

Fisher's busy pace at the Hayden Planetarium picked up after the Zeiss projection instrument arrived from Germany in late January. The opening was scheduled for October, and he was in charge of planning and implementing the grand opening. He was working longer hours because, despite the greater workload, no additional staff could be hired. In fact, according to one history of the AMNH, Fisher must have been counting himself lucky that the planetarium would be opening at all. The depression hit the museum and its wealthy trustees hard. In 1933 Henry Fairfield Osborn, the longtime and distinguished president, had retired out of frustration with the chronic shortage of funds and the elimination of projects that he had supported. The museum cut salaries, curtailed publications, and eliminated staff posi-tions. Beginning in 1932, fieldwork and expeditions had to be funded extramurally. This was the start of a period during the depression years when the museum was infected by an "atmosphere of pessimism and defeat," according to anthropology curator Clark Wissler.[17]

Meanwhile, Te Ata was touring during much of the spring and summer. The couple kept in touch through letters, most of them accompanied by newspaper clippings that often included the obser-vations of famous Oklahoman and Cherokee, Will Rogers. Two such clippings dated August 7 were tucked in with one letter from C.F. One was about the arrival of Rogers and Wiley Post in Juneau, Alaska, in Post's new red pontoon-equipped monoplane. The other was Rogers's

Te Ata stands with Sioux interpreter, Frank Zahn, in South Dakota. In 1927 Fisher had been adopted by the Standing Rock Sioux and named Mato-kokipapi, meaning "Afraid-of-Bear." Photo by Clyde Fisher. Courtesy Dept. of Library Services, American Museum of Natural History, neg. no. 284232.

letter in the *New York Times* about the upcoming flight from Seattle to Juneau. He said he thought the embattled President Roosevelt would like to be with them on the trip. But Post and Rogers were both killed on August 15 when their airplane crashed in a storm while they were flying across interior Alaska.

Te Ata and Fisher got together in early July for a short trip to visit six Indian reservations in Wisconsin, Minnesota, and the Dakotas.[18] Fisher took some wonderful photographs of his wife in front of a Sioux tipi near Bullhead, South Dakota, at Sitting Bull's grave in Fort Yates, North Dakota, and by a replica of a Mandan earth lodge near Bismarck. Inside the lodge, Te Ata sat on the floor with her legs folded in front of her, pretending to be grinding corn. Gazing at the lens, her expression was as inscrutable as Mona Lisa's.[19] Fisher returned to New York, and Te Ata, after meeting Ataloa in Chicago, went on to New Mexico. She visited one of Fisher's assistants, Dorothy Bennett, who was participating in an archaeological dig near Jemez. Bennett said it was in that setting that both of them felt comfortable enough to lower their normal reserve. "She performed a program around a camp-fire one night and afterwards we sat and talked," Bennett said. "Although she was still the wife of my boss, I considered her to be a friend."[20]

After Te Ata returned from her western trip, she stayed in New York for a few days before heading to Franklin, Vermont.[21] After she left Fisher wrote her a letter in which he said he feared he was the cause of her recent tears. Although the exact cause was not revealed, C.F. asked her, "[Please make allowances] for my racial inheritance and bringing up, so different from yours. Maybe I am not entirely grown up yet. I hope I may yet change and develop." He closed by writing that living with her the past two years had been a "grand privilege." He said that he wished it had been he, not Alexander, who had written of her: "She is the spirit of the beauty of her race, intense as a flame, splendid as the wind-swept plumes of the eagle."[22]

While she was in Vermont, she was featured in an issue of the popular national magazine, *The Liberty*. In her regular column titled "To The Ladies," Princess Alexandra Kropotkin introduced Te Ata as a Chickasaw-Choctaw who had entertained at the White House. Then, from her interview with Te Ata, Kropotkin extracted three short Indian anecdotes that fit the writer's pithy style: (1) An old Indian grandmother had once told Te Ata, "All my life I have been trying to learn as the chickadee learns." How? she was asked. "By keeping still—and listening." (2) When Indian travelers would come to a strange village, it was customary for the village women to soil their clothes so the visitors would not feel ashamed of their travel-stained clothing. (3) To keep peace among themselves, Indian women every year would dig a deep hole in which they ceremoniously buried all their unkind thoughts.[23]

✧

As the date for the grand opening of the Hayden Planetarium neared, Te Ata was still away from home, probably intentionally to give Fisher more unencumbered time to work. She spent mid-September at Loon Island reading about the Natchez tribe and adapting and adding Natchez material to her repertoire. The Natchez had historic ties to her own tribe, the Chickasaws. In the eighteenth century, both tribes were located in the southeastern part of what would become the United States and both tribes were in conflict with the French, which had established settlements and forts on their lands in the lower Mississippi Valley.

Following terrorist attacks from both sides, the Natchez launched a surprise attack on two French garrisons, nearly wiping out the forces there and taking three hundred women and children hostage. With Choctaw allies, the French retaliated by nearly exterminating the entire Natchez tribe. About two hundred Natchez managed to escape and were accepted as refugees into Chickasaw settlements. The French demanded that the Natchez be handed over; the Chickasaws refused. The French successfully sought allies from other tribes, which periodically harassed and raided Chickasaw villages. The Chickasaws, armed by their English allies, gave as good as they got and stood their ground. In 1736 the French attacked the Chickasaw village of Akia and were defeated decisively. Three years later French forces were again frustrated in their attempt to defeat the Chickasaws, and a peace treaty was signed in 1740. By that time the Natchez had scattered with the winds, their life as a tribe at an end.[24]

Aside from this eighteenth-century chronology, Te Ata learned that Natchez life had centered on religious ceremonies. Their "Ancient Word," the story of their tribal origins, was passed down through generations in a form that allowed no alterations. It told how Coyocopchill, the Infinite Spirit, had fashioned man out of clay and created some small spirits who were his "free servants." Coyocopchill contained the Evil Spirit so that he could not do much harm, but he also had minor spirits who did his bidding. When the people had gone astray, Coyocopchill sent a man and a woman from the sun to give them a code that contained his rules for proper behavior. Kill only in self-defense.

Do not commit adultery. Do not be greedy; share everything "liberally and with joy." The people built a temple to show their devotion to these teachings and the sacred fire, the sun, became the symbol of their religion. Inside a mound, their temple contained the eternal flame, its guards and a chest containing pearls worn by the elect, the sun caste, on ceremonial occasions.[25]

When a member of the sun caste died, the spouse and several others might choose to accompany the deceased to the spirit world. The French tried to dissuade them from this practice, but the Natchez explained that this was a joyful not a dreaded journey. They wanted to be with their friend on his journey to a better place. Although the Frenchman Antoine Simon Le Page Du Pratz found them to be the "enemies of falsehood, faithful to their promises, true to their word . . . and . . . never the first to give offense," their basic belief in sharing and giving were too much at odds with European avarice and materialism.[26]

Inspired by what she read, Te Ata was "teeming" with creative ambition. She loved projects like this, harnessing and shaping a body of material into a theatrical format that was appropriate to her and her audience while remaining faithful in spirit to the original source. Apart from the tribe's creation story, Te Ata adapted several pieces of Natchez folklore. One she titled "The Adoption of the Human Race" took place at the beginning of things and involved a council between the Up-Above-One with the moon, sun, rainbow, thunder, fire, and water. One by one they requested from the Up-Above-One the right to adopt Man. He refused them, telling them that they would be helpful nonetheless. To the thunder, he said, "You can warn them [humans] if anything dangerous comes along. Man will throw a sweet smelling plant upon the fire so that you may know they thank you. To the sun, "You will give them light to go by and warmth to make things grow." To the fire, he said, "You will always be close to them. They will bring you food and keep you alive and you will take part in their ceremonies." He told the rainbow that "you can help them by preventing floods. You will come to them as hope and they will admire you for your beauty and goodness." Water "will keep them clean. When they build their lodges it will be near you and they will call you LONG-PERSON because you will help them to have long life."

Te Ata could do this sort of work anywhere, but she felt especially inspired in special places like Loon Island. Often, however, Loon Island

Te Ata never made the short trip out to Loon Island in anything but a canoe. Located in central New Hampshire's Lake Winnipesaukee, Loon Island was Te Ata's sanctuary after each long season of touring. (Photo by Clyde Fisher.)

was "teeming," as she put it, with guests. When she arrived in September, Mona Woodring immediately took her to dinner at a house on the lakeshore owned by colleagues at Columbia's Teachers College. Everyone expressed regret that Fisher could not join them, but they partied on into the night. The next day Te Ata sent C.F. a couple of descriptive postcards. On one, a snapshot of rural New Hampshire on a crisp, lovely day, she wrote about seeing "[b]eautiful road-side stands [stocked] with . . . richly colored squashes, pumpkins, great sacks of shiny yellow onions, toe-sacks of potatoes, red tomatoes, yellow and green cantaloupes, green striped watermelons, fresh corn and other delectible [sic] things."[27]

Talking Leaves and Repertoire Building

The second note depicted Loon Island abloom with silver rods. "Should you come to Loon Island now and walk down the tiny trail to the studio out toward the point, thence right past the home of the summer ice, on over the bridge leading toward the boat house—before you, you would see a great splash of color, a small green bench upon which rests a red typewriter[,] . . . a bit of a talking leaf in it; behind this you would see a southern Indian, in summer clothes—a halter and shorts made of many colors. Over her black hair is a red cloth. Her legs, and arms and shoulder are bare. She is seated upon a red cushion and diligently . . . pecking at this machine, writing to perhaps— her lover. She wears no rings upon her hands . . . so she must be a young maiden—waiting for romance."[28] After Fisher read this tempting note, probably the only thing that kept him from leaving immediately for Loon Island was that Te Ata would be returning to him in three days.

As the domed room grew gradually darker, Clyde Fisher stepped to the control panel before the audience of seven hundred fifty invited dignitaries for this October 2 premiere performance at the Hayden Planetarium. A moment later some three thousand "stars" flashed upon the dome, and the audience gasped. No one was prepared for anything so realistic and dramatic. With no pillars or posts to inhibit viewing, the illusion of limitless space was virtually perfect.[29] That gasp must have been music to Fisher's ears. For the next forty-five minutes, the audience witnessed a celestial extravaganza. Using other features of the Zeiss projector, dumbbell-shaped and about twelve feet long, the operator varied speed, latitude, and date in history so that he could show, for example, a view of the sky from the South Pole, the course of Donati's comet in the northern hemisphere in 1858, and the meteor shower of 1833.[30]

Facing the planetarium's main entrance was a striking and unique mural, a painting by Charles R. Knight depicting the astronomical mythology of the Blackfoot Indians. The Sun God—a young warrior with hand outstretched—pursued the Moon Goddess across the heavens. Also featured are an old man seated on a mountain rising from the sea. Desiring more earth to complete the world, he sent a duck, a beaver, an otter, and a muskrat to the bottom of the ocean to bring him more earth. Only the muskrat succeeded. The top of the mural was a night sky with two constellations separated by the Milky Way. Did Fisher and Te Ata have anything to do with the planning of the mural? It was probably no coincidence that the planetarium's mural depicted Indian folklore and that the planetarium director's wife was an Indian folklorist.[31] In any event, Fisher was the museum's indispensable man in getting the planetarium constructed.

During its first year of operation, the new planetarium in Philadelphia attracted two hundred thousand visitors. The Hayden Planetarium drew more than fifty thousand people in only its first eleven days. By October 24 Fisher wrote Te Ata that he had been working too hard and was "extremely tired." It showed in his letters, which contained churlish comments about her not acknowledging each and every one of his letters. He wrote that he was "ashamed" of his letters but noted that he had never been more rushed in his life. For example, on one recent day he had given two lectures at the planetarium, taught his New York University astronomy class, rushed to dinner in Brooklyn, where he spoke on the planetarium, and then escorted his audience to the planetarium for the 9:00 P.M. lecture given by his assistant, Bill Barton.[32]

Such reports must have been quite worrisome to Te Ata, for she surely knew by then that C.F. had a heart condition. It is not known if this diagnosis was made before their marriage, but if it was, he likely would have told her. There is no mention of his heart ailment in their letters during this period, and his medical records at Johns Hopkins University Hospital cannot be found.[33] Dorothy Bennett said she learned about Fisher's heart ailment in 1935: "We were in Chicago to visit the Field Museum and as we were making this rather long walk toward the building, Dr. Fisher told me not to be alarmed but that he needed to lie down. Well, I was alarmed; I was scared to death because he looked so drawn. He stretched out on the grass and rested quietly for about five minutes. When he got up, he had recovered. Then C.F. apologized, saying he should have warned me. He said, 'I have to do this every once in a while, but I'm fine.'"

Instead of confronting Fisher about his health, Te Ata chided him for working so hard and devoting so much of his attention to his "new toy," the Zeiss projector. He replied that had she been at home, he would not have worked so hard. Although he may have been trying to make her feel guilty, it would have been uncharacteristic of him.

Returning to Oklahoma every chance she got to see her family and perform, Te Ata visits two of her sisters, Avis, left, and Selena, center, in Tishomingo.

At any rate, he apologized to her in the same letter for any perceived petulance in his recent letters.[35] Still, he maintained his frenetic schedule, as visitors poured through the planetarium's doors.

Spending nearly all of October in Oklahoma, Te Ata had a crowded schedule too, but in contrast to Fisher's, nearly all of her engagements were social. It appears that she had only one program in Oklahoma, at her alma mater, OCW. It was a pleasant extended vacation; October's

Te Ata: Chickasaw Storyteller, American Treasure

weather was beautiful and invigorating. Her parents were in good health for a change. For the first time in what seemed like ages, Bertie had managed to gain weight—about 20 pounds, up to 140. The only work-related project of Te Ata's was a trip to the Mohonk Lodge in Colony, Oklahoma. She coveted a Wichita Ghost Dance costume, but the price for this original was out of reach. Reece Kincaide agreed to see if an artist like Acee Blue Eagle could make a copy of it at an affordable price. If so, Te Ata could obtain one to use in some of her sacred numbers. She also admired a fan of eagle feathers wrapped at the end with the "most perfect and delicate beading" and a papoose carrier that was selling for $75. She walked away empty-handed but hopeful that some purchases could be made as soon as she had earned the money.[36]

Her next paying dates were scheduled on her way back to New York. She had run short of cash in Oklahoma even though C.F. had sent her the money he received from a book review. He added that he would deposit the $35 he got for a lecture in his nearly depleted savings account. However, after he received her letter saying that one of her scheduled programs had been canceled, he sent her another check for $50. In her letter railing about the cancellation, she said she had previously turned down two other paying jobs to take the job that fell through. Writing the letter had a cathartic effect. Midway through it, her anger seemed to fade. "Isn't this a happy, lovely letter," she wrote sarcastically. "But the day is a mean one and I am so far down, I wonder if I shall ever soar again. Mebbe I shall get over it by the time I see you, Meester Fisher of the Hayden Planetarium of New York City."[37]

On her last day in Oklahoma, she turned contemplative. She noted signs of the changing season: Indian summer days giving way to the rain gods and the first sting of winter; great flocks of birds migrating south and crows congregating in the old cornfields by the roadsides; orange persimmons hanging on small yellow-leaved trees; the tall feathery grasses and the dark green of the cedars; bare trees with clusters of nuts silhouetted against the sky; the bois d'arc trees shedding their leaves and their great green milky balls. To walk among all this on an autumn day is to feel contentment and peace, she wrote to C.F. She ended her typewritten letter with a handwritten postscript a day or two later by noting that the weather was cold and rainy and that she would use his check to get Miko ready for the trip home.[38]

CHAPTER 10

Sailing Big Waters

Charles Hayden's donation was not his only philanthropical contribution to his namesake. In spring 1936 he sponsored the planetarium's participation in the study of a rare scientific event: a total eclipse of the sun. In May it was announced in the New York papers that Clyde Fisher would be traveling to Russia to make motion pictures of the solar eclipse scheduled to occur on June 19. Fisher would be among a group of scientists coordinated by Harvard University and the Massachusetts Institute of Technology that would be studying the eclipse from what was considered to be an optimum vantage point, a small town in Kazakhstan called Ak-Bulak.

Fisher would also visit colleagues in Scandinavia. One of them, the explorer Peter Freuchen, and his wife had met Te Ata, and after seeing her perform, they had become big fans. Mrs. Freuchen had shown Te Ata's publicity material to a Danish impresario named Frede Skaarup. In April Skaarup wrote to Te Ata saying he was interested in engaging her in Scandinavia.[1] Since he mentioned the lack of a summer season in Scandinavia, it is probable that Mrs. Freuchen had specifically mentioned the summer months, knowing that Fisher would be in and near Scandinavia that summer. The idea was to arrange some summer engagements so that Te Ata could also spend time with her husband in Stockholm and Copenhagen. If their schedules could be coordinated conveniently, it would be a wonderful, memorable, and economical way to see the Scandinavian countries together. Moreover, she might be a big hit there, which could open up new career avenues. The putative downside, however, was Skaarup's remark that in Scandinavia the traditional concert season began in September. He noted that Scandinavians like to make the most of their brief summers by staying outdoors. If Te Ata wanted to further her career, she would be better off waiting until the fall.

Skaarup's letter was a feeler. He already knew she was interested, but he wanted to know her rates and more information about her performances and repertoire. Would she be bringing her own accompanists? If her performance charges were "reasonable," he would pay her way over and her travel expenses in Scandinavia. Te Ata must have replied promptly to Skaarup's letter, because within a month a deal was made. Unfortunately, Skaarup's letter is the only known existing correspondence between himself and Te Ata at that time, so the financial details are not known. She decided to depart on July 11, so that she could spend about a month touring Scandinavia with Fisher. The concert season, however, would still be more than a month away.

Meanwhile, Te Ata and a crowd of friends saw Fisher off on May 16. As bon voyage gifts, Te Ata gave him a wristwatch, monogrammed handkerchiefs, a red tie, and a coyote figurine representing a stowaway. Many who could not attend the send-off had letters or telegrams delivered to the *Drottningholm*; it was his third time sailing across the Atlantic on that ship.[2] Some of the New York papers ran the announcement of the trip and photos of Fisher and Te Ata at the pier; the *Herald Tribune* mistakenly reported that the couple was sailing together.[3] Would that it were true, Te Ata must have thought. To have accomplished that, they would have had to secure a loan, and Te Ata probably decided against this because she knew she would not be bringing in any money until late August or September. She still managed to have a fine time at Fisher's bon voyage gathering. The next day she wrote him about two passengers she had observed as the ship was leaving the pier. Standing near his mother was a young boy waving good-bye to his father. The boy was "weeping copiously and loudly into a large white kerchief and trying to smile and wave" and intermittently issuing "piercing little cries of 'good-bye.'" In response to this poignant yet comic scene, Te Ata wrote that she was "continuously on the road between laughter and tears." In contrast, she noticed an elderly lady standing nearby who had "the most complaisant, resigned, self satisfied, cow-like look on her face as she rested one elbow on the window glass and fanned herself occasionally with a bunch of flowers." Referring to herself as "your attorney," Te Ata wrote that she was happy for any bit of humor at their parting, "for the Scientist looked so lonely" on the upper deck and she felt "so forlorn and abandoned!" "Your admirers stayed until you were a wee speck [standing] against the pipes," she continued. Then she brightened with the thought that "sad partings between friends mean glorious meetings and joyous anticipation."[4]

The voyage from New York to Stockholm took ten days. Fisher was selected to sit at the captain's table at dinner along with the American consul to Sweden and some Swedish tycoons. Dinner at 7:00 P.M. was one of six daily servings aboard ship. Perusing the ship's schedule of events, Fisher immediately decided that three meals a day would suffice. He played shuffleboard, took warm salt baths, went to ("too many") cocktail parties, read four or five books for pleasure, wrote letters, and tended to his diary. In the evenings everyone at the captain's table "dressed" for dinner. The conversations were convivial, and short speeches generally followed dinner. Often a Hollywood film (such as *Louis Pasteur* starring Paul Muni) was shown. At least two dances and a masquerade ball were held. Wearing a swallowtail coat, a top hat, white kid gloves, and a mask, Fisher went to the ball as a bridegroom and danced with every woman at the captain's table. That afternoon he had won $12 playing keno (the money brought to him on a silver plate). He used his winnings on May 22, his fifty-eighth birthday, to buy champagne for the captain's table, where he told his companions, "A woman is as old as she looks, and a man is old when he stops looking." To Te Ata, he wrote: "I must be purty old for I stopped looking several years ago," but his diary observations indicated otherwise.

As the ship neared Göteberg, Fisher was interviewed by a Swedish newspaperman who had been aboard. Just before landing, several other reporters interviewed him about his visit and his astronomical projects. Before he reached Stockholm by train, someone showed him a copy of a Stockholm morning newspaper, *Dagens Nyheter*. He was surprised and pleased to see his picture and an accompanying story on the front page.

He was ecstatic to be there. "Dearest Indian," he wrote Te Ata. "Arrived 7:45 this morning in Stockholm, my favorite city of Europe, in Sweden, the cleanest country I have ever visited, and with Norway

Te Ata: Chickasaw Storyteller, American Treasure

the most beautiful. You will like it much, I am sure." Although she would be joining him in less than a month, he told her he regretted not bringing her with him—as if it had been his decision. But even while he was lamenting the decision, he was asking her to bring all the money from his checking and savings accounts.[5] He sailed the next day for Helsinki. On arrival he had dinner and then left by train for Leningrad. A stream marked the Finnish-Russian border. The Finnish side of the bridge was painted white; the Russian side, red. In Russia everyone's baggage was inspected.

After touring Leningrad in a Lincoln driven by a Russian girl who spoke English, Fisher took a night train to Moscow and checked in at the Metropole Hotel on June 1. He went sight-seeing the next day and found Moscow clean (traveling New Yorkers in the 1930s could not fail to notice a clean city) and a blending of modern and old. For example, the transportation facilities, including a new subway, were excellent, but the universal instrument for calculating business transactions was the abacus. On June 4 he left by train for Ak-Bulak. When Fisher awoke the next morning, he observed that the terrain reminded him of the plains of the Dakotas. As they reached the Volga River, a passenger cranked up a phonograph and played a recording of "The Volga Boatmen." He arrived in Ak-Bulak on June 6 and sent Te Ata his last postcard: "Arrived here safely this morning. Everything all right; feeling fine. Nearly 100 degrees in the shade today and no shade."[6]

Ak-Bulak, located on the steppes of Kazakhstan in western Asia, was a transition point between the Occident and the Orient. Its nine thousand inhabitants mainly consisted of Slavs, Cossacks, and Mongols. They got about by truck, oxcart, and camel. In fact, the team's water supply was hauled nine miles outside of town to their expedition camp by "a Siberian camel complaining every step of the way," Fisher wrote. During the Wild Rose Moon (June), he picked and pressed a wild rose for Te Ata and tucked it in with his letter.[7]

The expedition's campsite was located on a hill, which Fisher learned was one of several ancient burial mounds in the area. During the Stone and Bronze Ages, the region had been a resting point on a migratory route linking Europe and Asia. The area was inhospitable, with almost constantly blowing winds, nearly daily dust storms, and temperature extremes and wild fluctuations. It was above 100 degrees for several days, then rainy and cold, then sizzling once again. The only reason the expedition camp was there was because Ak-Bulak lay on a thin horizontal strip across the Soviet Union that represented the viewing area for the full eclipse. Twenty-eight scientific expeditions from the Soviet Union and eleven from other countries also had camps within the strip.[8]

The eclipse was to last two minutes. According to the Science Service of the *New York Times*, the intensity of the eclipse would enable telescopes and cameras to capture information about the sun that otherwise would not be detectable. Fisher, who would be recording the eclipse on his Akeley movie camera and still camera, had several days to knock around town. On June 11 he was in Ak-Bulak when he heard a train approaching. He walked closer to the tracks to get a better look and saw a long chain of boxcars crammed with prisoners on their way to the Soviet gulags. Men in some cars, women in others. Armed guards rode between cars or on the roofs.[9]

Everyone spent the night at the eclipse camp on June 18. As the sun's crescent became thinner, "the eerie darkness became more pronounced." A little more than an hour later, the moon had moved entirely between the sun and earth and the two-minute phenomenon began. Fisher had hypothesized that the darkness would cause songbirds to stop singing, but he was so busy with his cameras that he failed to notice. He did notice Venus, however, "shining brilliantly about two degrees above the sun. The exquisite corona became visible as a five pointed star with very long streamers." Fisher wrote ruefully that many inhabitants of the USSR probably interpreted the corona as "a symbol of the Soviet star."[10]

After Te Ata received a radiogram from C.F. on May 27, she took out her red typewriter on a rainy day at Loon Island and complained about the weather and the inconvenience of having to renew a driver's license and leave for the city days ahead of schedule to entertain her brother Snake's wife, Maude, who was arriving in New York unexpectedly early. But as was so often true when she was in a bad mood, the act of writing seemed to lift her spirits. The letter's second page extolled the beauty of the island's flowers, Mona Woodring's recent purchases—car, furniture, and bathtub—and Ataloa's good fortune to be leaving soon for Hawaii, where she would be a visiting lecturer. Buried in the letter was the news that she had yet to hear from the

Freuchens or her presumed manager, Skaarup.[11] Her passage to Sweden was paid for in early June, although she did not say by whom. She also made arrangements for a September 26 return trip. She gave Maude the cook's tour, including a walking tour of Central Park South, a visit to the planetarium, dinner at John and Margaret Ball's house, and a trip to Bear Mountain and Lake Te Ata. Although her departure was still more than a month away, she wrote C.F. that she was already excited about making her first visit to Scandanavia with him. She reminded him, "[Do] all the things I would make you do were I there."[12]

A few days later Te Ata and Maude began a leisurely trip back to Oklahoma, so leisurely in fact that in mid-June Te Ata realized to her shock and dismay that to be on time for her first program in Oklahoma she would have to drive seven hundred miles in a little more than twenty-four hours. After driving twenty-four hours straight and dealing with two flat tires, they arrived at 4:00 A.M. Te Ata slept for four hours, drank a glass of milk and gave her program at 10:00 A.M. The stress was such that before her performance she grew a fever blister "as big as the lunar alps." Later her parents received the news of her planned sailing to Scandinavia with little response, prompting Te Ata to write Fisher about their reserve: "How contained they are about their likes and dislikes. They are proud of me . . . but they probably think I am a little off that I am so keen to go." She was worrying more seriously about the possibility that C.F. had not received any of her letters containing the news that she would be arriving in Göteberg on the *Drottningholm* on July 11. She sent him several more letters, all postmarked to different destinations, hoping that he would receive at least one. On June 18, the eve of the eclipse, she looked out her window at the night sky and, recognizing the Scorpion constellation, wondered if it looked as big and clear to C.F. in Russia as it did to her. As for her, she and her fever blister would be presenting a program the next day in Weatherford at the teacher's college.[13]

On June 23 she finally received a letter from Skaarup, practically dripping with anxiety. First, he suggested that she take a different ocean liner and that she leave for Scandinavia not in July but August. Skaarup reminded her again that the concert season would not begin until at least mid-September (which was only a few days before she was scheduled to return to the United States). Then, in no uncertain terms, he told her that she had to succeed "the very first evening," or it would become "practically impossible to continue." He went on to underscore that Copenhagen (where the first performance would be held) "is a difficult city," meaning if the audience does not like you, you are through, for all intents and purposes.

Skaarup advised her to bring everything she could lay her hands on in terms of costumes, music, accompanists (preferably Indian), and repertoire. Then, at the rehearsals, Te Ata would need to throw everything at him but the kitchen sink and he would select what he thought the Danish people would like. Finally, in return for paying all her continental transportation costs, she would give him exclusive rights to manage all of her performances in Scandinavia and Europe, if an expanded tour should develop.[14] As Te Ata had been clear that she was sailing home on September 26, Skaarup evidently believed she would change her mind if programs in Europe could be arranged. In his letter Skaarup wrote that he would not be able to pay "more than 50$ per concert. " Te Ata crossed out the "50$" and wrote "No" in the margin, meaning it was not enough. She also stuck to her original plan to leave in July. If she departed in mid-August, as Skaarup wanted, she and Fisher would be sailing across the Atlantic at the same time but in opposite directions.

Although American Indian artists and performers were popular in Europe, it appears that Te Ata and only a few other Native Americans had the opportunity to perform there during the 1930s. The Great Depression doubtless prevented some who otherwise might have put together a tour or been invited to make appearances. Coincidentally, one who traveled and performed extensively in Europe was a Chickasaw woman born and raised near Ardmore around 1900. The daughter of a white man and a woman of Chickasaw ancestry, Tessie Mobley grew up in both white and Indian cultures. She was particularly close to her maternal grandmother, who, it was said, spoke no English but taught her to do beadwork and to identify useful herbs and foods.[15] Tessie became interested in opera in high school and exhibited a beautiful singing voice in college. Her big break occurred in 1929 after she auditioned for the Indian Ceremonial at the Hollywood Bowl in Los Angeles. She not only performed there, but did so with Charles Cadman, who earlier had toured with Tsianina, the Creek-Cherokee singer. A promoter invited her to perform in Germany. As a result, she received scholarships in the early 1930s to study opera in Berlin and Rome. She also performed on radio and in concert in many European capitals, including a concert similar to the one Te Ata was scheduled for in Copenhagen and Stockholm. Though Mobley was known as an opera diva, her Indian heritage brought her additional notoriety. She had adopted the professional name Lushanya, which she understood to mean "Songbird." Before returning to the United States in 1935 to continue her career with the Chicago Opera Company, she starred in the role of Minnehaha in the operatic production of *Hiawatha* by Coleridge Taylor at the Royal Albert Hall in London.[16]

She was one of several Indian singers to star in the annual Albert Hall production of *Hiawatha*. Oskenonton, a full-blood of the Mohawk tribe, had starred in the title role so often that Londoners had come to associate his name with Hiawatha. Oskenonton, or Running Deer, had been discovered one night in the early 1920s in the Hudson River valley by some campers who overheard him singing by his own campfire. Struck by his exceptional voice, they persuaded him to move downriver to New York City to study music. After a few years in New York, he was invited to perform in London and in several European countries. He was much more successful in London than he was in his home country.[17]

The *Drottningholm* arrived on July 20 at 8:00 P.M., and Fisher characteristically understated the reunion in his diary. "Te Ata fine. To Hotel Eggers for the night."[18] Since Te Ata had not received his letter about his Finnish bath in Helsinki, he related that adventure in hilarious detail. After paying twenty-five cents at a ticket booth, he repaired to the dressing room where he disrobed. He was led into a small steam room and instructed to lay down on an elevated wooden platform only a few feet from the ceiling. A stout, sixtyish woman poured a dipper full of water into an oven holding hot stones, and steam was produced. Steam and heat gradually permeated the room. The woman exited but returned periodically to pour more water over the stones and perhaps see that Fisher had not been cooked. "I have never been in such a hot place," he said. "My perspiratory glands worked as I had no idea they could." The woman returned with a large bundle of fresh green birch switches with the leaves still on and proceeded to thrash him from the soles of his feet to his neck. "Then," he recalled, "she used the switches sideways as a scrub-brush. After a most thorough scrub-bing, I was directed into another room for another scrubbing with a Luffa sponge and soap." Then she shampooed his scalp with tar soap and administered a full-body massage. During the tub-bath phase, he remembered Stansbury Hagar's story of the Dominican who prayed for rain and got much more than he wanted. After the bath, he was given a cold shower and then slipped into a bathrobe made of towels. Madame attendant led him to his dressing room "where she dried [him] by pressing and rubbing the robe."[19]

Fisher and Te Ata awoke on their first morning together in Göteberg to find Te Ata's picture in three daily newspapers. She had been interviewed and photographed on the *Drottningholm* shortly before landing. At the Göteberg Museum they were both interviewed and photographed for an evening newspaper. Fisher could not wait to begin showing Te Ata around. He had been a devotee of Scandinavia since 1924 when he journeyed to Arctic Lapland to study and report on the Lapp people for the AMNH. They lived in the northern parts of Norway, Sweden, Finland and the northwest corner of the Soviet Union. The nomadic Mountain Lapps, Te Ata noted, were much like the migratory Plains tribes of North America. Instead of bison, the Lapps followed the vast reindeer herds, which supplied most of their needs. Unlike the Indians, as Te Ata was acutely aware, the Lapps had been largely left alone to live their lives in isolation. While to outsiders their existence seemed like unrelieved deprivation, tedium, and toil, Fisher and Te Ata found much to admire. The Lapps were family-oriented, self-sustaining, and self-reliant and in touch with, if not bound by, their history and tradition. They knew who they were and who they were not. They were not progressive, Fisher allowed, but in "the disturbed world of today, one can not help wondering whether the Lapp, quietly living out his way of life, insulated from our excited culture, is really at a disadvantage."[20]

The next day they sailed to Stockholm where they joined their friends, Samuel and Anne Tucker, for two days of sight-seeing, that included, of course, the planetarium.[21] At Uppsala they made what was for Fisher, the Ph.D. in botany, a pilgrimage to the Cathedral, because it was the final resting place of Carolus Linnaeus, the eighteenth-century Swedish botanist who founded the modern classification system for plants and animals. They called on the artist Bruno Liljefors,

Arctic explorer Peter Freuchen and his wife, Magdalene, were responsible for bringing Te Ata to Denmark to perform. Though the couples had a great time at the Freuchen's island home before Te Ata's performances, Te Ata had difficulty pleasing Magdalene during rehearsals. Photo by Clyde Fisher. Courtesy Dept. of Library Services, American Museum of Natural History, neg. no. 290925.

who was, by Fisher's reckoning, the country's greatest painter of birds and animals. At 76, Liljefors was still working in a studio filled with paintings and sculptures, one of which featured the face of former heavyweight boxing champion Jack Dempsey. For Te Ata, he inscribed a copy of a drawing of American Indians that he had made when he was 12.

They were met by the Freuchens in Copenhagen on August 8. After lunch they were introduced to Te Ata's Scandinavian manager,

Frede Skaarup, who took them to Denmark's principal newspaper, the *Politiken*, for a little advance publicity. Skaarup and Te Ata agreed to get together to begin rehearsals after Fisher departed on August 15. Then they spent a few days with the Freuchens at their island home, Enehoje. In the evenings Freuchen, a prodigious talker, regaled them with tales of his Arctic adventures, including those of special interest to Fisher, in which Freuchen had played a role in securing the three-ton Cape York meteorite for a Danish museum.

Fisher greatly admired explorers like Freuchen and was proud to be a member of the Explorers Club where he could rub shoulders with them when they were in New York. Although Fisher was considered a distinguished member of the club and thought of himself as an explorer of sorts, he did not think he was in the same league as, for example, Captain Freuchen or Captain Bob Bartlett who ventured into harsh and perilous environments. Like his late mentor John Burroughs, Fisher preferred to explore settings that others took for granted. He might sit still watching bees pollinating flowers or observe and collect specimens from a forest floor. Even though he trod the same ground on his hikes through Central Park, each one was an adventure because he always knew that he would see new, fascinating things. Te Ata was also an explorer, and, like Fisher, geography was often of secondary importance to her. She loved venturing into new settings not so much to understand how things worked or developed but how something stood in relation to the things around it. These were the things that Native Americans had been observing and recounting for countless generations.

After Copenhagen, Te Ata and C.F. sailed on to Oslo, Norway, and then back to Göteberg. They spent Fisher's last full day there with Henry Wassen, a curator of the city's museum. He had organized a credible display of artifacts from South American Indians. As Te Ata admired the collection, she had no idea that within a year she would be seeing similar objects in their natural setting in Peru. It would have buoyed her spirits, for at 4:00 P.M. on August 15, Fisher boarded the *Drottningholm* for the return voyage to New York.[22] He wrote the first of eight daily letters to Te Ata during the voyage home: "Dearest Dawn Girl: Just waved a tearful goodbye to you a few minutes ago. Lovely One! Will think of you often. . . . [M]ake the most of every opportunity, and let me know if I can do anything to help. My tenderest love to you. Bless you. . . . Always, Mato-Kokipapi." The reference to help meant financial help, although extrapolating from comments made in his letters about his depleted savings account, Fisher would have had to borrow money, something Te Ata knew he would never do for himself. Then, in what constituted an exposition on fiscal responsibility, he mentioned in his letters from the *Drottningholm* how he had refrained from spending money on drinks and entertainment and smoked only one pack of cigarettes on the voyage.[23]

Fisher was writing only what was on his mind, perhaps to stiffen his own resolve, not to chasten Te Ata. He did not need to; they both realized that she had ongoing financial responsibilities. Moreover, he would not want to do or say anything that would increase pressure on her since only the first program in Copenhagen was set. They understood that she needed as many programs as she could get. In a letter to him, Te Ata wrote that his economizing on his trip home "almost made [her] weep." "I had meant to insist that you take some of the money I had and then neglected it. You always spend too much on me, insisting that I buy things and you never have anything."[24]

There is no telling if Magdalene Freuchen had a specified role in the arrangement between Te Ata and Skaarup, but Te Ata's rehearsals in Copenhagen did not start until Mrs. Freuchen arrived. At some point it was decided that there was no money to pay Margaret Ball to come over to accompany her best friend, so it was likely that Mrs. Freuchen was asked or volunteered to beat the drum. Te Ata's first rehearsal was held on August 20 at the Royal Concert Hall with Mrs. Freuchen, Skaarup, and the hall's director on hand. Te Ata performed for two hours and showed her husband's films on Indian pottery making and Indian dancing. Te Ata was relieved when Skaarup turned thumbs down on the films; she thought they were incompatible with her program, but Skaarup had wanted to see them. Then Skaarup decided that Te Ata ought to wire Fisher for her big drum and masks. Instead, she wrote to him: "They [Skaarup and Magdalene] are like the old cow that sees more grass over the fence—afraid it might be better." During the long rehearsal, Skaarup and the director were both "delighted with my work until they got tired," which she said underscored her point that "nothing should be too long—even if a manager asks to see *everything*. People should always leave, wanting more."[25]

After another lengthy rehearsal the next day, Skaarup and the others seemed even more pleased. Skaarup told Mrs. Freuchen he thought Te Ata's performance would succeed but was disappointed she was not staying longer. Her first concert date was set for September 14. On the eleventh, she would perform a dress rehearsal in the hall for the press. "The manager now seems much sold on the program—perhaps his wife had much to do with this for she cried when she saw the program 'because it was so beautiful.' Made me think of Mother McClure who broke her glasses once weeping over something in one of my programs."[26]

With almost two weeks before the dress rehearsal, Te Ata could relax. She stayed with the Freuchens in their island home, venturing out some to sight-see with Magdalene, whom she liked very much. "We laugh together a lot and that brings us closer."[27] Still, the first program had to succeed. If it did, there would be another performance in Stockholm on September 18, then one in Göteberg and another in Copenhagen before she departed for home on September 26. It seemed she was planning to leave on schedule no matter what. She wrote that she missed C.F. greatly and thanked him for "bringing such experiences and memories to [her] store-house." "Without you, it could not have happened and had it happened without you it could not have been so satisfying."[28]

As the concert date drew near, Te Ata's mood changed. At a rehearsal two days before the program, she became annoyed that everyone was speaking in Danish and ignoring her. "I'd wait and wait and wait and sometimes walk out—to keep from screaming." Still, she and her accompanist and benefactor, Magdalene Freuchen, managed to work "like Trojans" going over and over several of the numbers. Afterward, on the eve of the dress rehearsal, they stayed out until 2:00 A.M. Te Ata woke up five hours later and could not return to sleep. All that anxiety, and then, according to Magdalene, the important writers did not attend the dress rehearsal. Fortunately, those who showed up wrote laudatory reviews and Skaarup seemed pleased. Writing in the *Politiken*, the Danish actor Carl Alstrup said: "Te Ata was a beautiful experience. . . . [I]t was difficult to come back to reality; the rhythm sings in me still. She is a vision, a wild rose, a lovely representative for this sad and proud race."[30]

The Scandinavians who saw Te Ata perform in 1936 were uncharacteristically demonstrative. The critics' praise was extravagant and numerous encores were demanded though many in the audience knew no English. Photo by Delar Studio, Rockefeller Center, N.Y.

After the dress rehearsal, Alstrup had bemoaned the fact that he was too old to fall in love with Te Ata but said he must see her again. An artist came backstage and tried to sketch her but gave up, saying she was hard to capture. He asked if he could try again the day after her program. She agreed, and wrote to Fisher, "Mebbe you will like it—if it doesn't look too much like me!" She sent him several write-ups that had been translated into English. One told of how "a famous scientist came down to Oklahoma and found this little Indian princess—took her East and civilized her and urged her to become a great artist." Te Ata punctuated that sentence with a great flourish of question marks.[31]

Her public performance was the next day, September 14. She had never before presented a program under such circumstances. It was not that her audience understood little or no English—she had performed on Indian reservations—but that her immediate future was controlled by the size and enthusiasm of the audience and by the reviews. As always, she was nervous, but not unusually so. She noted that the seven-hundred-seat hall was "pretty full" and that the audience was very enthusiastic. She was asked for eight or ten encores and received several bouquets of flowers. About a party afterward in her honor, Te Ata wrote, "Many lovely things were said to me." In the morning, an actress brought her a newspaper containing a long review in Danish; she had appended to it her own one-word translation: "victory." In a letter to C.F., she got a bit carried away: "How I wish you could have been here with me for all this—for it was about my greatest success."[32]

It may have seemed that way, with people telling her that no new artist had ever generated so much favorable publicity, but the concert lost money. "Only the cheap seats sold," she wrote to C.F. Moreover, she learned that many in the audience had gotten in free because Skaarup had hedged his bets by giving away tickets. It also did not help—or maybe it did—when she learned that a group of "mediocre Gypsy musicians" had sold out a fifteen-hundred-seat auditorium. Nevertheless, the Stockholm concert was on.[33] When she arrived in Sweden on the September 17, she was exuberant to be there, for she much preferred Stockholm to Copenhagen; she and Magdalene went on a shopping spree, and Te Ata managed to spend the equivalent of her Stockholm concert fee.[34]

The concert was another critical success. From *Svenska Dagbladet*: "Te Ata is a great artist. She has within a narrow frame united a piece of unspoiled nature, traditionally satiated culture and great powers of acting to a remarkable unity." She offered "love songs, lullabies, hymns to the Sun Rise and Sunset, legends, and incantations, ritual and cult and tuned to a deep folk-like poetry, where the strong rhythm of the desire for life compel one to dance and the final unavoidable premonition of death only press forth a prayer that death might become like a tremendously beautiful song."

What happened between that performance and her departure on the September 26 is unknown. She may have performed another program

Te Ata: Chickasaw Storyteller, American Treasure

or two, or she may have continued basking in the glory of the Swedish reviews. At any rate, her only letter to survive that period was written to Fisher on board the *Drottningholm* on her way home. She missed him terribly, as she had mentioned in every letter to him. In this one she elegantly captured the most meaningful and spiritual elements of their three-year marriage.

Three years of togetherness on the trail—and we have known the tang of the desert sage-brush and seen the gnarled strength of pinon and cedar. We have talked together under green hemlock boughs and marveled at the dignity of the Northern Pine. We have sailed "big waters" and have felt drawn and fascinated by the knowledge of the Ancient One. We have loved the smoke and the beauty of the camp fire and have felt the warmth that comes from companionship with real friends. We have felt our aloneness and the sadness of parting, but always knowing we would feel as much, the keen joy and the sweetness and strangeness of coming together again—and—we have caught a photographic cloud or two and had an occasional dance among the stars.

The 28th Sun of the Hunting Moon and an Indian on the Atlantic sailing back to you![35]

CHAPTER 11

Peruvian Expedition

In early 1937 Dorothy Bennett learned that a total solar eclipse would be visible in the southern hemisphere that June. She mentioned this to Fisher, noting that she understood it would be the finest and longest solar eclipse (seven minutes) until the year 2004. She asked Fisher what the museum planned to do about it. He said he was not aware of any plans. "Well, I told him we ought to do something," she said, and she set to work.[1] "I traced the path of the eclipse and found that the mountains of Peru would make an excellent vantage point from which to observe the eclipse. After learning that there were American-run mining camps in Peru, I looked up one of the mining companies in the phone book and called for an appointment. I told this executive all about these distinguished astronomers setting out on this important scientific expedition and asked if the mining company would be willing to put them up."[2]

Actually, as there was no written proposal, the "distinguished astronomers," other than Clyde Fisher, had yet to be identified. That was an insignificant point at the time, Bennett knew. If the support materialized, so would the astronomers. The next question was how to get to Peru. Fisher contacted a New York–based shipping company, the Grace Line, and offered it the "prestigious opportunity" to provide the round-trip transportation. When the company accepted and details were worked out, the Hayden Planetarium–Grace Expedition was announced in the newspapers.[3]

The AMNH press release noted that the June 8 solar eclipse would be viewed from the coastal region of Peru where the Incas had built temples and offered sacrifices to their sun god. The opportunity to visit Incan and even pre-Incan ruins and the ancient ones' modern-day descendants was a powerful lure to Te Ata. In due course, the name "Mrs. Clyde Fisher" was added to the list of expedition members, designated as "photographer."[4] Though Fisher had taught Te Ata how to use both still and movie cameras, and she would shoot stills on this trip, he must have exercised something like executive privilege to have his wife included in the expedition's official party. He also selected two eminent astronomers who agreed to join the expedition, two painters who would render oil paintings of the cosmic event from different locations (artists may be a sign of Te Ata's influence), and an aerial photographer who would capture the eclipse on film from a Pan American airplane flying at thirty thousand feet. Fisher had filmed eclipses from airplanes twice, in 1930 and 1932, and would have loved a third flight, but according to Bennett, his heart condition made the flight too risky.[5]

๛

The ocean liner *Santa Lucia* shoved off on May 7. Te Ata was especially anxious to see the descendants of the Incas. She believed they might be her distant relations because some archaeologists had speculated that part of the tribe had migrated north. And according to a version of the Chickasaw migration legend, the ancestral Chickasaws had followed the leaning pole to the north, then east, winding up in the Southeastern United States.[6] The ship crossed the equator as Te Ata was finishing a book called *Peruvian Pageant* by Blair Niles. Later, after she and Fisher had cocktails with the vice president of Grace Lines, a Bolivian Indian named Jorge Zalles, Te Ata performed folklore in the lounge. They docked at Guayaquil, Ecuador, amid flying pelicans and floating hyacinths and were immediately swarmed by street vendors. The outdoor market displayed richly colored fruits and vegetables, and the river was crowded with dugout canoes and bamboo rafts supporting little inverted V-shaped shelters, mostly ferrying stalks of green bananas under the protective drape of banana leaves.

On May 18, as they approached Peru, Te Ata wrote that they were "sailing into winter."[7] After landing in Trujillo, they drove to the ruins of Chan Chan, a pre-Inca city dating to about A.D. 900. The capital of

Te Ata on the deck of the *Santa Lucia* heading to Peru. Although the trip was an expedition to photograph and study a solar eclipse, Te Ata's main purpose was to see and meet South American Indians. (Photo by Clyde Fisher.)

the Chimu empire, the city once covered six square miles and was protected by a wall up to thirty feet high. Although, the Chimus were conquered by the Incas in the fifteenth century, Chan Chan's buildings were left standing long after the city's inhabitants were gone. Located in the desert and constructed entirely of adobe, enough of the buildings remained—despite weather, earthquakes, and looting Spaniards—to "show what a grand and imposing" city Chan Chan had been. Fisher took a picture of Te Ata holding a relic from a Chimu burial ground that had emerged naturally from the shifting sands. Kneeling amid scattered fragments in the sand, she gazed intently at the object in her right hand, as though by concentrating she might have divined the story behind it. The photograph reveals that Te Ata was not afraid to touch burial objects, as were many traditional Indians.[8]

Te Ata: Chickasaw Storyteller, American Treasure

After two days of sight-seeing in Lima, which Te Ata found to be "a beautiful and cosmopolitan city with wide boulevards and lovely plazas," she left Fisher on May 22, his fifty-ninth birthday, to fly south to Arequipa. Dorothy Bennett and Charles Coles, the expedition's official photographer, accompanied her on this trip that would culminate with visits to Cuzco and Machu Picchu. Te Ata described the six-hundred-mile flight in detail in her journal. As they flew from one region to another, she described landscapes of isolation and desolation, the variety of topographies and a kaleidoscope of colors. In a desert that would not support a single blade of grass, they saw a lone human being walking, miles from anywhere or anything. He did not signal for help and his stride was purposeful. How did he get there? Where was he going? He apparently carried neither food nor water. Was the trekker delusional, had he been expelled by his tribe, or was he on a vision quest? Further on, they flew over immense fields of cotton and fertile river valleys and saw teeming flocks of pelicans and seagulls. To the west was the Pacific, which Te Ata noted was first "turquoise, then aquamarine, then the deeper blue that cemented it to the horizon." Later they flew over miles of "cream color sand dunes that resembled meringue," sands of "varying textures and shapes and soft colors of mauve, lavender, rose and blue."

After landing in Arequipa, they boarded a train for a trip through the Cordillera Occidental, a branch of the western Andes, to Cuzco. Te Ata awoke on the train with a headache, for in the night they had climbed to an elevation of more than fourteen thousand feet. "The trip today was perfectly gorgeous—until I became so tired with the excitement and color and strangeness that I could absorb no more. The magnificent mountains along our route and the herds of llamas and alpaca[,] . . . the natives more [and more] unspoiled as we get farther away from the city and tourist beat. . . . I have never seen so much color in Indians, costume, in buildings and the mountains."

Their train arrived in Cuzco at twilight, but the three travelers had no desire to see the city that night; their excitement had given way to exhaustion, in part from the elevation, 11,200 feet above sea level. They bounced back the next day, on the eve of the feast of Corpus Christi, watching parades of Indians from the surrounding mountain communities congregate at Cuzco's great square.[9] Te Ata and the others spent half a day at the square amid the color and pomp, but wherever Te Ata went, "all eyes were on her," according to Bennett. "She stood out because she was so beautiful, statuesque and tall, almost towering over the people. [Following her around] I felt like the tail of the kite."[10] Although she must have felt frustrated at not being able to talk to the people, Te Ata managed to get one group of Indians to perform a traditional dance. She probably reciprocated in some way. That afternoon they were escorted about Cuzco by a guide with a perfect blend of attributes. Señor Cardemas was part Indian and part Spanish, spoke English, and was an employee of an archaeological museum. As they walked, the remnants of the once-formidable Inca civilization were everywhere, the famous Temple of the Sun, arches, doorways, segments of the wall that once surrounded the city. When the Spanish came, they erected structures on foundations built by Inca labor. Te Ata implied that modern labor had not changed much over the centuries: "The Indian carries the load of Peru upon his back and for almost nothing. [Economically] even machines and horses cannot compete."[11]

In the afternoon Te Ata sat on a bench in the plaza, looking through a colonial arch leading to the market and saw "the life of Cuzco moving in and out." "Now here comes a mother wrapped in a beautiful homespun manta [rough cotton blanket] with her baby on her back, moving in a little trot-like gait, and with her is another woman carrying a great load of pottery and merchandise on her back." This led to a brief discourse on the appearance and fashion of Cuzco women generally. "[They] are rather small in stature but stout and buxom and can carry many pounds on their backs, which is what they usually are doing, be their load children, food, fire wood, pottery or fabrics. [They] wear many wideskirts [sic], usually falling to the ankle and one worn over the other; the top one is looped back to show its gayer sister just beneath. A waist coat is worn over a cotton blouse and a beautiful shawl is worn around their shoulders. If they are not barefooted, they wear primitive thongs or more rarely, hightopped shoes. The hat they wear depends on the province they are from; one of the most colorful is large-brimmed and upturned, the underside of red flannel and the top of dark blue wool, gayly decorated with colors and silver braids." Men, she wrote, were very strong—sometimes carrying loads on their backs of up to four hundred pounds—but they were not as industrious as women: "Sometimes, the men are idle; the women,

Te Ata: Chickasaw Storyteller, American Treasure

Te Ata with Peruvian Indians. Te Ata said she felt a real kinship with the Indians wherever she traveled in Peru. And according to her friend Dorothy Bennett, as they walked about Cuzco, "every eye was on her."

never." Men's fashion matched women's in color: "They wear llama wool ponchos, neck scarves, woven caps with ear flaps that sometimes bear beads and designs, and over these caps they wear large hats or sombreros."[12]

After two or three days in Cuzco, the group traveled seventy miles by rail to the mysterious ruins of Machu Picchu, one of the seven latter-day "wonders of the world." They made the last link of the trip on ponies, ascending from the Urubamba River valley to the ruins, built on the impregnable horseshoe spur of a mountain rising abruptly almost two thousand feet above the river. To the north, the majestic Huayna Picchu towered above the ruins; the Incas probably used it as an observation point. Almost all information about Machu Picchu was speculation. Since the Spanish apparently never saw it, there was no written record. According to one theory, it was built by Incas fleeing from the Spanish. Still, there had been no consensus on whether the city was Incan or pre-Incan or on when or how it had been abandoned. The terraced ruins were discovered by an American archaeologist, Hiram Bingham, in 1911, just twenty-six years before Te Ata's visit.[13]

Unfortunately, she and her party of seven had little time to explore the ruins and take pictures. "We walked thru room after room, thru ceremonial chambers and to the place where the 'sun was tied'" (a large sun dial carved from rock by which the Indians could mark the solstices and equinoxes). She also mentioned two extraordinary engineering and building feats, the water system, whereby water was circulated through the city via seventeen fountains interspersed on the various terraces; and the rock staircases, which permitted relatively easy perambulation in a city that was literally carved out of the mountainside.

After their return to Cuzco, Te Ata spent her last afternoon, May 30, sitting in a plaza "watching the world of Cuzco pass by," happy as a lark.

⨾⨾

Fisher split the expedition, headquartered in Lima, into five groups. The only one sure to be free of cloud cover was led by Major Albert Stevens, of the U.S. Army Air Corps, who would be flying and photographing at nearly thirty thousand feet. The other groups were dispatched to preselected sites in different parts of Peru. One was composed of a CBS radio crew that would be broadcasting a description of the eclipse live over the network. Fisher and Te Ata were going to Huanchaco, the first port north of Trujillo. Accompanying them would be an artist, Agnes D. Johnson, of Lima. Instead of flying, they decided to drive the four hundred fifty miles through the desert, as Te Ata wrote, "to really get acquainted with it." Since they would be traveling most of the distance over sand, they hired a driver, who enlisted two companions just in case they got stuck.[14]

They departed on June 3. Before the first hour had expired, they were stuck, and the three hired men spent the second hour dislodging the Ford station wagon. Even if there was a paved road between Lima and Trujillo, the desert's shifting sands must have covered up large segments of it. They got stuck several more times the first day.[15] At least they were not likely to get lost; Lima and Trujillo were both on the coast. The travelers stayed overnight in a tiny village in a house without electricity. They slept fitfully on canvas cots; their host's burro occasionally wandered up and down the hallway outside their room. Te Ata thought it was amusing only in retrospect. On the next day, their driver was much more successful at keeping the Ford going. He had discovered that to avoid being devoured "by the hungry sand" he needed to travel at a fairly rapid speed.[16] Even so, there were many close calls. Once they suddenly found themselves hurtling down a steep sand dune, with the wheels of the station wagon serving as runners. They arrived in Trujillo on the night of June 4, feeling that they had not only seen but experienced Peruvian deserts.[17]

Though they were housed in Trujillo, their eclipse station was an old hacienda fifteen miles north in a virtual ghost town, Huanchaco. They shared the hacienda with two other teams, one from Peru and one from Japan. Every day they drove to the hacienda, which faced the sea and was located only a hundred yards from the breakers, to test their instruments. A few clouds over Huanchaco at the wrong time on June 9, and all of the money, effort, and time would be wasted— at least as far as Fisher's observations were concerned. But the Fisher luck held; this was his fourth cloud-free solar eclipse.[18] The first contact of the eclipse came on June 8 at 4:14 P.M. Since the moon always comes from the west in every solar eclipse and since the sun was already low in the west, Fisher noted that the moon seemed to come up out of the sea. Within minutes, Te Ata recalled, "there was a perceptible darkening of the heavens; the water took on a leaden color; a chillness was in the air as well as expectancy." For a ghost town, quite a sizable contingent had gathered at the hacienda, but they were quiet, probably like the Kazakhs in Russia the year before, not quite sure what to make of these crazy foreigners. The total eclipse began at 5:18 P.M. Using the Akeley camera with a foot-long telephoto lens, Fisher shot movie film. Te Ata shot Kodachrome photos of the corona, and Agnes Johnson began what turned out to be, according to Fisher, an excellent painting of the corona. The corona was unusually beautiful and showy, as the streamers of silvery light from the eclipsed sun radiated out uniformly from the poles and equatorial regions. Te Ata was so overwhelmed that she did not even try to describe the beauty and majesty of the eclipse in her account. Nor did Fisher, but he did describe the final moments of the eclipse: "The sun set, still partially eclipsed, sinking into the Pacific Ocean, with the tips of the crescent pointing upward."

To escape the heat in the city in July 1937, Te Ata and Fisher vacationed in Maine, Vermont, and New Hampshire and at a tony resort called Yama Farms in the Catskill Mountains.[19] To her, these were havens similar to Loon Island, scenic spots owned or used as getaways by their well-to-do friends. Could Fisher and Te Ata afford lengthy vacations in such desirable places? It is difficult to estimate their income. Neither left behind any financial or tax records from this period. Fisher's salary was $6,250, and he earned additional money in lecture fees, but how much and how many cannot be determined. Te Ata was charging clients between $100 and $250, plus expenses.[20] But it is not clear if she got, for example, $100 for each of six performances in Pittsburgh or if she was paid, say, $250 for the lot. Whatever their income, it is likely that in most years their expenses just about matched it. They made periodic references in their correspondence to their small or dwindling savings. They probably spent little of their own money on these getaways. Because they were a popular and stimulating couple, many members of the New York social elite were pleased to add them to their eclectic mix of party or house guests. Te Ata performed informally during many of these stays. She was glad to do it; the other guests, who were invariably charmed by the Indian legends and her talent, were potentially good business contacts.

In the fall Te Ata hit the road again, traveling to Pittsburgh, Cincinnati, and Chicago.[21] Publicity was generated in every city, and despite her experience with reporters and her intention to provide accurate information, many erroneous statements were attributed to her. For example, her mentor, Frances Davis, was named as a Bloomfield teacher who had sent Te Ata from Bloomfield to Columbia University. In an article in Lexington, Kentucky, she was identified both in the headline and in the text as an "Indian impersonator."[22] Other errors were more egregious and potentially embarrassing because it might appear that she was not well informed. Te Ata was quoted as saying that the Chickasaws and Choctaws were "enticed" to give up their southeastern lands for lands in Oklahoma. Surely she did not say "enticed"; she had known since childhood that the tribes had been coerced to move by the federal government and the state of Mississippi.[23] She also was misquoted as saying that the Chickasaws used to live in tipis before they came to Oklahoma. Historically, the tribe had never been nomadic or lived in tipis.

The authenticity of other statements attributed to her are more difficult to evaluate. For example, did she really say, "I would not advocate a marriage between the races if one of the contracting parties is full-blooded Indian. But in my own case, I'm a half-breed; there is white blood on both my father's and mother's sides." There was no elaboration, so the statements attributed to her are provocative but not very informative. When she was asked about her philosophy, she said it had nothing to do with theology: "My cathedral is the great out of doors. I must have periods of solitude and quiet. At least twice each year I go back to my people for a mental rest. It is only in the great silence of the woods and fields that I am able to find it. I always return from these visits ready to tackle any problem." While she did find solitude refreshing, the implication that she could reap its benefits only in Oklahoma was not true. In discussing her recent travels, she said there had been times when she felt she was "on the outside looking in." "It happened when I visited Scandinavia. I liked them [Scandinavians] immensely but there was an intangible barrier." In South America: "The minute I stepped off the gangplank I felt at home. In Cuzco, if I could have spoken their language, I would have 'belonged.' It is a feeling one cannot explain in words. You just know it is there."[24]

What upsets you? she was asked by a reporter. She handed the reporter a clipping from another newspaper, filled with inaccuracies and misstatements, and said, "Look at that. When I read that story I felt like scalping somebody!" Then she chuckled, probably to put at ease the reporter, who fervently promised to quote Te Ata verbatim. But when the story was printed, it contained errors too. When she was quoted accurately, valuable insights into her character were revealed: "I am not and never was interested in 'things,' but I am tremendously interested in human beings. Fundamentally we are not different. We all have our little grievances, our petty jealousies, our great happiness. I believe we would be better off if each attempted to understand the other's point of view."[25] Despite her comment about wanting to "scalp" inaccurate reporters, she considered such errors as nothing more than fleeting annoyances. She apparently never wrote a letter to the editor about such mistakes; she did correct some clippings with a pencil or fountain pen, but she thought, why be angry over stupid and unintentional mistakes. She tended to look forward, to her next performance, to her next audience. Her bond was always with the audience, including the newspaper reporter, for even though the article might contain errors, the reporters uniformly praised Te Ata and her programs.

～

In November Te Ata twice profited from her association with the AMNH. She was paid $100 to present a program to the members' children. She was reminded by Hazel Muller, secretary of the education department, that her first children's program, "Indian Songs and Stories," had been presented eight years earlier, after her new friend Clyde Fisher had arranged it.[26] Her second assignment for the AMNH was published in the November issue of *Natural History*. Under the byline "Te Ata of the Chickasaw Tribe," her article was titled "Native American Thanksgiving." Because of space limitations, about 800 words of the original 3,400 had to be cut, but the editor, Edward Weyer, offered Te Ata the opportunity to shorten the "excellent" article herself. She made the cuts and returned the manuscript, which Weyer found "skillfully shortened."[27]

In the article she used a busk festival to represent an example of Indian Thanksgiving. Many of the Muskogean tribes in the Southeast, including the Chickasaws, had busk festivals (sometimes called green corn ceremonies) long before contact with the colonial powers. But as Arrell Gibson wrote, "By the beginning of the nineteenth century, the Chickasaw Nation was in the throes of a comprehensive metamorphosis from the natural state to a general acceptance and application of the ways of Western civilization."[28] Te Ata knew that in her head and heart, and in a sense her article was a lament. But it was also true that many elements of the busk festival celebrated by other tribes, such as the Creeks, had survived. That is why Te Ata used the Creek festival as her primary model. Not only was information easier to obtain, but here was an important ritual that still existed.

Still, making the busk festival analogous to America's Thanksgiving was a stretch. Although it involved giving thanks for the past year (irrespective of blessings), it lacked many dimensions of the American holiday. It marked the spirit of renewal celebrated at the beginning of the new year, starting with the corn harvest in July. The busk festival also had a political element, as the people brought gifts to their chief.

Furthermore, it was quite elaborate, with various ceremonies and activities lasting between four and eight days. Te Ata's point, however, was not to compare Thanksgiving celebrations but to take advantage of the holiday season to educate readers "about an ancient, versatile and beautiful Indian tradition."

That is what she did, simply, without overloading the reader with too much detail:

> After the corn became ripe, the Chief set a day for the ceremony to begin; as the sun appeared above the horizon, he came to the door of his cabin, situated on elevated ground, and greeted the "Giver of Life" with three long calls. Then, after lighting his calumet, he wafted the smoke three times, to the sun, to the earth-mother, and in a circular movement to the four corners of the earth.[29] People cleansed themselves and their dwellings. The houses received new plastering and cane mats; the tribal members drank a black-colored emetic as a purgative.

Then, tongue in cheek, she wrote, "Some less violent medicinal treatment might well be prescribed for the modern American community as an aid to surviving the annual digestive ordeal." The article continued:

> [The busk festival] restored man to himself and his family. It absolved the Indian from all crimes, murder excepted, and gave him a chance to start anew. It was the season for moral and physical purification, general forgiveness . . . and united thanksgiving. At the corn ceremony the men danced all night, until the coming of the dawn. Then they retired and did not come forth again until summoned by the call of their Miko, just before the sun reached the middle of the sky. The remainder of the day was spent in speech-making, preparing tobacco for their ceremonies, tending the fire [built in the center of the square and to burn for the entire new year], ball playing and other games. On the last day the great Chief usually made "big talk," exhorting everyone to be exact in the performance of duty, to instruct his children carefully, to remember to venerate their dead. If anyone had distinguished himself during the year by an act of great bravery, this would be recounted that all might hear and think about it.
>
> Some of the dances of the ceremony were done by both men and women, the men in one circle and the women in another. Gourd rattles and beautifully decorated pottery-drums were brought forth,

and to their rhythm, while singers chanted their songs upward to the ear of the Great Mystery, the men, women and children danced their old patterned rituals. A well-known ethnologist once said that the Indian did not preach his religion—he danced it.

The article had no bibliography or citations, but this was consistent with Te Ata's performances. She wanted to speak directly to her audience, and this perhaps reflected the idea that she was an artist rather than a historian or a culture bearer. She wanted her offerings to have the ring of authenticity, and her artistry would convey trust. Her writing was merely serviceable, intended to convey the richness and beauty of the busk ceremony. That is why she did not address more parochial or academic concerns, such as when busk festivals flourished, how they changed, and why and when for most of the Southeastern tribes they had died out. Writing the article was a good exercise in self-discipline and it was nice to have a byline in a prestigious magazine, but she was probably not satisfied. Expository writing was too confining for her. And while she was an excellent observer, she undoubtedly realized that her writing skills for public consumption were only adequate. At any rate, Te Ata never again wrote another piece like "Native American Thanksgiving."

A month before Te Ata's article appeared, Fisher's book for lay readers, *Exploring the Heavens*, was published. As his friend and former employee Marian Lockwood wrote, " Here is the book . . . representing the years of experience which have gone into the making of a teacher and an astronomer."[30] Technically, Fisher was not an astronomer; he was not formally trained as an astronomer and did not practice astronomy. But his general grasp of the subject was exceptional, and his reputation as an astronomer was stellar after the opening of the Hayden Planetarium in media-rich New York. Fisher not only explained astronomy in terms the public could understand, but he looked like an astronomer right out of central casting. By 1937, when his book appeared, he was being referred to as the dean of American astronomy. More than Fisher's "friends and acquaintances" read the book. Soon after it was released, the book went into a second printing.[31] It received favorable reviews in many newspapers, including the *New York Times* and the *New York Herald Tribune*. He also received a letter from Albert Einstein lauding the book.[32]

Te Ata: Chickasaw Storyteller, American Treasure

Meanwhile, as 1939 dawned and Europe was hovering on the brink of another Great War, Te Ata, at forty-four, was entering one of the best, most rewarding years of her life. It began in January with a letter that she wrote to Eleanor Roosevelt, whom she apparently had not seen since 1933, and culminated with a trip to the ancient ancestral homeland of the Chickasaws and Choctaws in Mississippi. Even so, this productive and fulfilling year in her life would not be without considerable pain.

CHAPTER 12

Hyde Park and the Mississippi Homeland

More than five years had passed since Te Ata's performance for the Roosevelts at the White House. She knew she had been a big hit and in her excitement had predicted she would be invited back. But now, well into Roosevelt's second term in office, no invitation had come. In fact, there is no evidence that Te Ata and Eleanor Roosevelt corresponded at all between 1933 and 1939, though Te Ata likely offered written congratulations to the Roosevelts on Franklin's reelection in 1936.[1]

Why had she not been invited back? Probably because Eleanor Roosevelt did not play the traditional role of First Lady, planning and hosting White House entertainments. As the historian Doris Kearns Goodwin wrote, "Eleanor was able to forge a new role for herself, as a new kind of first lady, an activist role never practiced or even imagined before."[2] Furthermore, Te Ata had not lacked bookings. Although she would have been delighted to entertain the Roosevelts again, the most important factor in promoting her career had already occurred. She had been the featured entertainer at Franklin Roosevelt's first State Dinner in the White House. Since then every promotional brochure and nearly every news clipping had mentioned that historic April evening in 1933.

But in January 1939 when Te Ata read a newspaper item announcing that King George VI and Queen Elizabeth would be the Roosevelts' guests in the spring, she wrote to Mrs. Roosevelt: "A program of American Indian folk-lore might be quite appropriate to one of your social affairs, while the King and Queen of England are here. Those of other countries always seem greatly interested in *native* [emphasis hers] culture."[3] Just two days later, Mrs. Roosevelt's secretary, Edith Helm, thanked Te Ata on behalf of her boss but noted that no plans had been made.[4] The prompt response was a plus, but the wording of the note did not seem promising.

Meanwhile, Te Ata received several requests that demonstrated her prestige in the Native American and arts communities. The director of the National Folk Festival, based in Washington, D.C., wanted advice on selecting Indian groups for the festival to be held in April.[5] Leland Stowe, editor of the *New York Herald Tribune*, wrote that he had been asked to be a sponsor of the National Gallery of the American Indian and wanted her opinion of that project. She responded, "I must admit that I would be more enthusiastic about a museum to be placed *in the Indian country & for the Indians* [emphasis hers]; so much of his art has been carried to big cities and placed in boxes or in files. . . . But I am deeply interested in any worthy movement that will acquaint America in general with the beauty of the Indian creative mind."[6] Oliver La Farge, who was president of the corporation that would be running the Indian Concession at the World's Fair in New York later that year, asked Te Ata if she would serve on the advisory board.[7] The plan was to centralize control over the Indian objects exhibited and offered for sale and the Indians employed and their performances.

Thomas Thompson's health, especially his cardiopulmonary health, declined in the late 1930s, but there is no account of his last days or of his death. It is known that Te Ata was with her father when he died, at age seventy-four in an Oklahoma City hospital on April 23, 1939. Bertie mentioned her husband's death only parenthetically in her unpublished memoir. Te Ata probably wrote to Fisher before and after her father's death, but none of the letters were included in her papers, and there is no evidence that she talked or wrote about his death with anyone. She bore grief privately. She survived all of her immediate family members and apparently did not share her deepest feelings about their deaths.

Among the condolence letters from friends was one from the famous Arctic explorer, Bob Bartlett, a friend of Fisher's and fellow member of the Explorers Club for many years: "You are one of the not-too-

Thomas Thompson, posing for Clyde Fisher on Te Ata's wedding day.

numerous people in the world, whose happiness means a lot to me," he wrote. "All I can say is that I am thinking a lot about you and wishing I could really ease your sorrow by sharing a part of it with you. When you come back East I hope you will let me see you and try to help cheer you up." Another was from John Ball, who sent a poem titled "The Conversation."

> I asked the spirit, "what will you employ
> To keep immaculate the perilous joy?"
> And the spirit cried,
> "The brain's silver shall dissolve

Te Ata: Chickasaw Storyteller, American Treasure

The heart's music shall decline.
But from their going will resolve
The single purpose that is mine.
These two are shadows that I sow
Before I come . . . and as I go."

Thompson's granddaughter, Helen Cole, said his death probably had to do with weak lungs: "Weak lungs were part of that side of the family." If he had weak lungs, he abused them all the more by smoking pipes and cigars, which he did with relish over many years. There are a few references in his earlier letters to Te Ata about "heart problems." His grandson, Hiawatha Estes, who lived with his grandparents through most of his youth, was attending the University of Oklahoma in 1939 and living in Norman, just twenty-five miles from his grandparents. "The last time I saw Granddad, he was in the hospital here [Oklahoma City]," Hi said. "He hadn't been sickly at that time, but he developed pneumonia, I think, and was hospitalized. I asked him, 'How are you feeling, Granddad?' 'With my fingers,' he said. Though he was quite weak and ill, he was still Granddad. I didn't appreciate him enough while he was alive. When I was 16 and 17, little things he did used to irritate me." One thing: "He didn't have any teeth and when Grandma gave him meat, he would have to beat the hell out of it with a knife so he could swallow it. Well, sometimes I'd find all that noise very annoying." Another thing: "He would drag me to Saturday afternoon Westerns, and he'd insist that we sit on the front row. So I would some-times say belittling and insulting things to him. I remember once Te Ata overheard me and she said, 'Some day you are going to regret this.'"[10]

The day before Thompson died, a letter was mailed to Te Ata from the White House. A few days later the letter arrived, and Te Ata learned that she had been invited to entertain the king and queen of England at President Roosevelt's Hyde Park home on June 11.[11] How bittersweet the moment must have been. About the same time, Thompson was being laid to rest in Oklahoma City. On April 28 Te Ata wrote to Mrs. Helm, accepting the invitation. She remained in Oklahoma first to support her mother and then, after she took sick, to look after her during her illness.[12]

Arrangements for the new program were more complicated than those for the White House performance in 1933. Mrs. Roosevelt had much less time for details and left much of that to others. Correspondence went through secretaries, and a New York impresario, Henry Junge, was in charge of coordinating entertainment for the Roosevelts. Even so, Mrs. Roosevelt worried that "it might be too hot for Te Ata to go in the sun and do her part," so she suggested that Te Ata perform under the trees.[13] Initially, Te Ata was to have shared time with entertainers identified only as "a colored quartet," but that fell through. Then a Choctaw baritone, Wesley Robertson, known professionally as Ish-ti-Opi, began lobbying to get onto the program with Te Ata. Fisher told Te Ata in a May 2 letter that he had gotten a call from Ataloa, who said she had talked to Ish-ti-Opi. Quoting her, Fisher wrote: "He asked me to help him get the appointment to appear before the King and Queen when they visit the Roosevelts—saying it would be such a help to him when he goes to Europe." Ataloa told Fisher that the Choctaw singer was "so full of himself that he cannot think of anyone else."[14]

When Te Ata had not returned to New York by May 10, Junge had worked himself into a state of high dudgeon. Speaking to Fisher, Junge insisted that Te Ata wire him immediately on the date of her return so that she could present her intended Hyde Park program to him. Fisher told him that Te Ata was in Oklahoma and would return "in good time." "But," Fisher wrote to Te Ata, "he said he could not take my word for it—that he must hear from you directly. . . . He talked like a Prussian; maybe he is one. Anyhow, he is a damn fool. But I was very polite to him. . . . [Y]ou had better wire him immediately, or he may have apoplexy."[15]

After that call, Junge wrote to Mrs. Roosevelt that he had learned from Fisher that Te Ata was in Oklahoma with her mother, "who is suffering from a fatal illness, with anticipated demise." The stress may have caused Junge to exaggerate, because by then Fisher knew that Bertie was recovering, not dying, and as a gentleman, first, last, and always, he would have reassured Junge.[16] At any rate, Te Ata must have put Junge straight, for as Fisher noted: "[Junge] called me on the telephone this morning—as sweet as sugar. . . . He asked about your mother and was most considerate in every way. He did not seem to be disturbed about your coming home as late as May 28th (But gosh, I was). I had been counting the days."

In mid-May Te Ata wrote Fisher that she was "very much upset" to learn that an article had appeared in the Duncan, Oklahoma, newspaper "about . . . entertaining the K and Q." Te Ata was upset because she apparently had promised not to announce the engagement in advance. Hoping for more detail, the Chickasha newspaper called Frances Davis who—tipped off by Te Ata—persuaded the newspaper to hold off. Te Ata wrote Fisher: "I'll be killed if it gets back East." She nervously checked the Oklahoma City newspapers every day, and to her relief, nothing about the Hyde Park program appeared. She figured her brother Snake must have been the source. "More and more I'm learning to keep within myself what I do not *want* told. About the only ones I'm entirely willing to tell anything, is Mamma, C.F. and F.D.D. [Frances Dinsmore Davis]."[17]

Henry Junge and Mrs. Helm continued to fuss intermittently over details. Will Te Ata have twenty minutes or thirty minutes? Will she be sharing time with someone else? Even Mrs. Roosevelt finally got involved. What about the etiquette regarding royalty at picnics? she was asked by a reporter. Replying that she did not know anything about it, Mrs. Roosevelt said she would learn by June 11.[18] Apparently Ish-ti-Opi finally got through to Eleanor Roosevelt, who told Junge: "I feel rather sorry for Ish-ti-Opi and if he would like to come up with Te Ata and she is willing to share her time with him, I think they could take a half hour between them. Perhaps they could do something together and each have a chance to do something separate. If not, you may be able to work him in down here next winter."[19] Junge responded that the Indian baritone impressed him and would "make a notable and attractive addition to the program," adding that he and Te Ata would both "audition" before him on June 1 and that he would report the results to Mrs. Roosevelt. The "audition" probably was arranged so that Junge could determine if the Chickasaw and the Choctaw complemented one another or if they could or would perform together. Junge forwarded his impressions and proposed programs to Mrs. Roosevelt and asked her to decide the length. After Te Ata's audition, he wrote, "One need not be a great ethnologist to derive pleasure from such a lecture on the American Indian." He said he mentioned Mrs. Roosevelt's suggestion to Ish-ti-Opi and Te Ata that they "do some ensemble work," and while Ish-ti-Opi was willing, Te Ata declined.[20]

Less than a week before the performance, Te Ata wrote a long letter to her mother, and although she mentioned lectures she had attended, dinner at Margaret and John Ball's house, family news, questions about her father's childhood, the weather, and so on, she wrote nothing about what would surely be a milestone in her career.[21] Neither did she mention anything about two feature stories on her that were printed that week—an account of the royal picnic—in the *New Yorker* and in the *New York Herald Tribune*. The *New Yorker* piece, a biographical sketch, may have helped to dispel what the magazine reported as "fanciful tales" about the marriage of Te Ata and Clyde Fisher: that "Dr. Fisher found his bride, untamed and primitive, in a native hut and educated her himself."[22]

The *Herald Tribune* reporter called her a "modern-day Pocahontas," noting that both Indians married white men and that both had met British royalty in London. Stretching the comparisons a bit further, the reporter observed that both Indian women "carried themselves like a daughter of a king." Te Ata was "slim, beautiful, delicate in manner and speech. . . . King George and Queen Elizabeth will have seen many Indians in Canada, but it is safe to say that they will not have seen one who better reflects the highest potentialities of her race." In the interview at her apartment at 41 W. 72d Street, Te Ata said she had been too busy to be excited or nervous about the upcoming performance. She said she would present several dramatic vignettes, combining song, dance, and sign language to enact folklore of her people. "All of my material is authentic Indian lore but I have to adapt it to theatrical forms. For example, an ancient legend which perhaps would have required hours for the telling in Indian ritual, must be compressed into a few minutes. Modern American audiences wouldn't wait to hear it in its original form. Sometimes I go back to old, old stories which were translated long ago into English, but so crudely that they had no charm."

Calling Te Ata a "loyal champion of her people's traditions," the story also pointed out her belief that it was possible for Indians to adapt to the white man's world without losing the peculiar qualities of heritage. For example, it was noted that Te Ata lived in a modern New York apartment, "but its decorations are effectively Indian—pattern rugs and table runners, Indian basketry used as sconces for the wall lights, tall pottery vases filled with pampas grass and a highly

Te Ata: Chickasaw Storyteller, American Treasure

decorative beaded gadget in the corner." Gadget? Te Ata told the reporter that her clothes, most of which she designed herself, always included some touch that was symbolic of her people. Almost all of her jewelry was made by Indians or was Indian in design. As she traveled across America, the article continued, Te Ata sensed "a great rebirth of interest in all phases of Indian lore." She credited the "Indian Bureau" (under John Collier) for "encouraging the Indians to reverence what is beautiful in their heritage, while . . . preparing them to live in the white man's world." She noted that the bureau schools on the reservations no longer deprecated the old ways and tribal elders were being encouraged to teach native dialects to children. "Our people have great potentialities and it is remarkable what they have done despite the shabby treatment they have received."[23]

Last-minute details were addressed. For the printed program, would she be Te Ata or Princess Te Ata? When she dealt with the matter publicly, she always pooh-poohed the phony title. But after a decade of being identified as Princess Te Ata, the title may have taken on a life of its own. On the Hyde Park program, she was Princess Te Ata.[24] President Roosevelt himself decided that Te Ata and Ish-ti-Opi would have fifteen minutes each with additional time for encores.[25] Both performers had to cut some fifteen minutes out of their original planned presentations. Te Ata removed two numbers but added one. She would perform first, as she had requested.

Making the three-hour drive with Te Ata from Manhattan to Hyde Park on the appointed date, June 11, was Fisher, Margaret Ball, and Kuruks Pahetu. Margaret Ball drove, and while giving an animated review of a movie she had just seen, Walt Disney's *The Ugly Duckling*, she missed a turn and the quartet wound up in Connecticut. Fortunately, they had started so early that they arrived in plenty of time.[26] The picnic menu featured several kinds of meat, including hot dogs. In his written note accepting the picnic invitation, the Roosevelt's son, Franklin Jr., made a "formal request to handle the Hot Dog Department, especially the eating of them." And he closed: "Yum-yum to you all!" The Roosevelts thought it would be fun to introduce the king and queen to one of America's culinary mainstays, but the press, according to Margaret Ball, made it seem like serving hot dogs was an insult to the monarchy.[27]

The picnic and performance were held not at Springwood, the Roosevelt's thirty-five-room mansion on the Hudson River, but at the president's Hill Top Cottage, which he had designed and which was aptly located on a hill some three or four miles distant. Te Ata found the gray stone cottage "simple and sturdy." She and Margaret agreed that they could design a much more interesting and convenient one.[28] After dressing, there was time to contemplate the upcoming performance, and if Te Ata had not been nervous previously, she felt then like a "caged tiger." "Too many people going in and out of my dressing room," she said. "Too much talking and running about trying to see the people gathered on the lawn and the great ones sitting on the porch[,] . . . just too much noise and excitement for me."[29]

At nearly 2:45, Mrs. Roosevelt came for Te Ata. Taking the makeshift stage, she began by facing the porch, where seven tables had been set up. At table one sat President Roosevelt, Queen Elizabeth, Mrs. Lehman (wife of the New York governor), and Secretary of the Treasury Henry Morgenthau. King George VI sat at table two with Sara Delano Roosevelt, the president's mother, Governor Lehman, and Mrs. Morgenthau. At the other tables were various and sundry British earls, lords, and ladies as well as other British and American dignitaries. The rest of the audience was arrayed around Te Ata on the lawn.[30]

Te Ata was dressed in a full-length buckskin ceremonial Dakota dress that was more than one hundred years old. She waited for dramatic effect; only the rustling of the leaves from the trees overhead were audible. She began with Hartley Burr Alexander's "The Last Song":

Let it be beautiful when I sing the last song—
Let it be day!
I would stand upon my two feet, singing!
I would look upward with open eyes, singing!
I would have the winds to envelope my body;
I would have the sun to shine upon my body;
The whole world I would have to make music with me.
Let it be beautiful when thou wouldst slay me, O Shining One!
Let it be day when I sing the last song![31]

During her second selection, a Seneca romance legend, Te Ata noticed that the king and queen smiled and laughed spontaneously—and appropriately. In another number, "The Song of the Maiden

Te Ata: Chickasaw Storyteller, American Treasure

Though not a good photograph, it is one of the only two accessible prints of Te Ata entertaining the Roosevelts and the king and queen of England at the president's Hyde Park home in 1939. Some home movies of the performance (unfortunately silent) are available for viewing at the Roosevelt Library in Hyde Park and at the Chickasaw Council House Museum in Tishomingo.

Weaving," Te Ata used a beautiful Salish basket loaned to her by Clark Wissler.[32] She bowed, acknowledging the applause, and left the stage, giving way to Ish-ti-Opi, who sang three songs he had either written or arranged. She undoubtedly resented his apparent horning in on her Hyde Park performance, but instead of being critical, she simply ignored him. He is not mentioned in her memoir or in any of her other written references to Hyde Park. In her accounts, she was the only performer that day.

By her second group of selections, Te Ata's nervousness had vanished, but the conditions were not ideal. The time limit made her feel rushed, the wind was stronger than she liked, and because the audience surrounded her, she felt her voice was scattered. As a further distraction, the king started taking motion pictures of her and continued throughout her second set. But she soldiered on, focusing not on these minor disturbances but on the task of matching a great performance to a great occasion.

Afterward Te Ata presented Queen Elizabeth with two Indian dolls for her children, the princesses Elizabeth (the present queen) and Margaret.[33] The queen asked about the preservation of Indian culture and Te Ata's adaptations of the folkore. She responded at some length and doubtless mentioned her own trip to England in 1930. They were then joined by King George, who offered his hand and congratulations. His boyish, clean-cut features, deep blue eyes, and handsome tan must have tongue-tied Te Ata, for she only remembered saying, "It is my pleasure, Your Majesty," before bowing and moving away. She also talked with President Roosevelt, who introduced his mother and other guests, including Britain's ambassador to the United States. She greeted Governor and Mrs. Lehman, who had had Te Ata entertain in the executive mansion in Albany twice during his administration. Eleanor Roosevelt and Te Ata chatted for a while and then parted; it was their last time together.

Although they referred to one another as friends, their relationship had been professional. The only time they were together not as entertainer and entertained was the day at Bear Mountain when Mrs. Roosevelt dedicated Lake Te Ata. Whether their relationship would have continued or perhaps deepened, no one can say. But by the time of the Hyde Park picnic, the beginning of World War II was only two and a half months away, and from that day forward, the focus of both Franklin and Eleanor Roosevelt narrowed markedly. The Roosevelts still often traveled to Hyde Park, but it was a retreat, a brief refuge from the crushing burdens of the job. One of those retreats occurred exactly a year after the famous picnic. A reporter noted that the weather "was much the same as it was on that historic weekend last year and the hills across the Hudson River stood out as clearly against the backdrop of the Catskill Mountains to the north. But there remained only a memory of peace which existed in the world at that time."[34]

After Te Ata's party left Hyde Park that day, they drove to Pelham, New York, to have a gala dinner with Margaret and John Ball and their young daughter, Ann. The next day Te Ata and C.F. were back home, where Te Ata wrote to her mother that she was "setting things straight and getting back to earth and to the simple things." Two days later the last artifact of the Hyde Park picnic arrived: a thank-you note from Eleanor Roosevelt.[35] She was not at home to receive it, however; she was heading north to Loon Island, to rest and prepare for the new season ahead.

≈

Te Ata apparently needed an extended rest. She wrote to Fisher from Loon Island on June 22 that she had been feeling so tired she "could hardly drag [herself] about." It was her practice to take the summers off; she worked and traveled from fall into June. Sometimes, she would accept invitations in the summer but not many and usually only if they were in or around New York City. This exhaustion she writes about feeling in the summers accumulated following months of traveling and performing. Although she had the repertoire to vary her performances considerably, and it is evident from the newspaper write-ups that she did to some extent, she probably felt constrained to include in most of her performances "God's Drum," "The Last Song," and several others that the public had come to associate with her. To perform those same pieces over and over and consistently stir the emotions of her audience took great energy, pride, and dedication. No matter how many miles she had just driven to be in a school auditorium, she felt she could do no less than her best for the audience, any audience. It might be the only time in their lives that some of them would see an Indian performing culturally relevant material, and she wanted to leave the audience with sterling memories of herself and her people. Such was the pressure that she took on herself.

That July, only two months after her father's death, Te Ata suffered the death of another man near and dear to her. Hartley Burr Alexander, author of "God's Drum" and an early and major admirer and supporter, died at the age of sixty-six.[36] Beyond liking and admiring him, Te Ata owed Alexander a lot: through referrals, he helped her to book many performances during the early part of her career. She mourned his passing and probably regretted not having spent more time with him. Alexander was an authentic Renaissance man, one with an immense breadth of talent and skill as a writer, poet, teacher, researcher, historian, anthropologist, and philosopher. Te Ata understood that for an artist even to be noticed by a man like Hartley Alexander was a worthy tribute, but to be openly and unceasingly promoted by him was a high compliment indeed. She had not relied on his help for several years, and it is likely that in 1939 Te Ata's fame may have eclipsed his own. But like his fellow Nebraskan, Thurlow Lieurance, he was a special friend who played a pivotal role in Te Ata's career, and in that sense, Alexander's passing marked the end of an era.

Te Ata spent much of the rest of the summer of 1939 entertaining out-of-town guests. She noted in a letter to her mother that a steady stream of guests from both sides of the family had paraded through the couple's small apartment. "Dr. Fisher and I came home last night and breathed a great sigh of relief to once more (at long last) be alone with each other. It seems to me we have not been alone for two minutes since last March when Ataloa arrived on the scene." In the same letter, she echoed the sentiments of millions of Americans just two days after Germany invaded Poland by saying that she hoped the United States could stay out of the European war." "But," she wrote, "I am fearful that we cannot." Moreover, the hope following her performance at Hyde Park that King George or Queen Elizabeth might have invited her to England surely disappeared in the early days of September, after England and France declared war on Germany. In reference to the war in Europe, she wrote it was "shocking that people are not more civilized today." Te Ata betrayed either a poor word choice or a naïveté that was almost shocking itself, given the wholesale slaughter and carnage of World War I. She concluded her remarks about the European war by pointing out the irony of people referring to Indians as savages.[37]

Later that September Te Ata and C.F. traveled to Mississippi to visit the descendants of the Choctaws who had not emigrated to Indian Territory following the signing of the 1830 removal treaty of Dancing Rabbit Creek. Under a provision of that treaty, Choctaws who declined to emigrate received land allotments in Mississippi and were made citizens of the state and the United States.[38] In other words, their lives under Choctaw sovereignty were over. Assimilation did not take place, however. To the contrary, the Choctaws who remained generally had more Choctaw blood and were much less acculturated than the Choctaws in Oklahoma. To see Choctaws who still observed the old ways would be like looking through a window to her past, since she had a little Choctaw blood and the Choctaws and Chickasaws had shared so many customs and traditions. For years, she had been wanting to visit the Mississippi Choctaws to see firsthand how they lived and which of the traditional customs were still practiced. She had been corresponding with the tribal chief, the Reverend E. W. Willis, for some time, and when a big Choctaw celebration was planned for late September, the visit was arranged.[39]

En route, they visited Tupelo, Mississippi, in the heart of what had been the Chickasaw Nation before removal. The Chickasaws had lived mainly in north-central and northeastern Mississippi, while the Choctaws had lived just to the south in central Mississippi. Those who had elected to remain still lived there in small enclaves and communities in and around Philadelphia. At their Tupelo hotel, Te Ata and Fisher were greeted by an unnamed resident who took them on a tour of the area. The tour included a visit to an Irish farmer named Byron Kelly, who showed them a number of Chickasaw artifacts that he had found or dug up on his land over the years. Most of the artifacts were European trade goods (via the British or French, who in the eighteenth century were in competition for a Chickasaw alliance). Other artifacts were Indian-made shell beads, gorgets, and shell-tempered pottery, and Kelly presented Te Ata with a shell-bead necklace that had been made by an eighteenth-century Chickasaw. The disturbing part about this to many Indians then and today is that the necklace had been recovered from a Chickasaw's grave, according to Fisher, who reported that Kelly "had examined about 100 Chickasaw Indian skeletons."[40]

Many Chickasaws agreed with the traditional tribal stricture that graves—whether historic or prehistoric—should not be violated in any manner for any reason. Even digging up remains to advance science was a desecration. But once remains and artifacts had been unearthed, opinions seemed to diverge. Some Chickasaws believed strongly that immediate reburial was the only correct option; without proper burial, it was believed that the spirit of the deceased Chickasaw would wander eternally. Others felt no such strong compunction or belief. They gave the impression, without saying so directly, that once the objects had been unearthed, the sacredness of the grave and its contents had been dispelled. (The two perspectives persist today.)

Te Ata seemed to fit into the latter group. If she were an absolutist, she most likely would not have accepted the necklace and her writing would have reflected a revulsion of Kelly's avocation, if not the man. Did she know that farmer Kelly had disturbed ancient Chickasaw graves? He probably did not own up to it. If he was unsure of Te Ata's sensibilities, he probably would have told them that many of the artifacts and some remains found on the ridgetops of Tupelo had not been buried deeply and had worked their way naturally to the surface.[41] This was true and is likely how Kelly first discovered that part of his land was, in effect, a two-hundred-year-old cemetery. But it would be naive to believe that this man of the soil, displaying hundreds of artifacts, did not dig up at least some of them. On the other hand, he undoubtedly presented himself not as a looter but as a sensitive and knowledgeable collector. Perhaps he thought he was.

If Te Ata once had been an absolutist, her conviction might have been weakened by her associations and experiences with scientists, particularly at the AMNH, a highly respected institution that exhibited the remains and burial goods of numerous Native Americans as well as ancient peoples worldwide. Te Ata had seen such bones there and probably had attended related lectures by her husband's anthropology colleagues. What was more likely to capture her attention were the feelings of being there—in her ancestral home. Although she knew nothing about her direct ancestors who lived in the area, Te Ata's senses would have been highly attuned to experience everything that forms an indelible sense of place. Walking along a ridgetop, she could imagine herself in 1739, smelling cedar from the trees that grew in abundance in the thin, sandy soil, looking in all directions for any sight of French soldiers before hiking down to a nearby creek to fill a pot with water. Having seen drawings of Chickasaw camps, it was no great feat for Te Ata to imagine in detail the entire village arrayed around her. She, of course, would be one of the tribe's storytellers, a position not only of importance—communicating history and culture to younger Chickasaws—but also of reverence.

What she did not see in Tupelo were Chickasaws. In contrast to the Choctaws, many of whom remained in central Mississippi, only a few Chickasaws refused to migrate, and most of them either were intermarried or soon would be. One hundred years later, in 1939, the quantum of their ancestors' Chickasaw blood was quite small; probably none of their descendants would be recognizable as Indian.

Te Ata: Chickasaw Storyteller, American Treasure

Te Ata and Fisher arrived in Union, Mississippi, the site of the Choctaw event, on September 26. Although it was billed as a Choctaw Council Meeting, the name was misleading, for the two-day program was social; in fact, it was sponsored not by the tribe but by the Lions Club of Union. The printed program directed persons wanting more information to "Sitting Bull" Joe Kasden and "Shooting Bull" Ernest Tucker. A copy of the program showed that on September 27 at 11:30 A.M. an address was given by "Miss T.E. Ato [sic], a Choctaw Indian [sic], New York, N.Y."[42]

Te Ata's journal, composed as a letter to her mother, was full of detail. At the stickball game, she noted that while the whites sat in the bleachers the Indians "sat, stood and squatted over among the trees and what a lovely sight it was." It would be "almost impossible to pose such a group with such perfectness for line and color." It is characteristic of Te Ata that instead of mentioning the segregation of the two races, she pointed out the perfect composition and beautiful colors displayed by the Indian people watching from the trees. She went on to describe in detail Choctaw fashion and style. The men still wore feathers in their hats, beaded straps around their shoulders, and colored kerchiefs about their necks. But they were eclipsed by the women, who wore long multicolored percale dresses, four-inch bands of broadcloth with beaded designs worn around both shoulders and the waist, white aprons, beaded ornaments around the neck, and earrings. Their hair was waist length and bedecked with beaded combs and ribbons.

Te Ata was a bit disappointed that the stickball game and dancing were held at night, since she had wanted to record them on movie film. But she was impressed with the "grace, beauty and fleetness" of the stickball players and the insouciance of girls who periodically brought water to players while the running, jumping, and colliding bodies continued unabated around them. The dances, named for the snake, tick, and war, were "simple, the movements were rhythmical and strangely beautiful." "They made me think of wind running thru tall grass, wave upon wave[,] . . . slowly, rhythmically[,] . . . the repetition like that of a drum beat, surely and slowly weaving its spell."[43]

About two thousand Choctaws lived in Mississippi in 1939, according to the superintendent of the Choctaw Agency, H. K. Meyer. They

Te Ata and Nannie Willis, wife of the Misissippi Choctaw chief, in Philadelphia, Mississippi, in 1939. Te Ata, who was part Choctaw, was invited to address a tribal social event. She and Fisher were surprised and dismayed to find that the chief and his wife were refused service in many of the town's businesses. (Photo by Clyde Fisher.)

had six or seven schools and a hospital, where a large number of cases of tuberculosis, hookworm, and malaria were treated. In addition, the federal government was building a few houses with indoor plumbing as models of proper sanitation. (How Choctaw families would afford their own new sanitary houses was not clear.) Wanting to see inside some of the typical Choctaw homes, Te Ata and Fisher drove Chief Willis and his wife, Nannie, to their house in Philadelphia. On the way they stopped at a Philadelphia drugstore. Although Chief Willis told Fisher that the Willises would not be welcome in the store, Fisher assured them that everything would be all right.

Te Ata wrote, "C.F. was so distinguished looking, and so authoritative in his quiet, gentle way, that the shop owner, embarrassed, could not refuse to serve us." Te Ata and Mrs. Willis ordered ice cream, which the latter consumed with considerable delight. Then Fisher ordered orange juice and the chief looked somewhat crestfallen. He had anticipated ice cream but felt that to be polite, he should also order orange juice. Though the chief was clearly disappointed, he could not be persuaded to change his order. Afterward Te Ata suggested that they stop at a dime store, but Mrs. Willis gave a firm shake of her head. Indians were not welcome there, and she did not want to court humiliation. The chief's home was not one of the newer ones with indoor plumbing; it was "very poor," had few furnishings, a fireplace for heat, and a few chickens scratching around out in the yard.

Te Ata and Fisher left Philadelphia on September 28, their sixth wedding anniversary. As an epilogue of sorts in her journal, she wrote that the thing that had impressed her most about the Mississippi Choctaws was that after one hundred years of contact with other races and all their trials and tribulations, they were still together and still Choctaw.

CHAPTER 13

Heart Loaded Down and Heavy

By 1940 Te Ata's programs were arranged by Colsten Leigh. Leigh was Fisher's manager as well, and in one of his journals, Fisher noted that Leigh received 40 percent of his speaking fees.[1] A big-time manager who commanded big-time rates, he had offices in Chicago, Oakland, Detroit, and Buffalo, as well as on Fifth Avenue. On the left margin of his letterhead was a long list of clients, including Malcolm Cowley, Mortimer Adler, Jim Thorpe, Eleanor Roosevelt, Abraham Flexner, Will Durant, Clifton Fadiman, and Te Ata.[2] That winter Leigh arranged Te Ata's extensive tour of the Deep South.

Meanwhile, Bertie was on her way to Virginia. After her husband's death, she no longer wanted to live in Norman, so she moved to Oklahoma City to be near her son Tom, who was thirty. But after ten months of illness and unhappiness, despite the best efforts of Tom and his wife to care for her, Bertie moved back to Norman to be with Hiawatha. She continued to suffer from an nearly unremitting pain. When Avis was visiting from Virginia, where her husband was stationed in the navy, Bertie asked if she could go back with her, thinking that the change might do her good. Hiawatha thought the long trip would only exacerbate his grandmother's poor health. To help her decide, Bertie, a lifelong believer in the power of prayer, said she prayed for direction: "One Saturday night God came to me. . . . He was standing beside me with His arms stretched out over me. . . . He never spoke a word. After I woke up I could still see Him and then He went away." On Monday

God appeared again to Bertie while she was propped up in bed at 10:00 A.M. reading the Bible. "[He] put out his arms and said Go in Peace. I never heard anything plainer than those words. So I knew it was all meant for me to make the trip." Bertie and Avis left for Virginia two days later, and Bertie said she "stood the trip fine."[3]

Te Ata spent almost three weeks traveling down the Florida peninsula, appearing in several locales from Gainesville to Miami Beach. She stopped at several Seminole encampments and communities, mixing pleasure with business. She loved observing and talking with members of the more unacculturated tribes. Several songs and legends that she identified as Seminole are contained in her papers. One of them, "Story of the Turkey," marked "retold by Te Ata," tells how Turkey used to be chief of all the birds until he was captured by some people, one of whom, a medicine man, worked some strong medicine on him, shrinking him down to his contemporary size. This was done because it was felt that Turkey had abused his great power by killing too many of the people—snatching them up into the sky and carrying them away. Now Turkey's size and way of life was changed. "You will not be able to fly so high again," she said, quoting the medicine man. "If the Seminoles catch you, they will eat you. You will be allowed to fly as high as the top of a tree. The Indians will shoot you with their bows and arrows. You will be good food and useful to the Indians. You will have to use your wits to keep away from them."

"Old Man made it so," the medicine man continued. "He took pity on us. He showed us how to help ourselves. But he will help you, too. He will make it so that you can go quietly among the grasses and in the woods. There you can hide from Man and rear your young. It will always be hard for them to find you. Old Man will allow you to wear the scalplock at your breast. It will remind you and your clan why you are no longer the King of Birds."[4]

Although Te Ata wrote the story in narrative form, she probably never performed it exactly the same way twice. That would be in keeping with the tribe's oral tradition. Although the story belonged to the tribe, the adaptation and the words were the storyteller's. She was free to improvise as long as she remained faithful to the story's essence. Te Ata was always mindful that a tribal story she was enacting had been a gift to many generations. When she seemed completely lost in her role as the old woman left behind on the trail by the tribe, it is because she was there. So it was that charming, humorous, instructive, poignant, heartbreaking stories— many hundreds of years old— were replenished and reached a much wider audience through Te Ata in 1940 than ever before.

∽

In a March 22 letter, Fisher wrote, "Bring your mother home with you. I am anxious to see you both." Evidently, Te Ata had written her husband about the possibility of picking up Bertie in Virginia and bringing her to New York. Te Ata sensed that her mother was nearing the end of her life, and she wanted this hardworking, modest, provincial, and good woman to see New York City before she passed away. So on March 25, Bertie's seventieth birthday, they set off for the biggest and glitziest city in the country. The sight, sounds, and smells of such an utterly foreign yet compelling city must have been almost overwhelming to Bertie. But if so, she seems to have adjusted by the time she started writing her short autobiography a few weeks later. After her arrival, she got "awful sick" for a prolonged period. She says she probably would have died had it not been for "the Doctor" (Fisher). She surely understood that Fisher was not a medical doctor, but his "bedside manner" may have helped her to feel better.

When Bertie improved, Te Ata suggested she write the story of her life. According to Te Ata, the subject had come up one day at breakfast. Fisher had been quizzing Bertie about flora and fauna and was amazed at the depth of her anecdotal knowledge. Te Ata left a writing tablet and pencil by her bedside and asked her to write her story for her children. That was the motivational key, for as Bertie wrote in the introduction, "I have lived for my husband and my children. They want me to write down the stories I tell them of my early days. I am used to doing the things my children ask. . . . And even tho I have had no education nor any of the qualities for writing a book, for them, I will try it."[5]

Bertie concluded her autobiography (typewritten, it was thirty-nine single-spaced pages) with an account of her nearly four-month stay in New York. Although she was quite ill part of the time, she was so impressed with New York that she quipped her life was just beginning at 70. She must have felt that way on the ferry to Liberty Island, for this was, she wrote, her first boat ride (with the possible exception of taking a flat-bottomed ferry across the Red River).[6]

Bertie Thompson. This photo was taken by her son-in-law on the day he married Te Ata.

Another time, they drove through the majestic Hudson River valley to the U.S. Military Academy at West Point and to Bear Mountain and the beautiful little lake that was named for her daughter in 1932. Recalling the ceremony, Te Ata pointed out where Kuruks had paddled her across the lake in a canoe to the waiting throng, including Eleanor Roosevelt who had christened the lake in her honor. How proud Bertie must have been, and fortunate to be standing there overlooking Lake Te Ata.

In the city Bertie liked walking and having lunch in Central Park and going to the Central Park Zoo. She was impressed by the majesty of St. John the Divine Church and the immensity of the skyscrapers. Referring to one of her son-in-law's lectures at the planetarium, she wrote: "I feel like if you don't see or hear anything else in New York, this one thing is worth the trip up here." She tried Chinese and Hungarian food and found them a little too exotic for her taste. Perhaps Te Ata and Fisher were trying to do too much. While visiting the Balls in Pelham, New York, Bertie again took sick and a doctor was summoned. Instead of spending the night, they stayed a week, until Bertie could travel again. The Balls treated her so kindly and attentively that she said she came to think of them as her children.

They went to the World's Fair on Long Island twice during Bertie's stay. She seemed to be most captivated by the exhibits housing Elsie the Borden Cow and an all-electric kitchen. She listed seeing an "electric clock, percolater [sic], ice box, mixer, wafle [sic] irons, dish washer." Then, tongue in cheek, she added, "I didn't see any electric cook tho, but guess she was there somewhere."

Bertie finished her autobiography with these words: "Well, my time is near up in New York and will go back to Virginia but must say I have enjoyed every minute I have been here and the ones I have been with and they have done everything in their power to make me happy and to show me a good time, which they certainly have. I never will forget the New York trip which I never dreamed I would ever take. But who can ever tell what will happen."

Te Ata was included as one of ten Indian career women featured in the December 1940 issue of the periodical *Independent Woman*. Others included the famous potter Maria Martinez, whose annual income was said to be $20,000; Pop-Charlee, a painter from Taos Pueblo; and

Lushanya, the only Indian who had succeeded in opera. The writer of the article noted that "a number of girls [sic] from the different tribes are helping us to understand the beauty and mysticism of their folklore. . . . [N]o one can do this more delightfully than the lovely Te Ata."[7] In January 1941 Te Ata was invited to be the guest of honor at the Decorator's Club on Fifth Avenue at a tea previewing an exhibition of Native American designs adapted for fashion and decoration. In the invitation letter, the exhibitor, a blueblood named Elizabeth Blomquis Symonds, wrote: "You have done much to further interest in all that we owe to Indians in art and music."[8]

Te Ata was working as much as she wanted to—with the exception of taking time off to be with her sick mother. While her siblings, Selena, Gene, Avis, Gladys, and Tom, all pitched in to help out with the increasingly frail Bertie, Te Ata did her share of the caretaking in addition to providing the bulk of the financial support. According to her ethos, writing a monthly check in no way absolved her from spending lengthy periods with her mother—and this was often time away from her career and her husband. She had always arranged her schedule of programs to include a lengthy stay in Oklahoma, and since her father's death, Te Ata had spent even more time with her mother. Her visits were a tonic to Bertie. There were times when Te Ata arrived and Bertie could scarcely lift her head off the pillow, but within a day or two she would be up cooking and sewing. Was she using her physical condition to manipulate her children? Probably not. She had never been dishonest or devious. Rather, as a woman who had always "lived for her children," she was not as happy when they were not around. Situational depression probably exacerbated her physical problems.

Missing from the scene entirely from sometime in 1939 through 1941 was Te Ata's older brother, Gene (Snake). His niece, Helen Cole (Avis's daughter), said that Gene left a note for his wife saying he was leaving and "just disappeared." Helen had no idea what prompted him to leave. Apparently the matter was not discussed with the children of the Thompson clan, because Hiawatha (Gladys's son) also did not know why his uncle disappeared. Years earlier Gene had graduated in animal husbandry from Oklahoma A&M (now Oklahoma State University), took a faculty job at a college in Lawton, married Maude, a prominent woman and musician from Duncan, and settled in nearby Comanche to raise a family.[9]

Gene and Te Ata, very close as children, were not so close as adults. They apparently did not see each other much and almost never corresponded after Te Ata left home. Te Ata's letters often contain references to her other siblings but not to Gene. This alienation from the family was uncharacteristic of the children; even Gladys, who often exhibited paranoid tendencies, remained closer to the rest of the family than Gene did. "Gene's son, Ross, looked for his father for pretty near two years," Helen Cole recalled. "Finally, Ross found his father in late 1941, living on 'Skid Row' in New York City." How long he had been in New York is not known. He seems to have made no attempt to contact his sister despite knowing that she was living in an apartment building just a few miles away. Perhaps he had been watching her, waiting for the right opportunity to approach. There were family stories circulating about Gene's drinking. It is implausible that he had drifted into New York City by happenstance; more likely, he was looking for help but had not found a way to ask for it. No version of the father and son reunion exists, but Gene was persuaded to return to his family. After a time, he returned to his job at Cameron, the college in Lawton. Then he resumed his life with the family as though nothing had happened.[10] He lived another thirty years with no apparent relapses.

Te Ata performed in New Orleans on February 6, 1941, and for the first recorded time, she tailored part of her program to the war in Europe. In the next morning's *Times-Picayune* an article led with her story of the contribution of the Indian sign-talkers to the Allied cause in World War I. "The armies were fighting in France," she was quoted as saying, "when they discovered that all the messages they sent were finding their way to the enemy. . . . They tried using different languages. But the Germans were good interpreters. Finally they appealed to the Indian soldiers. The messages were sent in the Indian language and for once the Germans were stumped." She also noted pointedly that fewer Indians than any other group had to be drafted to fight that war and that while so many had enlisted, many of them were not even citizens of the United States. Citizenship had been conferred on various groups of Indians, such as the Five Civilized Tribes, beginning with the Dawes Commission at the turn of the century. But not all Indians were made U.S. citizens until Congress enacted legislation to that effect in 1924.[11] "Evidently," she said, "they weren't considered intelligent enough to vote, though just why they had to be formally declared citizens of the country that was taken away from them will always remain a mystery to me."[12] She understood perfectly well why. But expressing bafflement underscored the irony.

On February 10, Te Ata arrived in Durant, Oklahoma, to visit her uncle Greenwood and aunt Minnie. Hardly had they started visiting when a telegram arrived for Te Ata from Maude, Gene's wife, who was looking after Bertie in Oklahoma City. According to the wire, Bertie had a very bad cold and was becoming agitated because Te Ata had not arrived. Although Te Ata was worried, she seemed to savor the drive through south-central Oklahoma, the old Chickasaw Nation. At one point she crossed the Washita River near her land allotment. She recalled, "I found myself at an old spring I had not visited since Daddy drove me there on one of our Sunday excursions," in the buggy pulled by the two mares, Blaze and Ginger. Before she reached Oklahoma City, "night was creeping along the middle of the earth—leaving the edges all aglow with orange and blue." "And I seemed almost alone upon the earth and above it—for at this time of night . . . there is a distinct lure in the prairie for me. Stars came forth one by one and I became less tense and drew in deep fresh breaths of good Oklahoma air."[13]

Te Ata stayed with her mother for two weeks, during which she made a pot of pashofa. In the old days the cracked corn and pork stew was made by Chickasaw healers as part of an elaborate ceremony they conducted, also called Pashofa, which was intended to cure the critically ill. When Bertie felt better, Te Ata traveled to North Texas to present some programs arranged by her manager. During one performance, she recalled visiting a small community and learning that some mothers had warned their children to stay inside because the Indians were coming. After reporting Te Ata's remembrance of this shameful example of bigotry, the newspaper reporter indulged in the same practice by assuring the readers that Te Ata will not "do any scalping. She didn't even bring a tomahawk with her."[14]

Sentiments like those must have frustrated Te Ata, but she rarely responded angrily, and never publicly. She could not do anything about obtuse reporters, nor would she permit such remarks to harden her heart. She was aware that racial intolerance and insensitivity were deeply ingrained in many Americans. Her way of handling insulting stereotypes and hatred, of winning friends and influencing people, was to keep on portraying the beautiful, the wise, the profound. She believed her way was successful. She could see this was so, when the curtain fell and the audience was on its feet applauding. She liked the applause, perhaps even craved it, but part of the satisfaction came from her hope that some of those who rose to their feet had undergone a small transformation.

✍

Back in New York, Fisher was about to set off on a five-week lecture tour of upstate New York and Pennsylvania. Why a 63-year-old man with a heart condition would willingly brave the often fierce, dangerous late-winter elements of upstate New York for weeks is puzzling. His motive probably was not money, because his fees, less Leigh's 40 percent, usually left him with hardly more than enough to cover his expenses. At the end of this trip's journal, as always, Fisher made a chart of his expenses. Gross fees for six weeks of lectures totaled $1,027. Other expenses totaled another $414; this left Fisher with a net income of just $201.49.[15]

More likely, his motive for embarking on the physically risky tour was a combination of the deep satisfaction he derived from teaching and denial of his diminished physical resources. Obviously, he knew that the upstate weather in March would be hazardous at times. If he had forgotten or hoped for better, he learned otherwise as the snow continued to mount as he drove between Utica and Pulaski. As he neared Pulaski that night, snow was piled up along the highway higher than his car.[16] He was accompanied by Te Ata's sister, Avis Fifield, whose husband's ship, the *Tuscaloosa*, was docked in New York. Within a few days, they planned to rendezvous upstate, and Avis would drive with her husband back to New York City for a week of liberty before he again shipped out.

Clyde had been scheduled to deliver two to three lectures per weekday—and he had to show up to get paid. On St. Patrick's Day, after his lecture at Ovid, New York, he was surprised to receive an overnight telegram from Te Ata: "Will you and your lady honor me by having lunch with me March 17 in Geneva at Hotel Seneca at 1 o'clock, or at your convenience?" He was surprised because he had not expected to see her until March 20, when she would have concluded her Pennsylvania programs at two teachers' colleges. But she had driven considerably out of her way north to Geneva in western New York to surprise him. "Her thoughtfulness puts me to shame," he wrote in his diary.

He had not seen his "tall and slender Indian" since he had bid her good-bye at the railroad station in Jacksonville six weeks earlier. After being apart such a long time, their reunion at the hotel restaurant was typically undemonstrative, no more so than if they been apart for the weekend. Despite their love for one another, both were naturally reserved and almost never exhibited displays of affection, such as kissing or hugging, in public.[17] Dorothy Bennett remembered one tender moment between them that was supposed to have been private. On the ship returning to New York from Peru in 1937, Bennett was about to knock on their stateroom door to summon them to dinner when she noticed the door was ajar. She looked into the small room just as Te Ata walked into Fisher's welcoming arms and they embraced. "They held onto each other, and I, quite embarrassed to be witnessing such a private moment, tiptoed away. That was the only time I can ever remember seeing them embrace, and of course I wasn't meant to."[18]

Te Ata arrived for the luncheon bearing a gardenia for Avis and a carnation for her husband. After their late lunch, Te Ata drove back to Pennsylvania—taking Avis along—for the last of her programs in Pennsylvania. Fisher left Hotel Seneca and checked into the more modest Styles Tourist Home in Geneva. Most of his overnights on the lecture tour were at tourist homes, ranging in price from $1 to $2 per night.

Te Ata finished the last weeks of her season with several appearances in the New York City area. Then, as was her seasonal practice, Te Ata went to Loon Island for a few weeks to rest and recharge her batteries. That June she and Mona were enjoying a rare event, being alone on the island before the heavy summer traffic of guests began arriving about the middle of the month.[19] Fisher was again burning the candle at both ends. He was delivering two to three lectures per day at the planetarium and developing fresh ones for the future, in addition to his other institutional duties. He was also plugging away on the book manuscript on the moon. According to his contract with Doubleday, the manuscript was to be delivered on January 1, 1942. In between these assignments, he wrote book reviews for *Natural History*.[20]

He was almost perpetually fatigued. In responding to one of his letters, Te Ata teased him about falling asleep during a radio talk by the broadcast journalist Lowell Thomas. Even so, she wrote that he simply must get some rest and relaxation; she practically insisted that he come up to Loon Island for a weekend party.[21] While driving seven hundred miles round trip for a long weekend may not have been exactly restful, it did get him out of the city and out of reach of the steady stream of invitations that he received from friends and colleagues. Though Fisher had been thinking seriously about retiring as director of the Hayden Planetarium for some time, he wanted to remain with the planetarium in some diminished capacity. In late May or early June, he broached the subject with AMNH vice president of finance Wayne Faunce, and after some negotiation the details got worked out. Fisher would have the title Director Emeritus and retain his office.[22]

In working out her tour schedule for the fall and winter of 1941–42, Te Ata again asked Colston Leigh to be mindful of her need to spend a substantial block of time in Oklahoma. He responded that the best time would be in November. He was already booking her in and around New York in December, in the Midwest in January, and on the West Coast in February and March; some $1,100 in bookings had already been arranged there. Leigh said he hoped to "run this up to about $2,000." He would then arrange for dates heading east, to reach New York by mid-April. At the end of June Avis drove Bertie to Omaha for a stay with Gladys. At this late stage of Bertie's life, her children were sharing the responsibility of caring for her. They felt she would probably not live much longer, but her death was not considered imminent. Te Ata and Fisher had previously decided to take a nostalgic six-week trip through the Southwest, covering much the same path as they had on their honeymoon in 1934. Te Ata would see her sister and mother both going and coming. On August 1 there was a short announcement in the *New York Times* that after twenty-eight years with the museum, Clyde Fisher had retired, effective that day. Roy Chapman Andrews, director of the museum, praised his versatility in science and said that "his progressive views of child education formed the cornerstone of modern visual education that has been a model for museum education throughout the country."[23] In one hundred words or less, it was not a bad way to wrap up a distinguished career of nearly three decades, except for one substantial omission: Fisher's primary role in the development of the Hayden Planetarium. The story ran on the same day that Fisher and Te Ata drove out of town heading west, just as they had in 1934. Only this time there was no fanfare.

And this time there were no lectures or programs to perform. They attended a Fisher family reunion in Ohio and visited Gladys and Bertie in Omaha and several friends and acquaintances along their route. In the Southwest they were drawn to all the old familiar places such as Seton's spread near Santa Fe, Maria Martinez's home at San Ildefonso Pueblo, Meteor Crater in Arizona, and the Lowell Observatory near Flagstaff. They spent three days in Gallup at the annual Indian Ceremonial, watching some of the best Indian dancers in the nation. Fisher indulged in his typical orgy of photography while Te Ata bargained for small crafts that she would later distribute as gifts to friends and family.[24]

Their lengthy, unhurried trip home was like a kaleidoscope of Te Ata's past. They spent time in Tishomingo with Te Ata's half sister, Selena; in Chickasha, with Frances Davis; and in Wichita, with Thurlow Lieurance, who gave Te Ata her first break by signing her with a chautauqua company more than twenty years before. Her old mentor Hartley Burr Alexander was deceased, but they observed some of his work on display in the state capitol building in Lincoln. They arrived in Omaha to find that Bertie's already frail health had worsened perceptibly. In his journal Fisher wrote that she was in "very bad physical condition." But as always, Te Ata's presence helped, and after three days her condition had improved and Te Ata and C.F. departed for home.[25]

The improvement was only fleeting. When Te Ata returned a month later she learned from Gladys that their mother had been in bed since Te Ata's last visit. She was in considerable abdominal pain, not able to eat and sleeping poorly, but was responsive if not talkative. After a week, Te Ata was on the horns of a dilemma: should she stay on, perhaps indefinitely, or should she leave to resume her performance schedule, beginning the next week in Massachusetts?[26] "Surely hate to leave Mamma. Each time seems the last," Te Ata wrote on October 27, a cold, raw day in Omaha. After a week with Bertie, during which her condition had not changed, Te Ata left the next day.[27] Six days later, on November 3, 1941, Alberta Lucy Thompson died. Her death certificate gave the cause as heart failure.[28]

Josephine Fisher, wife of Fisher's brother Otto, wrote Te Ata a note of sympathy, in which she expressed this poignant sentiment: "Those we have known and loved wait for us when we ourselves are facing the lonely road, knowing that no one can go with us. If anyone is there, if anyone waits, it is surely one's mother."[29] Only once did Te Ata refer in writing to the death of her mother. In mid-December, in a short, gloomy letter to her OCW classmates, she wrote, "I have spent a great deal of time going back and forth to see my mother. In November, she was eased of her great pain and so I am just returned from Oklahoma with a heart loaded down and heavy."[30]

CHAPTER 14

Loon Island

With Bertie's death and Fisher's retirement from a full-time role as director of the Hayden Planetarium, the couple was freer to take extended vacations and spend more time together. Fisher also had decided to give up his extended lecture tours. Was this decision health-related? Although his heart condition required him to pace himself, he never mentioned his health in any correspondence. Te Ata's increased freedom was bittersweet. She was no longer obliged to cancel performances or dash off to Oklahoma or Omaha to comfort her ailing mother. And it was a blessing that Bertie's pain and suffering had ended. But she was irreplaceable in Te Ata's life. The mother-daughter bond that was forged in Emet had never foundered. They had been devoted to each other, and Te Ata's grief was profound and prolonged.

She would mask it, however, because that was her way and because she, unlike her husband, was not retiring or even cutting back her work. In January 1942 she began one of the longest and most ambitious tours ever arranged for her by her manager. Fisher accompanied his wife to Oklahoma on the first leg of the tour that featured a route up the Pacific Coast almost to the Canadian border. Clyde accompanied her to Oklahoma to help bolster her spirits. The tour had been arranged before Bertie's death, and the inclusion of bookings in Oklahoma had been, as always, the means for Te Ata to have time with her family and Frances Davis. A newspaper photo shows the couple on the OCW campus during this trip. Fisher, in his customary three-piece suit, stands near the top of a flight of stairs, as though lecturing a gaggle of admiring students and Te Ata and Frances Davis, who are all neatly arranged on the stairs looking up at him.[1]

They also spent a day in Tishomingo. After she left home for good in the early 1920s, Te Ata probably never again returned to the former Chickasaw Nation capital city without beholding the stately pink granite building on the hill. She did not have a great many childhood memories of the building when it was the Chickasaw Capitol; it was erected when she was 3 years old and sold to Johnston County when she was 14. But she remembered being in her father's office on the second floor when he was the tribe's national treasurer. And in time she had come to understand and share the reverence with which most Chickasaws held the building. Since it had been constructed of large blocks of granite, its durability was practically guaranteed. No matter who occupied the building, most tribal members saw it as a permanent monument to the Chickasaw Nation.[2]

In 1942 the federal government still held in trust the mineral lands of the Chickasaws and Choctaws. That meant the Indian people could do nothing with the 350,000 acres without the federal government's approval. The government permitted coal companies to lease some of the land and paid the tribes a share of the revenue, but because the coal market was depressed, tribal expenses had been only meeting or exceeding revenue for years. From 1932 to 1941 the deficit of the larger tribe, the Choctaws, had grown to $131,000; the Chickasaw deficit was $77,800. Indians in south-central and southeastern Oklahoma formed the Choctaw-Chickasaw Confederation in an effort to wind up tribal affairs by selling the mineral lands. Its president, W. W. Short, a Chickasaw, claimed 9,800 members in the fifteen county units. On the strength of those numbers, Short was invited to testify before the Senate Indian Affairs Committee. "We have seen our estate grow smaller year after year," he said. "We have seen our money wasted on unnecessary [Indian] bureau officials and tribal officials until we have decided it is time to get together and do something. . . . The federal government should buy our coal and asphalt lands."[3]

Where did Te Ata stand on the matter of the mineral lands? Most tribal members seemed to favor selling them, so that they could receive their per capita payments. But once that was accomplished, the tribe's only source of income, mineral land leases, would be gone and there would be no means to pay tribal officials, even just one, the governor. The tribal governments, then, would cease to exist. It is unlikely that Te Ata, whose career was dedicated to the preservation of tribal life and lore, would have favored snuffing out the last vestige of tribal control. On the other hand, she undoubtedly applauded the efforts of the Choctaw-Chickasaw Confederation to band together to fight for a say over the final settlement of tribal property. Short also implied that the remaining restrictions on the tribes should be dropped: "There are hundreds of Choctaws and Chickasaws in service fighting in this war. What will those men think of their government keeping them [as] wards and guardian of their property? When they come back they want to be free men."[4] It was possible that freedom would be manifested in another way. Instead of advocating the sale of the mineral lands, they might see that they had other interests in common—revitalization of the tribe, for example, by electing their own leaders. In fact, this is exactly what happened, but the grassroots movement would take ten years to gain momentum.

Fisher left Oklahoma by train for New York while Te Ata headed west in the family automobile. They would be separated again for several weeks but planned to spend two or three months together later at Loon Island. Te Ata was thrilled to be driving north through California. The sights and scenery contributed to alternating states of bliss and frustration over not having enough time to stop more often. When she did pull over, she was enthralled by the vistas, sometimes even at night. While driving high in the mountains one evening around midnight, she described seeing a crescent moon set off by two luminescent planets and fleecy clouds, and she felt as though she could almost reach up and take "this shining necklace with [her] hands."[5]

What is notable but not surprising about her correspondence from this period is how much of it involved describing the scenery and how little involved human contact. On the one hand, she had always had a profound love of nature and was particularly moved by the grandeur on display along Pacific Coast Highway. On the other hand, the superficiality of the brief relationship with her hosts was not, in her opinion, worth noting, let alone describing. This is not to suggest that Te Ata was coldly impersonal in her dealings. In such settings she employed a persona that she had developed and was comfortable with. She was charming, witty, and approachable but never to the point of inviting undue familiarity. She liked questions calling for open-ended answers so that she could say what she liked. She guarded against being too remote or too friendly; she wanted to be liked and respected, if not adored, but she wanted to retain an element of mystery and unpredictability, to keep people a bit off balance. Taking on a persona connotes disingenuous behavior, but in Te Ata's case her persona mainly signified consistency.

Te Ata evidently did not visit any Indian communities on this lengthy West Coast trip. She had not been visiting tribal people as much in recent years. Often, as in this instance, her itinerary was crowded with appearances. Leigh had been arranging the schedules, and it was to his client's and his own benefit to pack them as full as possible. Of course, Te Ata could have directed him to leave open certain dates, but that might have led to conflict, which Te Ata studiously tried to avoid. Besides, she and Fisher could use the money especially now that he was retired.

On February 23 she wrote to Clyde that he might have to put $100 in her checking account if she did not receive a check from her manager or one associated with her land allotment (probably representing a lease payment) near Tishomingo. She said she had only $150 left and "you can't tell what may happen."[6] Indeed. On the five-hundred-mile drive from Red Bluff, California, to Portland, Oregon, she wrote, "the weather man emptied his whole bag before me[,] . . . snow, sleet, rain, ice and brilliant sunshine." She dared not stop, given the treacherous conditions and her obligations in Portland, but found the trip filled with "exquisite impressions," especially of fourteen-thousand-foot Mount Shasta, the crown jewel of the northern California Cascades.[7]

After two performances in Portland, one in Seattle, and one in Bellington , near the Canadian border, Te Ata set off diagonally across Washington to Walla Walla. That long trip was one of most gorgeous she had ever taken. Driving over the Cascade range, the snow was piled several feet deep, blanketing the vast evergreen forests. She told C.F. in consecutive sentences, "[I was] thrilled from head to toe," and "[I am] simply *ill* that you are not with me."[8] She proceeded through the Columbia River Gorge back to Portland. "The roads curve in and out for miles—one startling view after another, snow covered peaks, towering

Te Ata: Chickasaw Storyteller, American Treasure

waterfalls [and] rocky slopes that wear a business green coat of moss and ferns." She met C.F.'s sister, Ora, in Portland, as arranged. She was glad to have Ora's company with Bertie's death still heavy on her mind. "I feel so lost with Mother and Dad both gone," she wrote to her husband.[9]

Te Ata and Ora drove down the coastal highway: on one side, jagged cliffs dropped into the ocean; on the other, a cascade of majestic snowcapped mountain peaks. She called the magnificent redwood trees the "chieftains" of the forest. She was awed by the size of the General Custer and the General Grant, though she was "not an admirer" of their namesakes. She took pictures in the dark drizzly forests, where even the ferns stretched up and over her head, knowing that the photographs would not be any good. She told Fisher not to scold: "I know better, I just don't do better." Later they saw the devastation wreaked by the logging of old-growth forests, scenes that disgusted and depressed Te Ata. "How could man be so careless with such grandeur?"[10]

Before heading up to Loon Island in the fall, Fisher and Te Ata were visited in their Upper West Side apartment by E. J. Kahn, Jr., a staff writer for the *New Yorker*. Kahn specialized in doing profiles of prominent, sometimes eccentric New Yorkers. In a medium-length piece, Kahn did an adept job of reviewing Fisher's diverse science background and achievements—including his role in establishing the Hayden Planetarium—and incorporating informative and amusing anecdotes. He wove Te Ata into the narrative a few times, once noting, "She has appeared in programs at Bear Mountain so often that when a new lake was made there a couple of years ago, it was called Lake Te Ata. She occasionally points out to her husband that while she has had a fairly substantial body of water named after her, he has never done better than the Dr. Clyde Fisher Dahlia, a variety developed . . . by a Long Island lady horticulturist who belonged to a bird-and-tree club Fisher had organized."[11]

In another reference to Te Ata, Kahn wrote that the apartment was decorated with her professional "knickknacks," such as tomahawks and war drums. (If Kahn had been profiling Te Ata instead of her husband, he would have benefited from instruction in cultural sensitivity.) Kahn wrote that she was listed in the telephone directory as Princess Te Ata. He quoted her as saying that "almost all lady Indian

Te Ata and C.F. at Central Park, where they ice skated in the winter and hiked year-round.

entertainers adopt the title, much as prizefighters call themselves Kid." Kahn did not set off that remark in quotation marks, probably because she did not say it. She knew little and cared less about boxing. As for Fisher, Kahn provided very few personal details, but in one amusing anecdote about his ability as a nature photographer, Kahn noted that Fisher "is willing to go to some lengths to get what he hopes will be a striking picture . . . and once had some friends lower him on a rope part way down the side of a sheer 400-foot cliff in order to snap a duck hawk's nest. He was photographing a couple of young duck hawks when their mother returned in an angry, argumentative mood. Fisher merely swung around and photographed her, too, which startled her sufficiently to give his friends a chance to haul him up safely."[12]

Te Ata: Chickasaw Storyteller, American Treasure

Kahn included some of the couple's diversions, such as hiking in Central Park, but did not name their favorite getting-away-from-it-all spot: Loon Island. Te Ata and Fisher traveled there in late summer 1942, intent on witnessing one of nature's best shows, the fall foliage from beginning to end. Te Ata had been going to Loon Island frequently since 1924, when Mona Woodring had first leased the property. She always associated it with positive things: beauty, solitude, restfulness, good friends, creative endeavors, small adventures, and an ever-changing pageant of nature. It was as close to her vision of an ideal home as she knew she was going to get. A few years after she and Fisher were married, they were on Long Island and found what Te Ata said was her "dream home." Although the details of the occasion and the description of the house have been lost, she quickly came to realize that a Long Island home was impractical. Making a sizable investment at Fisher's age and precarious health and moving many miles away from his office (a five-minute walk from their apartment) were out of the question.[13]

In recounting the story to her niece, Helen Cole, Te Ata said she told Clyde that if something happened to him, she would not be able to afford that house alone. Furthermore, she insisted that if he died before she did, his material wealth should go to his three daughters, even though two were married and the third was living independently. She insisted, though she understood the consequence: she would probably never have the means to buy a house or retire for many more years, if ever. She was also beginning to realize, when she dared to think about the future, that very likely she would be spending many years alone.[14]

Such dour thoughts, however, were not in Te Ata's mind as she, C.F., Mona Woodring and Frances Davis traveled the 330 miles from New York City to Loon Island on August 16, 1942. Although Mona and Frances would come and go, as would many others during the next several weeks, Te Ata and Clyde intended to remain into November. The property had not changed much since 1924. Located in Lake Winnepesaukee—twenty-eight miles long by eight miles wide—Loon Island could only be accessed by boat. The two-acre island supported a remarkable variety of flora and fauna, a three-story house, a two-story cottage, an icehouse filled with sawdust, a boathouse big enough to accommodate two motor boats and canoes, and a swimming beach.[15]

In the late 1980s, more than sixty years after she went through the big house for the first time, Te Ata recalled the occasion. The living room, she said, was dominated by a large rock fireplace and mantle. Adjacent to the fireplace was a wood box stocked with firewood, which was burned for warmth or effect nearly year-round. On the floor was a white caribou rug, which guests liked to stretch out on until it got so old that it started shedding. Near the staircase was an old organ, which Mona immediately commenced to play—with a good deal of feeling. When Te Ata found some sheet music, they sat at the organ together, Mona playing and Te Ata singing, their interlude occasionally interrupted by laughter.

Adjoining the living room, the dining room was separated by several strings of glass beads and shells suspended from the top of the doorway. Walking through them produced clinking sounds. The pantry contained canned goods and blue and white New England–style China. A large icebox was empty but could be stocked from the icehouse adjacent to the house. In the kitchen next to the wood-burning stove was a large wood box. Three stairs led to a landing that opened to more stairs ascending to the bedrooms, three on the second floor and three more on the third, all painted different colors.

Mona stayed in the green room and Te Ata the yellow room, a third-floor "perch" among the treetops where she could commune with the birds and have a good view of anyone landing or standing on the sandy beach below. In later years Te Ata liked to work on her material in this aerie, because even when there were lots of guests, she could read, write, or rehearse there undisturbed. After the nearby cottage was better furnished, she or Clyde often would work there. Like the big house, it was nestled among the pine and deciduous trees, but it was nearer the shoreline, close to an outcropping called "the point," where an American flag hung from atop a tall pole.[16]

It was second nature to Mona and Te Ata to want to share such an idyllic place. Mona invited relatives from Nashville and colleagues from Columbia's Teacher's College. Te Ata invited fewer people, since Mona was the owner and overrunning the island with people would be defeating much of the reason she was there. Mainly she invited those closest to her, C.F., Frances Davis, the Balls, Jolly. To make the place more homey, Mona acquired more furnishings, decorations, and assorted stuff, which her guests complemented with their own offerings.

Following one of her western trips, Te Ata brought a Navajo rug to replace the balding caribou rug. Everyone was so pleased with it that she donated several more Indian rugs and Indian-made accessories and artifacts. One was a full-length Indian warbonnet of golden eagle feathers that Te Ata hung on a dining room wall. Mona also had large windows put in the living room, to "invite the outdoors to come in," as Te Ata put it. Outdoors, they planted dozens of rhododendrons, and though they were not indigenous to the island, they fared so well that they soon became identified with it.

In one of the early years, Te Ata built an outdoor fireplace near the point. She waded into the lake and gathered just the right stones and wedged them together (not having cement), applying damp sod between the cracks for bonding. Although she admitted that the fireplace was not much to look at, it was serviceable. She had constructed it in the open space of a ring of oaks, thus closing the circle, which as a sacred symbol to Indians made this an especially good place to prepare and share a meal with friends.[17]

The four friends arrived at about 9:00 P.M. on August 16, and a neighbor took them in his boat across to the island. They went for a quick swim and by 10:00 were starting a late supper. With the exception of several excursions around the lake and Fisher's three business trips to New York City, he and Te Ata stayed on the island until November 3. Apparently there was no telephone, but mail was delivered twice a day, except for Sundays, via a U.S. mail steamer called the *Uncle Sam*.[18] The idea was not so much to be productive as to enjoy the setting. Early on the second morning, Fisher was awakened by a single loon flying over the house, calling. As time went by, more loons seemed to visit more often, and in the evenings of late October, the guests were often serenaded by loon choruses. Te Ata mentioned how much the call resembled the "high-pitched song of the Navajo in the Yeibichai Dance."[19] The couple included many of these anecdotes and observations in a steady stream of letters and postcards; 116 recipients are named at the end of Fisher's journal together with totals for each. More than half of these relatives, friends, business acquaintances, and associates received more than one piece of mail; a few received more than ten each.[20]

As in the past, the guests would gather during the evenings, usually outside, to read aloud from a book or for storytelling. Everyone was expected to contribute. Guests came and went, keeping up a fresh supply of stories. Sometimes Te Ata would use the guests as test audiences for Indian folklore that she might add to her repertoire. Also in the evenings, Fisher, on request, would provide astronomical observations, including how various constellations got their names. He and Te Ata canoed every day and swam several times a week into October; the hardier Te Ata continued swimming into November. Her complexion was naturally light, but she tanned well and sunbathed frequently. On inclement days, she sometimes used a sunlamp; a tan enhanced her beauty and made her look more Indian.[21] Periodically, when they saw squadrons of flying fortresses over Lake Winnepesaukee heading northeast to England, via Newfoundland, they were reminded of how different and fragile their little corner of the world was.

Fisher had always been a book reviewer for the museum's periodical, *Natural History*, and after his retirement, he reviewed more books than ever, usually one or two per issue. Also, he had arranged for Te Ata to review a book in every other issue. Among the books they reviewed during this period was *The Road to Disappearance*, by the historian Angie Debo, and *The Changing Indian*, edited by Oliver La Farge.[22]

In Te Ata's three-paragraph review of *The Road to Disappearance*, she revealed little about Oklahoman Debo's impressive scholarship on the history of the Creek Nation. She called it "absorbing but sad." Fisher's equally brief review of La Farge's collection dispensed more information pertinent to the content of the book, which consisted of seventeen papers presented at the annual meeting of the American Association on Indian Affairs, of which La Farge was president. In quoting one of the authors, his AMNH colleague, the anthropologist H. L. Shapiro, Fisher distilled the book to its essence:

> There is more than paradox in the fact that the American Indian has become an alien in a country once his by possession, and more than irony in the fact that he is looked upon as a social problem where his ancestors reigned supreme. But whether or not we object to regarding the Indians as a problem, their status has been reduced to that of a minority group, and their success judged by the degree to which they can assimilate our culture or come to some working terms with it.[23]

By mid-September everyone had departed except Te Ata and Fisher. They meandered around the island photographing one another: here,

C.F. in a Colombian dugout canoe called the "Cayuga"; there, a chipmunk retrieving a nut protruding through the lips of the daring Te Ata. On September 27, the eve of their ninth wedding anniversary, they swam in the rain and went canoeing on "a stormy lake." That evening they took turns reading aloud from the best-selling novel *Green Mansions* by W. H. Hudson.[24] Later they drove twenty miles north into the White Mountains to see a stunning autumnal display.[25] Two weeks later Clyde and Te Ata, wearing her Cheyenne dress, paddled along Winnepesaukee's mainland looking for good settings in which to photograph her for publicity material. Clyde shot candids, stills, and movie film (unfortunately without sound) while she was performing "Song of the Maiden Weaving" and "Song of the Newborn." It rained hard on their last night at Loon Island. When it subsided a bit the next morning, they packed up and shoved off in a canoe for the mainland. As they drove south toward Manchester that November 3, they could see a light dusting of snow on the hills and mountain tops. Winter was coming and with it, Te Ata's next season.

Fisher and Te Ata were apart for lengthy intervals in 1943. Te Ata was back on the lecture trail, while Fisher, nominally in retirement from the planetarium, was lecturing there every day, sometimes up to three times. His motive for continuing such a relatively heavy schedule probably involved a combination of financial need, loyalty, and a desire to continue doing what he did so well. After presiding over the planetarium's birth and formative years, Fisher was happy to give up the administrative part of the job, the side he liked least and handled less well. He no longer had the headaches associated with trying to do more with less, flagging morale, or explaining why the planetarium was not more successful. He completed work on his book *The Story of the Moon*, which was published in February 1943. Fisher personalized the book in a way few authors could have by recounting his experiences searching for meteor craters and filming and studying lunar and solar eclipses.[27] The book seemed to be selling well at $3 per copy. Fisher's brother Otto ordered seventy-five copies to give away to friends.

As Te Ata was winding up her winter tour, a photo essay she had collaborated on with Fisher was published in *Natural History*. Titled "The Creation of an Indian Jar," the spread contained a text under her byline and eighteen photographs and captions chronicling the process from beginning to end. She received $58.50 for the lot. [28]Te Ata prefaced the photographs with a one-page essay on American Indian pottery, noting that women had been using the coil method to make pottery for many generations. In the past, she wrote, the agricultural tribes, such as those of the Southeast, had attained the greatest development. But in more modern times, the Pueblo Indians of Arizona and New Mexico had elevated pottery to "its highest art." Probably the most famous among them, she wrote, was Maria Martinez of San Ildefonso Pueblo.[29]

The magazine's cover photo of Julian Martinez Maria's husband and collaborator, was taken by Te Ata. The portrait, taken outdoors from an angle below and to his right, shows a man who appears barrel-chested, very strong, and dignified, the image that Indians say, with sardonic humor, would look good on a nickel. At 58, Julian's nut brown face was deeply lined around the eyes and mouth. Character lines, some call them. Or imprints of a hard life. About the time the magazine was printed and mailed, word came that Julian had died. No cause of death was included in the newspaper accounts, but Fisher's former colleague, Kenneth Chapman, surmised that Julian's death was alcohol-related.[30]

In spring 1939, Fisher had met John Kieran, a New York City sportswriter and host of a popular radio quiz show called "Information Please." A sports fan, Fisher had been reading Kieran's columns in the *Times* and the *Herald Tribune* for years, and after Te Ata gave him a radio, he rarely missed "Information Please." They took to one another from the original meeting, a Sunday morning nature hike in Westchester County. They continued their Sunday morning hikes for almost a decade, until Fisher became too ill to continue. Kieran proved to be an eager and intelligent student, Fisher, a thorough but garrulous teacher, and both were skilled storytellers. Their friendship broadened to include attending various sporting events, where Kieran's insider's knowledge enhanced the experience, whether it was baseball at the Polo Grounds or Yankee Stadium or track meets at Randall's Island. By August 1943 Fisher bestowed on Kieran his highest compliment: he told Te Ata that Kieran was a "John Burroughs type of man—no pose, no bluff, genuine."[31]

On October 11, 1943, they listened together to the radio account of the fifth and final game of the World Series at St. Louis between the Yankees and the Cardinals. They were listening to the game in a roadster convertible owned by the Broadway actress Nanette Fabray, who was driving them to Princeton, New Jersey, to have tea with Albert Einstein. The meeting was arranged by Fisher, who had been acquainted with the great physicist for several years. The purpose of the visit was social, according to Kieran's account in his autobiography.[32]

It is likely, however, that Fisher had at least one ulterior motive for the meeting: to invite Einstein to address the members of the Amateur Astronomy Association. He had done so before by mail and been politely turned down. But if he asked the question and got an affirmative answer, surely he would have said so in the letter he wrote to Te Ata. Instead, he offered no details beyond the comment that the visit with Einstein was "the best [he] ever had." And, he said, "I want you to go with us on our next visit to Professor Einstein's home. You will like him, I feel sure."[33] Actually, Te Ata had already met Einstein at an extraordinary gathering. She and Fisher had been invited to someone's house to hear an informal performance by an interesting trio of musicians, two Russians and a German. Respectively, they were Misha Elman, one of the foremost violin virtuosos of the day, the great composer and pianist Sergei Rachmaninoff, and Albert Einstein. Te Ata recalled that Elman "allowed" Einstein to play the first violin part even though "playing second fiddle seemed to be hard on Mr. Elman."[34]

According to Kieran, he, Fisher, and Fabray arrived at Einstein's modest home on Mercer Street and were shown into the garden. Einstein was comfortably dressed in a baggy sweater and flannel pants. Kieran mentioned the physicist's famous mop of long gray hair but wrote that "truth compels the admission that they weren't quite up to the great white mane carried by Dr. Fisher. " Fisher made the introductions and then took out a camera and began taking photographs of the great man with Kieran and Fabray. Then Kieran took pictures of Fisher and Einstein and so on. Kieran wrote that Einstein took it "like a lamb, moving forward, backward and sidewise as directed." At one juncture, Einstein pointed the stem of his pipe at Fisher who was photographing the group and said, "It's a mild form of insanity in this country." Finally, Einstein directed the group inside for tea and conversation. When he was asked about his violin playing, he said he had almost totally abandoned the violin in favor of the piano. He had not taken any lessons and did not intend to; he just liked to amuse

Clyde Fisher and Albert Einstein at Einstein's Princeton home. As founding director of the Hayden Planetarium, Fisher occasionally asked the famed physicist to lend his name to the institution's public education efforts.

himself at the keyboard. Someone brought up the afternoon's World Series game, but Einstein said he was not a fan. He said he found baseball too complicated. In response to Fisher's request, Einstein explained something simpler: the continuous expansion of the universe. Kieran said that while Fisher may have understood the explanation, he and Fabray "were thrown off at the first curve."[35] After their nearly two-hour visit with Einstein, they returned to the city for dinner at the famous Algonquin Hotel.

Te Ata arrived in Manhattan to begin the new season of programs in 1943 and to be at home with Fisher for a couple of weeks. Then he left in early November for an ambitious, month-long trip to Mexico with Otto. Fisher took a train to Detroit, where he met his daughter, Beth Elinor, her husband, navy ensign Oliver Johnstone, and their daughter, Fisher's only grandchild, Sieglinde. After photographing Sieglinde, Fisher spent the day with Otto and their sister, Ora, who was still recovering from breast cancer surgery. Early the next morning, Clyde and Otto flew out of Detroit in Otto's Cessna with his pilot at the controls. They took a commercial flight from Dallas to Mexico City, arriving on November 10.[36]

The main purpose of the trip to Mexico was to observe the erupting Paricutin Volcano. Otto, quite well-to-do, picked up the tab. They got close to one of the volcano's four active cones and to within a few feet of a lava flow. The "explosions . . . sounded like cannonading [irregular explosions every second or two]." In a fever of excitement, the brothers shot still and movie film day and night. Their only disappointment was the cancellation of a flyover of the volcano because of bad weather.[37]

Fisher mentioned the highlights of the trip to his other brother, Howard, in a letter of December 21.[38] Obviously, if he had known that he would be returning to Paricutin in less than two months, he would have said so. Therefore, his return trip to Mexico must have come about and been arranged after the first of the year. This time Te Ata went along. Although February was the middle of her performing schedule, she did what she had to do to go along; it was almost inconceivable that she would miss out twice on such adventure.

CHAPTER 15

Final Journeys

When Clyde and Otto visited the Paricutin Volcano in November 1943, its thirteen-hundred-foot cone was a nine-month-old infant. It had begun as a small hole in a Mexican cornfield, emitting smoke. A Tarascan Indian who was plowing the field thought he might have inadvertently started a fire, though no flame was visible. When he covered the hole with a rock, the smoke continued to curl up from underneath. Alarmed, he ran to fetch the priest. Within a week a five-hundred-foot cone of volcanic rock and ash emerged. The rare opportunity to observe the birth of a volcano attracted an international array of scientists.

During the Fisher brothers' visit, the volcano's most violent activity was in the largest of its parasitic cones, Zapichu (Little Fellow). This two-hundred-foot cone, scarcely a month old, was producing "tremendous explosions . . . at the rate of one every few seconds."[1] The column of ash from the main cone climbed to 35,000 feet and blanketed several square miles surrounding the volcano, including two nearby villages, San Juan de Parangaricutiro and Paricutin.[2]

Although Clyde and Otto could stay only a few days, Otto decided to return to Paricutin and asked Clyde to accompany him once again. As the American Museum of Natural History had had a long and distinguished history of sponsoring scientific expeditions to study natural phenomenon, Clyde approached the museum's director about supporting a Paricutin expedition. The museum was willing to lend its

246

name and prestige to such an expedition, but most of the funding would have to come from another source.

Otto Fisher volunteered to be that source. It was a good match. He was going to return to Paricutin anyway, and his partnership with the museum transformed his return trip into a prestigious scientific expedition. The match provided the museum with the means to get its curator of geology, Frederick H. Pough, to where *the* geologic action of the moment was unfolding. And the expedition provided Te Ata, who was going as an extra photographer, with what may have been the greatest adventure of her life.

After spending a couple of days in Mexico City, the group traveled two hundred miles west to the state of Michoacán, where the volcano was erupting. The headquarters for their nine-day stay was a cabin placed at their disposal by the Geological Institute of the University of Mexico. The cabin was within walking distance of the volcano but apparently not close enough to be in harm's way. Fisher saw that during his four-month absence the terrain had undergone a remark./able transformation. The village of Paricutin was virtually unrecognizable. In November it had been thoroughly dusted with volcanic ash. Now, in March, "the only visible evidence of the [Tarascan] Indians' homes was mounds of volcanic ash." Pough wrote that it was possible to ride by horseback "over much of Paricutin without knowing there is any town there at all."[4]

After Zapichu played out, a large vent appeared on the opposite side of the dominant cone. Though it lacked the intense pressure that had fueled eruptions from the big cone, lava bubbled up from the vent like a roiling spring. Its flow extended around to the other side of the cone and then headed toward San Juan, four miles away. Pough noted that the surface of the flow quickly blackened into a "great aggregate of ropy black curds, while underneath, it continued to flow down a great tunnel, pushing forward a crumbling nose in a relentless plastic advance. The surface of the flow could be safely walked upon; the inner heat was only suggested by the numerous fumaroles and one- to five-foot-high volcanic mounds called hornitos, all intermittently belching subterranean toxic gases and debris."[5] Visibility was limited to less than twenty feet on some afternoons as high winds created dust storms that blanketed everyone and everything, even inside the cabin. Such harshness and sensory deprivation must have had the effect of amplifying the noise of the eruptions.

Pough intended to measure surface temperatures of the hot lava and photograph chunks of it breaking away from the lava flows. He also wanted to photograph a rare phenomenon associated with erupting volcanoes: the burning of hydrogen as it reached the air around the more active vents. Hydrogen was formed from water vapor by the removal of its oxygen as steam came in contact with molten rock. The blue-violet flames, however, were only visible at night. It was one thing to traipse around active fumaroles, vents, and hornitos in the daylight but quite another to attempt the same feat at night. So, Pough and Luis, his Indian camera bearer, made the trek on successive days and forged a trail of sorts that they could follow at night.[6]

The two men were joined the next evening, March 5, by Te Ata. If she or Fisher felt any trepidation about her going into a veritable minefield of volcanic activity at twilight, there is no record. Although Fisher must have been nervous if not fearful, he knew his wife could never pass up such an opportunity. All he could do was issue a lame but heartfelt request that she be careful. At 5:30 P.M., the trio departed, carrying cameras, film, and a radiation pyrometer for measuring surface temperatures. They headed toward a lava flow about ninety degrees around the base of Paricutin's cone.[7] Although the trip was not far, it was tough going, as their feet sank into the dry ash blanketing the former cornfield. To Te Ata, the billowy clouds of ash emitted from the volcano's peak overhead seemed an exaggerated version of the smoke billowing skyward from the old locomotives of her youth. Yet she was acutely aware that these clouds were not benign water vapor but an immense volume of volcanic ash. As she trudged ahead, the muscles of her legs tightened.[8]

Although the wind was almost calm, a dust devil as high as Paricutin itself danced by the hikers. As Pough noted, standing inside a dust devil was not an unpleasant experience. The whirling ash-filled mini-tornadoes caused a unique sensation, somewhat gritty but not abrasive. As the sun disappeared over the horizon, the western sky briefly turned salmon pink before darkness provided the backdrop for Paricutin's incandescent orange, red, and yellow lights. Above them the volcano was constantly hurling glowing boulders into the air. Several landed on the slope of the cone, most near the top, forming, by Te Ata's reckoning, "a magnificent glittering necklace of gold and red stones."[9]

Darkness also seemed to vitalize the ash-covered lava flows stretched out before them. By daylight they looked inert, but enormous subterranean pressure was constantly causing chunks to break off, exposing glowing lava inside the tubes. Te Ata described one flow as "a great black monster crawling its sinuous way over a desolate land." Pough lashed a pyrometer to a long stick and held it down as closely as possible to the exposed lava. The hottest reading was 1,740 degrees Fahrenheit. In the twilight the sight and heat of the glowing lava was accompanied by the crackling, hissing, and snapping associated with the fracturing of the flows. Looking increasingly concerned, Luis told Te Ata and Pough that he was going to double his price for guiding tourists to the volcano to fifty pesos.[10] In their excitement Pough and Te Ata ran out of film long before they had accomplished their objectives. They would have to return the next evening.

March 6 was for Te Ata both "the blackest" and the "most exciting" day of her life. Beginning at about 8:00 A.M., the wind picked up, and soon the atmosphere was darkened with ash. It was in the hair, mouth, and nostrils; everyone wore bandannas on their faces all day long except to eat. Finishing some soup, Te Ata noticed a layer of ash on the bottom of the bowl. Visibility was limited and mostly monochromatic. By late afternoon, however, the winds had calmed and the atmosphere was clearing. At 5:00 P.M. Te Ata, Pough, and Luis gathered up their equipment and set off for the volcano. This time Te Ata also took along an egg to fry on one of the hot boulders belched up by Paricutin.[11]

On the way they saw resilient blue jays perched on trees stripped of their bark and boulders that had been hurled out of the volcano, embedded in small impact craters. As they approached they heard rumbling and high-pitched hissing sounds as gas escaped from the fumaroles, the small openings in the lava bed. According to Pough's pyrometer, the temperature over one fumarole was 1,850 degrees Fahrenheit. Te Ata tossed a coin down into the hole and watched it melt. From there they hiked to a group of splatter cones positioned in a roughly circular formation at the base of the main cone. These ranged in height from a few feet to about fifty feet. Te Ata said they were "quiet but glowing."[12]

To photograph the inside of some of the cones, they climbed up the side of one of the larger ones. At its foot Te Ata had left the egg as a marker for their descent. Luis reached the summit first and excitedly gestured to Pough and Te Ata to hurry. No wonder. From an adjacent cone, red-hot rocks and large masses of molten lava were shooting up over the heads of the observers. Looking down into the cone they had crested, they saw "a bed of pulsating lava welling upward."[13]

Extremely excited but not consciously afraid, Te Ata began shooting still photographs as fast as she could snap the shutter. From the adjacent cone lava gushed up and sloshed out of the cone's mouth "in a glowing orange cascade, as explosive bursts hurled projectiles higher and higher above our heads," Pough recalled. Imperceptibly, the eruptions had become continuous. Then there was an ominous rumbling and shaking. They heard explosions behind them and realized that other cones in the area were coming to life. Suddenly, it seemed as though the valves of the entire subterranean plumbing system were now wide open.[14]

Realizing their peril, Pough shouted to his companions to get out fast. "Run!" he yelled. The urgency of his voice and the volcanic violence propelled Te Ata down the slope. They loped down the cone as best they could, carrying their equipment and sinking ankle deep into the ash. Te Ata led them down. "The faster I ran the more frightened I became. In my mind, I was flying like the wind, but underfoot I was tussling with the loose ash," she recalled. She fell down, quickly got up, and ran again. Glowing boulders were thudding down around her. From behind, she heard Pough—ever the detail man—shouting to forget the egg and keep going. Despite her fall, she reached the base of the cone first. As she retreated through this contemporary version of Hades, she was terrified that the earth would split open in front of her and she would plunge to a fiery, scalding death. At some point Te Ata turned around and saw that all seven small cones were erupting, throwing rocks in the air in "a most alarming way." She also saw that molten lava had obliterated the footprints they had made only moments ago.[15]

This would have been enough excitement for most people. But when the trio stopped to get their breath, and after admitting how frightened they had been, Pough decided he must return to the main cone, to ascend it partway so as to photograph all seven cones erupting.

Te Ata: Chickasaw Storyteller, American Treasure

Luis accompanied Pough, while Te Ata, her knees still weak, stayed put. Lava overflowed from the lips of the cones and within fifteen minutes the place where they had begun photographing was "a seething river of molten lava" heading toward Te Ata. But because the "river" was moving slowly, she did not leave her position, hoping that the two men would be rejoining her soon. She wondered if their view could be even half as thrilling as hers.[16]

Suddenly, Te Ata realized that this new "river" might cut off her companions' escape. Although she was pretty sure that they could not hear her, she began shouting for them to return. Sensing the absurdity of trying to shout above the noise of violent explosions, she nonetheless shouted at the top of her lungs to the geologist Pough to *"remember your darling son and charming wife at home, waiting for you."*[17] Meanwhile, the two men were climbing the main cone. Pough trusted Luis to watch for lava bombs while he photographed. Soon, however, it became obvious to Pough that they were witnessing the beginning of a general eruption of very fluid lava. The seven vents, as Pough called them, "were erupting forty-foot high fountains of liquid, with skyrocketing fragments of incandescent lava rising several hundred feet into the air, some landing almost at their feet." As Te Ata had feared, they realized that the merger of the seven flows might cut off their way out. Luis, in turmoil over his loyalty to his employer and his instinct to flee, began repeating, "Ay chihuahua, ay chihuahua." Pough may or may not have seen Te Ata gesturing frantically, but he did not need coaching. The two men began descending as rapidly as possible. As the crow flies, they were only seconds away from Te Ata, but to avoid the fiery obstacles, they were obliged to move along very cautiously. At times they seemed to trot in an almost zigzag fashion. Te Ata was extremely apprehensive that one or both of her companions would be horribly burned or killed right in front of her eyes. After what seemed to be several minutes of skirting disaster, both men reached Te Ata. They had miraculously managed to avoid serious injury both from the mortarlike bombs raining down on them and the various volcanic hot spots and lava flows on the ground. Luis announced that his price to act as volcano guide had now risen to one thousand pesos.[18]

After the trio climbed to higher and safer ground, they turned to watch one of God's most amazing spectacles. But within minutes the eruption of the seven cones had ended. A full moon lighted their way back to the cabin.

During the war years, gasoline rationing had severely limited the mobility of most Americans. So Te Ata was prevented from making her usual multicity and multistate tours. She relied more on contacts in New York, Pittsburgh, Philadelphia, and New England for work. She placed ads in *Program*, a monthly guide published in New York City for program and entertainment committees. And she had an agent, Roxanna Wells, based in Chicago. However, in a January 25, 1944 letter, Wells told Te Ata that, as they had discussed by phone, Te Ata was free to make any efforts she wished in her own behalf. That statement does not suggest a fruitful business relationship.[19] Though her travel and income were more limited, she and Fisher were not adversely affected because their monthly expenses were significantly lower. Her attenuated career during the war did not mean that she was idle, for idleness was not in her nature. Even when she spent weeks at Loon Island, always describing those intervals as restful, she seldom rested. She liked to write, both as a means of communication and as a vehicle for self-expression. But she rarely committed her anxieties, insecurities, and unhappiness to letters. That is precisely why many people keep diaries. There would be little point to filling up a diary with observations already contained in letters. Perhaps she believed that the only sure way to keep private thoughts private was not to write them down.[20]

Clyde was averaging about thirty lectures a month at the planetarium.[21] He had recently completed two manuscripts but received word from his publishers that publication would be postponed, due to the paper shortage, until after the war. One was a short illustrated biography for children on Audubon. The other was a two-part assignment for Simon and Schuster, where Dorothy Bennett was working as an editor. Fisher had agreed to edit a big book, *Wild Life of North America*, and contribute the chapter on birds. For that manuscript, he received $1,700 in September 1944. He had separate contracts providing for his work as editor and for royalties on the book.[22]

As often happens when siblings cross from middle to old age, they become closer, and this seems true of the Fishers during the 1940s. Fisher was corresponding regularly with his brothers, Otto and Howard. Fisher's letters to his younger brother, Howard, contained updates of current or recent activities and family information. The correspondence between Clyde and Otto was quite different, usually reflecting their scholarly pursuits and business interests. Although Otto had retired from the practice of medicine, he remained busy pursuing other interests. His letterhead identified him as a rare book collector, and his new passion for flying gave him the ready means to travel to interesting or even exotic places, such as Paricutin. In fact, he invited Clyde and Te Ata to join him for another expedition to the volcano in October 1944.[23] They politely declined.

Otto was actively playing the stock market. Clyde also was investing in the stock market. He had a broker or at least an unnamed adviser in New York and was getting regular advice from Otto. On July 5, 1945, Otto advised Clyde to invest at least half of his cash and savings in stocks. "You can take a broker's advice on buying," Otto wrote, "but not on selling—he will (may) want you to sell too soon, buy and sell too often."

Four of Otto's letters in summer 1945 suggest that he and Clyde might have had a mutually beneficial investing arrangement. Otto proposed that C.F. could make riskier and potentially more lucrative investments because he would agree to guarantee his account against loss.[24] This may have been a well-to-do brother's beneficent gesture. Or it may have been a quid pro quo, for in another letter Otto wrote, "The way I expect the stocks will behave in the next three years makes me want to put more invisible money in them. Would it embarrass you if you took some money & invested it for me? If so how much? I couldn't blame you if you didn't want to."[25]

Would Fisher, an accomplished man with a spotless reputation of honesty and integrity, knowingly have been a party to possible income tax evasion? Reflexively, the answer would seem to be no. But turning down the offer of his brother, endowed with considerable ego and pride, over such a delicate matter might have jeopardized their close relationship. Furthermore, the 67-year-old C.F. surely knew by 1945 that he did not have many economically productive years left. He cared nothing about amassing assets for himself but probably wanted to leave the biggest estate he could to his three daughters. Moreover, many otherwise honest, ethical people may behave differently when out of their element, particularly in an arena as murky as the stock market. A scientist who would never fudge data or misrepresent a colleague's work as his own might wink back at a preceptor conducting or proposing to conduct financial shenanigans.

In summer 1946, Te Ata and Fisher made a three-month, nearly transcontinental trip to the west and north into Canada. The planned highlight was to observe and film portions of the Sun Dance ceremony of the Blood Indians on their reserve in Alberta. The trip would be the last they would make together. Although Fisher's long-standing heart problem was not mentioned in correspondence from this period, Te Ata occasionally said or implied that he was working too hard at the planetarium. Moreover, this was their first and only lengthy trip free of speaking engagements or performances. As always, they could have used their fees to defray or offset expenses, but they evidently wanted to make this trip as enjoyable and hassle-free as possible. Furthermore, Otto had given his brother about $3,000 for the trip and the use of his Hudson automobile. Perhaps the understanding the brothers had was that Otto was financing another scientific expedition. Or perhaps Otto's generosity was, in part, his thanks to Fisher for participating in the stock market scheme. Other than getting to the Blood reserve on July 6, their journals reveal that they had few other appointments scheduled before the trip. That Te Ata uncharacteristically kept a journal covering the entire trip may have been due to a feeling that this would be their last trip together.

It was the longest trip they had ever made, excluding those involving sea travel; they put more than eleven thousand miles on Otto's five-year-old Hudson Commodore, not counting traveling the length of Lake Erie from Buffalo to Detroit by ferry.[26] They left Buffalo at 5:30 P.M., and soon, given the expanse of the Great Lake, could pretend they were on an ocean voyage. After an early dinner, they walked around the deck, watching the sun set and the moon rise. They turned in early, slept well, and awoke in time for breakfast and docking at 9:30 the next morning.[27] They spent three days with Otto and visited with Ora and sundry other relatives. One night, Otto showed his film of the Paricutin volcano, accompanied surrealistically by a tremendous thunderstorm that was passing over the city just at that time.

They made another boat trip through the Wisconsin Dells.[28] And Te Ata noted visiting a natural amphitheater where Indians used to meet for powwows and lately had been offering a nightly performance

Te Ata: Chickasaw Storyteller, American Treasure

that was to run to Labor Day. It was a thrilling setting, she wrote, with tipis and wigwams dotting the cliff sides against a backdrop of deep green woods. They intended to see the show on their return in late August.[29] On the first day of summer, June 21, Fisher and Te Ata visited Evergreen Tree, a Cochiti Pueblo Indian, whom Fisher had first met at the Indian Village of the Chicago World's Fair in 1933. Now living near the Dells, Evergreen Tree demonstrated some of his favorite bird and animal imitations. One was a dog fight in an Indian village; another was a bird catching an earthworm in the grass. He also played records of Southwest Indian songs and accompanied them with a rattle and his own singing and dancing. Te Ata said he was "delightfully uninhibited."[30] After a few hours of catching up and photographing their hosts, Te Ata and Fisher traveled to Red Wing, Minnesota, where they visited Frances Densmore, who for years had been recording songs of many North American Indian tribes for the Bureau of Ethnology at the Smithsonian Institution. She played recordings she had made in Panama, at Standing Rock, North Dakota, and at Santo Domingo Pueblo in New Mexico. Te Ata and Densmore had been acquainted for years, and though they had shared some information about Indian folklore and songs, they had had little professional influence on each other.[31]

In a reprise of their honeymoon twelve years before, Te Ata and Fisher visited the pipestone quarries in Minnesota. Although Congress had designated the quarries a national monument, the surrounding area was overgrown with weeds and brush. Their host was Winifred Bartlett, whom Fisher called "the moving spirit" behind the successful national monument drive. She pointed out that articles made from red pipestone mined most famously from these quarries had been found in mounds in Ohio, Florida, Louisiana, and California. She introduced them to George Bryan, a Chippewa and Haskell (Indian) Institute graduate who made pipes, little Indian faces, and other articles from the pipestone. Bryan said he learned the craft from a tribal elder. After fashioning the pipe with three files, from coarse to fine, Bryan heated it and then applied beeswax to produce the polished finish. Fisher filmed him working and bought one of his pipes with a sumac stem for $7. Later Te Ata learned that Bryan received only a miserly fifty to seventy-five cents a pipe from the Roes, who ran an Indian trading post in the area.[32]

On arriving in Bismarck on June 27, they received a telegram informing them that the Sun Dance of the Blood Indians would begin on "July 8 and continue for approximately two weeks." The wire was from the man who had arranged for Fisher and Te Ata to see and photograph the Sun Dance. He was the Reverend S. H. Middleton, director of the St. Paul's (Indian) School in Cardston, Alberta, near the Blood reserve. Since they decided to arrive by July 6, they had almost a week to visit people and sites in the area. Their hosts for these day trips were two old friends of Fisher's and prominent residents of Bismarck, George F. Will and Clell Gannon, and their wives.[33]

At the Fort Berthold Indian Reservation, northwest of Bismarck, Will introduced Fisher and Te Ata to Crow's Heart, a ninety-one-year-old Mandan, one of the last of the full-bloods, they were told. He was dressed in blue jeans and moccasins and wore his long iron gray hair braided. After the introductions were made in English and Mandan, Crow's Heart, who had been looking at Te Ata, said to his daughter, "She is Indian." Although Crow's Heart could hardly walk, his daughter, Mrs. Young Eagle, told Te Ata that he still enjoyed horseback riding and swimming. Only a few months before, when a case of the flu had lingered too long, he arose from his sickbed determined to handle his illness in the old way. Taking his grandson, who also had the flu, to the Missouri River, he broke the ice covering the surface, and without further ado, he and the boy plunged in. Crow's Heart pronounced himself well a short time later. During their visit, Crow's Heart showed his guests the extensive scarring on his back, which he said were remnants of the torture ceremonies of the Sun Dance.[34]

Next they traveled to Kenel, South Dakota, site of the annual Fourth of July Sioux dance. Te Ata met Alice Iron Necklace, who sold her a beaded belt for $10, a black velvet dress with elk teeth for $20, a pair of beaded boots for $6, and a bone breastplate necklace. Te Ata was so taken with the dress that she told Fisher she intended to wear it during some of her programs. At the dance, she was happy to see that many of the elder Sioux remembered Fisher from his adoption into the tribe as Afraid-of-Bear in 1927.[35]

Early on July 5 Te Ata and Clyde departed Bismarck for Montana. They entered the Blackfoot reservation at Cutbank, Montana, and headed northwest. It was a hot and dusty afternoon, and as they passed through another bedraggled little town, their spirits drooped.

Te Ata was driving and Fisher was on the lookout for a certain museum when suddenly she pulled the Hudson off the road and stopped. There, below them and to the west, was an Indian encampment: set against a backdrop of a magnificent stretch of the Rocky Mountains was a ring of twenty-two tribally decorated tipis adorning the valley floor. For a time they sat there taking in the sight. It was thrilling to both of them but for different reasons. Fisher was looking at a postcard from the past. Perhaps unwilling to disturb the integrity and sanctity of the setting, he took only a picture or two through the car window. Te Ata was touched in an elemental way. Although tipis were never part of Chickasaw culture, she considered them the most picturesque and beautiful of all Indian dwellings. The tipis also reminded her of the Indians' unfettered past. Moreover, such sites and sights (not all necessarily beautiful) were compelling and poignant symbols, she believed, of the affinity that Indians have with one another. "It lifted me completely out of myself," Te Ata wrote in her journal. "My heart sang the rest of the day."[36]

CHAPTER 16

Sun Dance of the Bloods

Nearing twilight, Te Ata and C.F. drove through the village of Cardston and got directions to St. Paul's, where they were greeted by their host, Reverend Middleton. Their connection was Long Lance, whom they had admired in life and whose memory they venerated still. Long Lance had visited Reverend Middleton many times after he began achieving fame and fortune in white society. His autobiography was dedicated to Middleton. Like Fisher, Middleton refused to believe that Long Lance had committed suicide in 1932, suspecting instead that he had been murdered. They also apparently refused to believe that in many respects Long Lance was an imposter. After Fisher and Te Ata arrived that first night, they reminisced about their friend in a room where a large oil painting of him was hung above the fireplace.[1]

The Bloods are one of three geographic-linguistic groups constituting the Blackfoot Indians of the United States and Canada. The others are the Northern Blackfoot and the Piegan, all traditionally nomadic hunter-gatherers who had lived in tipis and roamed over vast regions of western Canada and Montana. In the summer they came together to hunt buffalo and engage in ceremonies such as the Sun Dance.[2] Its main purposes were to affirm tribal unity and to renew the tribe's relationship to the supernatural powers. Because the Sun Dance was not mentioned by eighteenth-century explorers in their contact with the Blackfoot, some historians believe the ceremony originated in the nineteenth century.[3] According to Blackfoot oral history, however, the Sun Dance was an important ceremony long before white men appeared on the scene.[4] In time each tribe developed variations in the Sun Dance that made the ceremony more distinctly their own. The ceremony of the Bloods in 1946 was different in major or minor respects from its nineteenth-century predecessors, depending on who was writing the account. By the twentieth century one change that had been made in most ceremonies was the elimination of the element of ritual self-torture, whereby warriors sought to gain favor from the spirits.[5] However, Middleton showed Fisher and Te Ata some photos illustrating the torture ceremony taken on the Blood reserve as recently as 1892.[6]

The Blackfoot Sun Dance differed from similar ceremonies performed by other Plains tribes in that a woman played the leading role. As a request to the divine powers to cure a seriously ill relative, the Sun Dance woman vowed to erect a medicine lodge and go through elaborate ritual during the time of the Sun Dance. After this was under way, construction began on the medicine lodge, each stage of which was prescribed in detail by tribal custom.[7] The integrity and sanctity of the ceremonies had been maintained during the first half of the twentieth century mainly by the Blood chief, Shot-on-Both-Sides. Hewing to traditional tribal customs, the chief always wore his hair in braids, wore shell earrings, and spoke no English. Born in 1874, four years before Fisher, Shot-on-Both-Sides had become chief in 1913. He had refused several times since then to sell part of his people's land and through careful diplomacy had managed to keep tribal factions and the Canadian government satisfied.[8]

On July 8, their first full day on the Blood reserve, Fisher, Te Ata, and Middleton drove the twenty-four miles from St. Paul's to the site of the Sun Dance ceremony at Belly Buttes, which years before had been set aside expressly for the ceremony. As they drew near, they saw a single tipi outlined against a bright blue sky and endless prairie. The tipi's life poles, which poked through the smoke hole, shined pale in the sunlight. The tipi, painted with star designs near the smoke hole and along the base, belonged to the chief and his wife, Long-Time-Pipe-Woman. No one was home, nor was anyone or anything in the vicinity except for gophers and the skeletal remains of the last year's Sun Dance lodge—some sacrificial items still hanging from its rafter poles. As an adopted member of the Bloods, Middleton evidently felt he could take Fisher and Te Ata inside the chief's tipi for a look around. Te Ata thought it was simple but clean and charming. The tipi contained four beds complete with sitting backs that were laced together with leather thongs and decorated with beadwork on a red flannel covering. Trod-upon prairie grass provided a green carpet inside.[9]

They decided to drive to the chief's home on another part of the reserve. Again he was not home, but Long-Time-Pipe-Woman invited them inside the couple's one-room log house. Since she spoke no English, Middleton translated. She was old and crippled, she said, and exhausted from putting up the tipi on the ceremonial grounds. So she rested on her mattress during the short visit. Te Ata noticed that in contrast to the freshness and beauty of the tipi, the house was dark and not very clean. Inside, hanging on a wall but covered by a store-bought blanket, was the chief's medicine bundle.[10] Medicine bundles contained items, it was said, that originated from an encounter with a supernatural spirit—in a dream or a vision—often induced by fasting. The items in the bundles often were those associated with success in war, such as shields, knives, or lances.[11] The house also contained a four-cornered (representing the four directions) stone altar placed on the rough wooden floor, a long wooden table, and the bed where the chief's wife reclined. Te Ata noted in the dim light that the bedding and the old woman's clothing were quite soiled. Outside, Te Ata picked up and kept a memento of the visit: the feather of a golden eagle.

Later that day they met Chief Shot-on-Both-Sides in a little village, where he was buying food for the ceremony. At seventy-two, the chief was still handsome; he was lean and of medium height, and his hair was still mostly black. He had a high forehead and cheekbones, a prominent nose, full lips, and a square jaw. His eyes mirrored the intelligence behind them, while his skin, dark brown and deeply lined, reflected a life spent outdoors. With his appearance and dignified bearing, he looked every inch the chief. When Middleton introduced his guests to the chief, he greeted them in what Te Ata found a perfunctory way, which disappointed her, not because she felt slighted, but because she did not think his greeting was appropriate for a distinguished chief.[12]

Afterward Middleton took Fisher and Te Ata with him to an Indian camp on a creek near Glenwood to see Tough Bread, who was reportedly very ill. After Middleton talked with him inside his family's

Te Ata: Chickasaw Storyteller, American Treasure

tent, Tough Bread concluded: "Everyone else is preparing for the Sun Dance. I am getting ready for the journey to the Sand Hills. I am old and want to go." Later, out by the Hudson, Tough Bread's wife talked about her concern for her husband. Her "expressive gestures and low, rather guttural tones" reminded Te Ata of some of her relatives. And when the woman had finished talking, she slid her right palm over her left palm, a gesture her father often had used.[13]

The next day they visited Minnie Tallow in her home, which reminded Te Ata of her own childhood home. Although the Tallows valued their heritage, they wanted to live in a more modern way. They farmed several hundred acres and had a few modern conveniences and daughters who were decidedly ambitious; one wanted to become a nurse, the other a secretary. But Mrs. Tallow told Te Ata that her husband, Cecil, still had a medicine bundle and recently had joined the Horn Society, consisting of older and influential tribal men wedded to the old ways. He joined because his earlier refusal had displeased some of the men, and he figured that when a few of his cattle went missing some members were sending him a message. Then Mrs. Tallow showed Te Ata her beautiful buckskin dress and Pendleton blanket, which she would wear in the Grass Dance. She invited Te Ata to join in during that dance. Since Te Ata had packed her Cheyenne buckskin dress, she was happy to accept.[14]

On July 12 they returned to Belly Buttes to photograph more tipis being erected, to again pay their respects to the chief, and to meet a minor chief, Mike Eagle Speaker, who would be their interpreter while Middleton was away. Fisher noted in his journal that Eagle Speaker said he was a blood brother of Long Lance. Twelve tipis were now up. Te Ata saw an elderly woman emerge from a tipi next to the chief's, and facing the sun and raising her arms, she sang a song of prayer to the sun, asking that the people be granted long life. Te Ata was enthralled by the simple yet profound nature of the woman's plea, even before the woman's words were translated. She performed the simple ceremony with such reverence that she seemed oblivious to her surroundings. "Sun have pity on us," she sang.[15]

Over the next week Te Ata and C.F. drove out to the ceremonial grounds and saw more Indians arriving by horse-drawn wagons filled with lodge poles, bundles of bedding, groceries, supplies, children, and dogs. New arrivals were greeted, but the sounds seemed at times to be almost swallowed up by the vastness of the prairie. Families put up their tipis and tents, and members of the various tribal societies erected their tipis and lodges as well. Fisher and Te Ata captured much of this activity on still and movie film; although some Indians seemed somewhat annoyed, many were pleased. A few asked for copies of the photographs.

If it had been up to Fisher and Te Ata, they would have spent the entire week at Belly Buttes. But Middleton had arranged a schedule. One day Fisher was the guest speaker at the Cardston Rotary Club, and Middleton took them sight-seeing or visiting. He seemed to enjoy their company and conversation so much that these car trips might have been his way of having them to himself. As the time for the Sun Dance ceremonies grew closer, they spent more time at Belly Buttes. But if they had been feeling comfortable wandering about the camp taking pictures and talking with the Blood people, things were about to change.

Given their experience photographing Indian people, they must have known that they would have to pay to shoot film of the ceremonies. Probably Middleton had told them this as well. So they met with the chief and proposed to give him $100 for permission to photograph the ceremonies. It was their understanding that Shot-on-Both-Sides had accepted on behalf of four permanent societies, but perhaps the translation had not been clear. The Women's Society demanded a separate payment. The society's head, Mrs. Day Rider, announced through an interpreter that they would accept no less than $20. "You rich, you come a long way," she said. Fisher paid. Then Many Gray Horses, leader of the Horn Society, who had not been party to the agreement with the chief, announced that no photography of the society's ceremonies would be permitted, period.[16]

All of this confusion and unpleasantness upset Te Ata, and she blew off steam in her journal on July 17. "I am about to lose interest in these Indians! They make a bargain about pictures and next day say they want more. They seem a pretty mercenary lot. I feel I would like to forget the whole thing. I cannot bear being among people who do not want me around! And I know they tolerate us for money only! I'm not used to such treatment and I despise it."

Interspersed in her angry prose, however, were thoughts demonstrating greater clarity and understanding. "The people [Bloods] are treated badly by the townspeople [presumably Cardston] and exploited. Mainly, they do not want photography and for this—cannot blame them." Still, she supported her husband's efforts to film Indian people and their ceremonies as a means of educating the public about the richness of Indian culture—as she herself was doing in another way. On the other hand, she knew that the Bloods did not know Fisher's motives. To them, he was just another white man exploiting them. Others, she realized, did not care about motives; they were very poor and charging for photographs helped them to subsist in a culture that was becoming increasingly diluted despite the chief's best efforts.[17]

Nevertheless, the haggling and fussing went against Te Ata's grain, and the couple discussed leaving.[18] It was probably Te Ata who wanted to leave, but Fisher and Middleton met with the chief again, and an agreement on photography, excluding the Horn Society, was reached just in time, for the most signficant Sun Dance ceremonies were about to begin. Furthermore, Fisher and Te Ata were invited to spend the most important night, Saturday, in the tipi of the Eagle Speaker family.[19]

Te Ata was "hesitant" to even look into the tipi where the sacred Pipe Ceremony was being held by Jack Hind Bull—an elder whom she had met earlier in the week, so she missed "a great deal" of it. Her reticence may have resulted in part from natural shyness, but she also did not wish to go where she was not wanted. Eventually she slipped into the tipi with others and was immediately sorry that she had not entered sooner, for the tableau she observed was "thrilling." She saw a dancer moving toward the Pipe Altar, on which the sacred medicine pipe rested on a rack. He took a bit of tobacco or sage and rubbed it between his hands, then rubbed his palms over his body as an act of purification before starting to dance. Sometimes men and women danced together, facing one another, gesturing with their arms upward toward the sun. Each dance lasted about two minutes. The tipi was so crowded that it was hard to see individual dancers. Everyone received substantial amounts of food and tobacco, and some guests received gifts such as a blanket or a horse.[20]

The next day, July 19, the Horn Society's dance was "in full swing" when Fisher and Te Ata arrived at about 5:00 P.M. Some members wore

Te Ata and Chief Jack Hind Bull and his wife pose in their tipi during the 1946 Blood Indian Sun Dance ceremonies near Cardston, Alberta, Canada. Te Ata attended a sacred pipe ceremony held inside the tipi and called it a "thrilling" experience. The trip to the Blood reserve was the last and best that Fisher and Te Ata made together.

warbonnets with straight-up eagle feathers or feathers forming long tails. Several other members each held ten- to twelve-foot-long staffs decorated with feathers. Later, a social dance, the Owl Dance, was held. Behind several cottonwood branches stuck into the ground seven or eight men in unison beat a drum that was some five or six feet in diameter. Near them was a large heart-shaped sign nailed to a tree. Pinned to the sign were money, necklaces, and other gifts for the participants to collect after the dance.

This was a partners' dance, and Jack Hind Bull, dressed in a buck-skin outfit, asked Te Ata to dance with him. She could not gracefully refuse, though she wanted to because she was not dressed properly. The couples danced in a circle around a pole. Te Ata was enjoying her-self until an ugly scene ensued. One of the male dancers, whom Te Ata said had been drinking, confronted Fisher, demanding that he pay $30 for taking pictures of the dance. Te Ata would not let Fisher pay the man (even if he had been so inclined) on the grounds that it was a social dance with no religious significance and that all the proper arrangements had been made.[21]

The culmination of the Sun Dance ceremonies occurred over the next two days, with the completion of the ritualistic construction of the medicine lodge, four days after the Sun Dance woman had begun fasting and prayer in her tipi. By then the trees and saplings making up the lodge's framework had been cut, stripped, and positioned in the location that had been selected earlier at the Sun Dance camp. At this stage the frame looked like a circular horse corral.[22] By July the camp accommodated some twenty-six tipis and perhaps seventy-five tents. That afternoon, Fisher and Te Ata moved into Eagle Speaker's "earth-red [colored] tipi," becoming residents of the camp. Aside from Eagle Speaker and his wife, Red Otter Woman, and two of their chil-dren, her father, Tall Man, also lived in the tipi during the ceremony.[23] The two young daughters, Byrde and Marjorie, were very impressed by the statuesque and graceful Te Ata; they followed her about, observing her very closely and imitating her steps in the Owl Dance and her way of singing.[24]

Te Ata recorded every step of the ritual in her journal. She relied on Eagle Speaker for translations, background and perspective. That afternoon members of the Horn Society and the Women's Society went into the woods to preside over the cutting down of a cottonwood tree that had been selected to become the center pole of the lodge. Every element of the harvesting procedure was prescribed precisely and charged with religious significance. The center pole was brought into the camp amid much pageantry and fanfare. The singing and drumming of the procession were heard by those in camp before it became visi-ble. The western sky was suffused with unusually vivid sunset hues. Leading the procession was a horseman, John Cotton, naked except for a breechclout, his body coated with red medicine paint. He was followed by a lumber wagon driven by Chief Shot-on-Both-Sides, bearing the pole and the chief's flag, a yellow banner with the British lion in red. The other members of the Horn and Women's Societies rode on horseback or in wagons. Behind the chief's wagon, scores of others followed, some walking, others on horseback or in buggies, but all carried green boughs to pile onto the framework of the Sun Dance lodge.[25]

The procession circled the camp, and when the chief's wagon drew near to Fisher and Te Ata, they saw that three Horn Society men sat astride the pole beating on skin drums. These men and many others also wore only breechclouts; the women wore calico dresses and fringed shawls or blankets, and some wore Stetson hats ringed with leafy cottonwood twigs. After stopping at the four compass points for brief ceremonies, the medicine woman appeared, weak from fasting, wearing a feather headdress trimmed with ermine. She presided over the preparation and distribution of bits of buffalo tongue to everyone assembled, including children; all faced westward and offered prayers of supplication to the setting sun.[26] The Sun Dance woman was aided by several tribal women who one by one declared themselves to be living virtuous lives. This truth-telling included relating instances in which temptations were placed in their way by tribesmen, named individually in a loud voice.[27]

Following dinner, for which all had repaired to their own tipis or tents, the pole raising ceremony took place. The evening grew cool, and Byrde and Majorie snuggled up against their new hero, Te Ata, who drew her blanket close about them. In the gathering twilight, singing came, in turn, from the four directions. Te Ata thought the voices sounded "wild and impressive." Then groups carrying pairs of rafter poles tied together with cowhide thongs at one end about four feet apart converged on the Sun Dance lodge. The chief, minor chiefs, the Sun Dance woman, and Horn Society members appeared. Ropes were tied to the center pole, as were sacrificial offerings such as feathers and blankets, and the crier asked for volunteers to help raise the pole. Amid singing, drumbeats, and applause, the center pole was gradually raised vertically and placed in an anchoring hole dug at the center of the lodge. Other items of sacrifice were then tied to the upper part of the rafter poles, which were hoisted up and lashed into place. The framework of the Sun Dance lodge was complete.[28]

At about midnight Eagle Speaker's family and their guests retired for the evening. But the smoke singers continued to parade around the camp, singing and drumming and collecting gifts until about 3:00 A.M. That morning, Te Ata saw that the Sun Dance lodge was completely covered with the green branches. Everybody was up early and busy, except for Marjorie, the five-year-old, who was not feeling well.[29] A minor chief named Cross Child, dressed in buckskin and full warbonnet, came to Eagle Speaker's tipi and informed his nephew, Eagle Speaker, that Fisher and Te Ata were to be adopted into the Blood tribe. Te Ata knew her husband was going to be adopted and made an honorary chief, but word of her own adoption came as a surprise, "since [she] belonged by birth to another tribe."[30]

Te Ata was told to put on her skin dress for the ceremony. While she hurriedly prepared, Chief Cross Child had Fisher, doubtless to his embarrassment, drive him in the Hudson about the camp announcing the impending celebration of the "white man from the East and his Indian wife."[31] When Te Ata appeared at the Sun Dance lodge, where the ceremony was to be held, Chief Shot-on-Both-Sides looked her over carefully and then personally retied one of her braids. As she and Fisher knelt before Cross Child and Shot-on-Both-Sides, they were adopted by the "Blood Indians of the Blackfoot Confederacy." Placing a warbonnet on Fisher's head, the chief gave him the name Ape-kna-go-sin-nox-sin, meaning "Writes at Sunrise." To underscore the event, the chief told Fisher that this was a very high honor. Chief Joe Bull Shields interpreted Fisher's remarks, which were unrecorded. Later Clyde gave $5 to each of the seven chiefs present.

On behalf of Te Ata, Cross Child delivered what Fisher called "a wonderful oratorical presentation" during which he noted that the Indian blood in her veins made her a sister to the Bloods. Then, perhaps getting caught up in the moment, Cross Child told the gathering that Te Ata was "the most beautiful woman" he had ever seen on the Blood reserve. He placed a band with a single eagle feather on her head and named her Woman-Sa-sa-cha-ke, Eagle Tail Feather. After an introduction by Chief Bull Shields, Te Ata delivered a short program of Indian songs and tales told in sign language.[32] Although she did not record the program's composition, the Bloods were aware that Te Ata had performed before the king and queen of England, and it is highly likely that these Canadian Indians would have wanted a program similar if not identical to the one she presented at Hyde Park in 1939. Eagle Speaker later told her that she was the first non-Blood Indian who had ever performed in the Sun Dance Lodge. Fisher was the first white person to witness a ceremony there.

Why were Fisher and Te Ata honored by the Bloods? A major factor was their relationship to Reverend Middleton and possibly the late Long Lance, who lived among the Bloods for a time and was considered a brother by some of them. Although Middleton was primarily there to "save the souls" of the Bloods and to educate them, he appeared to have been a good friend of the tribe for many years and had himself been adopted into the tribe. It is noteworthy, however, that Mike Eagle Speaker harshly criticized Middleton in a letter he wrote to Fisher a few months later. He complained that Middleton would not share with the Indians the photographs and movie film that Fisher had sent. He said Middleton "looked down upon them [Indians] like dogs nowadays—even if they [Middleton] make they [*sic*] living out of them."[33]

How did their experience with the Bloods rank with their other adventures? Te Ata wrote Middleton that it was a high point in her relationship with Fisher. In her memoir she mentioned almost nothing about the unpleasant disagreements over money. As for Fisher, it was he, not Te Ata, who wrote about the uniqueness and importance of the honors accorded them by the Bloods.[34] At the end of the ceremony, Clyde and Te Ata left for St. Paul's; Middleton had arranged some last social events for them before they were to depart on July 24. Unfortunately, as far as Te Ata was concerned, that meant they would miss the rest of the day's dances and games at the Sun Dance and the closing ceremonies the next day. In the eyes of some, their departure right after their adoption into the tribe may have seemed mercenary or thoughtless. Undoubtedly, Te Ata and Fisher realized the spot they were in, but they felt indebted to their genial host.[35]

Te Ata and Fisher left St. Paul's in the early morning of July 24, heading north and west into the Canadian Rockies to Banff, Lake Louise, and Jasper. If the Blood's Sun Dance ceremonies had been their reason for making the trip, then the spectacular Rockies were dessert. The drawback for Te Ata was lack of time. Fisher had to get back to New York, and it is likely that their money was running low. Te Ata

Te Ata: Chickasaw Storyteller, American Treasure

would have liked "to stay indefinitely at the Banff Springs Hotel" and "was loathe to leave Lake Louise," the beauty of which "was unsurpassed by anything seen on the trip." The views were so awesome that twice they forgot to eat. They took photographs but not as many as they might have expected; nothing could capture the magnificence of the mountain peaks, the glaciers and deep blue lakes, the immense stretches of lodgepole pines and aspen.[36]

Within five days they had looped back to Cardston and then crossed the U.S. border at Carway. Heading home, they generally retraced their steps so they could again visit with friends and family, film Indian artisans at work, and give Te Ata the chance to buy Indian items she had coveted but passed up on the way west. They deviated from the familiar route to see Yellowstone National Park. Fisher had wired for a room and bath at the Old Faithful Inn, and according to Te Ata, they must have gotten the best room in the hotel. From their corner room, they could look out one set of windows and see Old Faithful; out another window they saw "hot beds of rising steam performing continuously." The price for the room with a view was $18, an "utter extravagance" for people used to paying between $2 and $4.[37]

Over the next several days they drove through the Crow reservation to its agency to see their friend Max Big Man, who took them to the rise above the Little Big Horn where Custer fought his last stand; visited, at Fisher's insistence, the graves of Calamity Jane and Wild Bill Hickok in Deadwood, South Dakota; and saw Mount Rushmore, which Te Ata thought was simultaneously a "stupendous work" and "a scar on the mountain." Whenever possible, they liked to look up people they had visited on their honeymoon trip in 1934. This was not only out of a sense of nostalgia. They enjoyed talking with interesting people and photographing or filming them in their homes or, in the case of Alex and Mary Le Sage, exhibiting their craft in the old tribal way. They found the La Sages at Grand Portage—a settlement of some two hundred Chippewas—digging spruce roots. Mary used the roots to bind baskets fashioned from birch bark. Alex used the root to bind the gunwales of his birch bark canoes. Later they visited the Grand Portage Chippewa Museum, where two of Alex's canoes were on display. The La Sages made a decent living from their work, and it showed; Te Ata noted that their living conditions had improved. Mary was able to sell all of her birch-bark baskets to the

Rodwells, a Chippewa couple who owned the trading post at Grand Portage. Despite their higher standard of living, the Le Sages, according to Te Ata, were as "unspoiled and gentle as ever."[38]

As Fisher wanted to do a film on Chippewas harvesting wild rice the old way in northern Minnesota, he and Te Ata set about trying to find a Chippewa man named Sam Yankee, whom Te Ata had visited some years before. Initially certain she could find his house, she and Clyde drove up and down roads that seemed increasingly unfamiliar to her. Suddenly she saw a small house with a flagpole attached to the front gable, and on top of the pole was an eagle feather. "That's the place," she said.[39] When they arrived, Yankee, a veteran of both world wars, and his wife were refurbishing their rice boat. They welcomed their visitors and readily agreed to help with Fisher's motion picture project.[40] Yankee told them they should return in a few weeks, as the rice would be ready for harvesting and many colorful ceremonies would be held. Te Ata and Fisher said they would return.[41]

About then, C.F. told Te Ata that he was starting to feel the need to return to New York. He had contracted with a publishing company to make editorial contributions to a book on trees, and he reminded her that he was already late. It is also possible that he was not feeling well or that he was nearing exhaustion. So they limited their return plans to calling on Fisher's family in Detroit and Ohio. Their brief stay in Detroit was the first time they had been exposed to traffic jams in almost two months, and Te Ata found it disquieting if not disorienting. At a family gathering at Otto's house, Te Ata donned her Cheyenne dress after dinner and gave a folklore program. It was the first time that some of Fisher's side of the family had ever seen her perform.[42]

Te Ata and Fisher arrived at their apartment on September 5, their adventure having consumed two and a half months. Te Ata wrote an emotional talking leaf to Reverend Middleton: "[T]hank you for the generosity of your time, hospitality and sharing your experience, which made our summer one of the most perfect ones we've ever had. Now the time we spent in Alberta belongs to the yesterdays, but our memories belong to all the todays and tomorrows."[43] The emotional letdown that often follows extended vacations was intensified by a letter from Mike Eagle Speaker. His five-year-old daughter, Marjorie, who had not been feeling well during the Sun Dance ceremonies, had died of an unspecified illness a few days after their departure. Eagle Speaker said the little girl's death had been very hard on his wife, Red Otter Woman. And though he did not say it directly, Marjorie's death had overwhelmed him as well. "It is really sad feelings," was his way of saying that his family was devastated.[44] Marjorie's death was an emotional blow to Te Ata, who had formed an unusually close attachment to both girls in the few days they were together. Not having children of her own, Te Ata loved to talk and play with children. This was especially so when there was enough time to establish real affection—as there had been with Majorie and Byrde. Te Ata also could not shake the disturbing visions of the family, Eagle Speaker, Red Otter Woman, and Byrde, going through the motions of daily living while mourning their incalculable loss.

Furthermore, Marjorie's illness and death, compressed into only a few days, proved to be a harbinger of what was starting to happen to Fisher—over a much more protracted course. Although they had planned to return to Minnesota to film the wild rice harvest later that fall, Fisher was not feeling up to it. Whether he or Te Ata would admit it to themselves or each other, his heart was beginning to fail.

CHAPTER 17

Alone

Te Ata had not been in the old Chickasaw Nation since 1942, the longest period she had ever been away. Gas rationing during the war was one reason. And "going home" was not like it used to be: her parents were dead and her siblings far-flung. Even so, she continued to think of Tishomingo as her home, where she might return to live out her days. But while C.F. was still strong enough to enjoy it, she wanted to spend a month or so in Oklahoma visiting relatives and friends. In spring 1947 they set out, visiting her people and performing in selected community and academic settings.[1] It was almost like old times before the war, when the couple would hit town, she appealing to the community's heart, he to the head. Her audience would be charmed and captivated. His would marvel at his color slides and erudition and plumes of white hair. Was there a more beautiful, dramatic, and commanding woman? Could there be a more dignified, articulate, and scholarly yet kindly man?

The photos of Fisher that appeared in the OCW student newspaper in May 1947 show a man who for the first time looked his years; his face had become heavily lined. And he moved increasingly like an old man. Yet he clearly charmed and impressed the student reporter who interviewed him and covered his program on meteorites.[2] Although Te Ata was 51 years old, her photos show a woman who appeared ten years younger. In one photo taken of the couple together, she looked more like Fisher's daughter than his wife. Moreover, she was still beautiful, maintaining her slender figure, youthful appearance, and lilting step.

Fisher was in the last phase of his professional life. He was lecturing a bit and writing textbook articles and overviews; he no longer conducted original research and apparently had no plans to participate in scientific expeditions. In contrast, Te Ata was still in her prime. At OCW, wearing her Sioux, Seminole, and Cheyenne dresses, she presented a program that was a blending of older and newer material. To the beat of the tom-tom, she began with a Zuni chant, "Hymn to the Sun," and then, using a papoose cradle made by an Oklahoma Seminole woman, followed with songs of a mother to her papoose. She finished with "Song of Greatness" and "Song of a Maiden Weaving." The audience demanded two encores, "Old Man Dancing" and "Northwest Coast Love Song," and urged her to do another. As always, she left them wanting more.[3]

As Te Ata and Fisher visited friends and relatives around the old Chickasaw Nation, they must have heard about the impending sale of the Chickasaw and Choctaw mineral lands to the U.S. government. Little progress had been made until 1945, when the Interior Department signified willingness to begin negotiating with the tribes after they had agreed on a price. Discussions dragged on through 1946. Quite suddenly all sides announced that they had reached an agreement on April 28, 1947, when the couple was visiting in Oklahoma. The federal government would pay the tribes $8.5 million for the mineral lands.[4] That worked out to a per capita payment for members of both tribes of approximately $315.[5]

The government had decided to make the deal because the executive branch had joined with Congress by 1946 "in a massive drive to assimilate the Indians once and for all and thus to end the responsibility of the federal government for Indian affairs." Preparation for the administration's policy of gradually terminating the government's responsibility in Indian affairs was enunciated initially in February 1947 by William Zimmerman, acting head of the Bureau of Indian Affairs.[6] This policy could not proceed efficiently until land deals were settled.

Whether this agreement was good for the Chickasaws and Choctaws was (and still is) highly debatable, but it was not hotly contested. There was no question that most voting tribal members favored the deal.[7] They had waited so long and become so pessimistic that for them the whole matter had boiled down to the belief that something was better than nothing. Te Ata probably opposed the sale for the very reason that the government wanted to buy the mineral lands: to terminate its treaty responsibilities to the two tribes. Nevertheless, she did not state her opposition publicly; this may reflect her physical isolation from the matter, her disinterest in nuts-and-bolts politics, and her relative lack of need for the money. While she could put her $315 to good use, she would not need it to make ends meet, like many Chickasaws and Choctaws living on their allotments. Did discussions of the mineral lands agreement during her trip home in 1947 increase Te Ata's sense of remoteness from the lives of her people? Was it clear that while she was principally concerned with dramatizing and promoting the beauty of Indian culture, most Chickasaws and Choctaws—culturally adrift and isolated in pockets of rural Oklahoma—faced the more mundane challenges of eking out a living day to day?

&

The beginning of the end for Clyde Fisher occurred in October 1947. He was hospitalized with "heart attacks," he later wrote to his friend Walter Campbell, a University of Oklahoma writer and historian.[8] No references to the incident appear in Te Ata's existing correspondence, but letters written by Otto mention that Fisher was in Detroit's Henry Ford Hospital for a cytotomy, a procedure in which a catheter was placed into his bladder through a suprapubic incision to drain the bladder to prevent infection. The procedure was ineffective, as Fisher continued to suffer bladder problems, and he became acutely depressed and anxious. Otto's letters detail his brother's prolonged, troublesome convalescence during the winter of 1947–48.[9] He also reported on their sister Ora's health. In July Otto had broken the bad news to family members that she had suffered a breast cancer relapse; the malignant cells had metastasized, and she was terminally ill.[10] Although he knew that his brother, Clyde, also was terminally ill with a failing heart, his letters reflected his hope that Clyde could still lead a reasonably productive life for a few more years, if he could come to terms with his diminished physical capability and take good care of himself.

Later in 1947 Fisher was admitted to Johns Hopkins Hospital in Baltimore; catheters were inserted and removed, and because his bladder condition did not improve as quickly as he expected, he

　　　　　　Te Ata: Chickasaw Storyteller, American Treasure

"complained bitterly" and was "a very poor patient," Otto wrote. Otto and Te Ata shared twelve-hour shifts at his bedside. "Nobody," Otto added, "but one who has been around him knows what it means to be at his beck and call. Sometimes not more than a minute would elapse between one request and the next one; and if I went out of the room and sat just 30 feet down the hall . . . he would send one of the nurses out for me. It has been that difficult for me and Te Ata to take care of him because he has never learned to be sick."[11]

Otto believed Fisher's depression exacerbated his heart condition. He again developed edema (swelling) of the ankles and fluid in the lungs. The Johns Hopkins doctors told Te Ata that the prognosis was not good. "Gloomy," was Otto's word.[12] Then, on December 22, Hopkins urologist Dr. J. A. Campbell Colston performed transurethral surgery on Clyde and removed an obstruction that presumably had been causing his urological problems.[13] On Christmas Day Te Ata told Otto that Clyde was definitely better, physically and emotionally.[14] He was discharged sometime in early January.

Despite this hopeful statement, Fisher's condition improved only slightly, and he and Te Ata spent an emotionally taxing January and February. To get Fisher to sleep in the hospital, Te Ata had to push him in a wheelchair; as soon as she stopped, he awoke. He wrote Otto that sitting resulted in constant pain. He was hospitalized in New York following a coincidental attack of tachycardia (a period of abnormally rapid heart rate) and blood in the urine. Despite warnings from his cardiologist and urologist that these events could occur and that in his case they should not be viewed with alarm, Fisher panicked, and Te Ata followed suit. As a result, he spent a few days in a New York hospital. Otto said he "scolded Clyde" for being alarmed at the tachycardia because "all of the heart specialists have told him that he doesn't have the heart disease of which people suddenly die[,] . . . the heart disease with coronary occlusion."[15] His signs and symptoms suggest that Fisher was suffering from progressive congestive heart failure.

By late January he was taking several medications daily, including a sulfa for his urinary problems, two heart drugs (Otto does not identify them), a sedative, and mercury to treat the edema. He felt a burning urge to urinate every few minutes, day and night, and although he had been told this was a temporary condition and an expected part of his surgical recuperation, he was continuously fatigued and in low spirits. In February Otto was happy to receive a postcard from Clyde but distressed to see two misspellings, suggesting "arteriosclerosis in the brain."

In late February Fisher was showing signs of gradual improvement, occasionally becoming engaged in conversation and telling stories with some animation. But he continued to demand Te Ata's almost constant attention. When she returned from occasional shopping trips, she would find him "sitting straight up in a small chair, just watching for [her], sad and disconsolate." Otto wrote a diplomatic letter to his brother telling him that he must start caring for himself. He told him to ask the doctor if it would be all right for Te Ata to sleep in another room. This was Otto's way of helping Te Ata without embarrassing or confronting his brother, who was so restless at night that Te Ata was getting little sleep. Toward spring, Fisher's health had gotten markedly better. Te Ata was taking him on walks outdoors. He cast these outings negatively, however, as "trudging along with Te Ata." He had to rest often and when he felt faint had to sit down immediately to avoid collapsing.[16]

Fisher had been elected president of the Explorers Club in late 1947. He felt greatly honored, and while the duties were little more than ceremonial, such as arranging for guest speakers and programs, even those could exceed the capability of a man who was suffering from brief episodes of insufficient oxygen to the brain. His election may have signified the members' recognition of the severity of his condition and been intended to convey their esteem and gratitude for his many years of devoted service. Fisher felt well enough in April to put in a few appearances at the museum. He probably resumed writing one of several manuscripts in varying stages of completion. He and Te Ata had written to thank Dr. Colston and to update him about his progress. Colston replied that he was happy Fisher's surgery had been successful and wanted Te Ata to know how much he appreciated the "devotion" she showed in caring for her husband: "I feel very strongly that this was a very important factor in getting him through the operation."[17] Fisher was well enough in May for a trip to Loon Island with Te Ata. This time they made the long trip in "three installments [days] on account of the cripple," Fisher wrote to John Kieran.

They stayed at Loon Island with Mona Woodring for about five weeks, which proved to be the happy twilight of the couple's marriage.

In July Fisher suffered an attack of tachycardia and nearly collapsed in the museum.[18] He was in a downward spiral from which there seemed to be no escape, in marked contrast to Ora, a model of acceptance and composure in her final days despite increased pain and suffering. She died in August and was buried in the Fisher family plot in Sydney, Ohio. Believing the trip would be too much for Clyde, Otto asked him not to come to the funeral, and he did not attend.[19]

Around Christmas Otto wrote that Fisher was "going downhill." What he needed most now, Otto wrote to his children, is Te Ata. But he recognized that Te Ata needed help and was happy that his younger brother, Howard, and wife, Eva, recently had arrived. The kindly man who never put anybody out before his illness had again become continuously whiny and demanding. The stress on Te Ata must have been smothering. Not only did she work slavishly in futile attempts to satisfy her husband, but she also witnessed the destruction of his personality during the final stage of his life. He had become a shut-in, then bedridden. He developed a bad cough. The cards, flowers, and baskets of fruit from all the well-wishers must have been small comfort in those bleak, long days of December. Yet, Te Ata never complained.

Kieran had been visiting Fisher weekly. On a visit just before Christmas, he wrote Otto that C.F. was "very weak," that it "[is] hard for him to control his face muscles and he speaks with difficulty. It is difficult for him to concentrate, too." Otto knew what he meant. Te Ata had told Otto that Fisher sometimes called out for help to people who were not there or people who were not even alive, like Ora. Kieran found Fisher a "restless and querulous patient, demanding much attention." "You know how it is," he told Otto. "Lingering illnesses are hard on everybody." Finding Te Ata on the verge of collapsing, Kieran helped her to arrange for a nurse to spend one shift a day helping to look after her husband.[20]

In a January 4 letter Otto warned Te Ata to take care of her own health; "Don't kill yourself for Clyde. You can't really help him much now." It must have been very difficult for Otto to write those words, an acknowledgment that the brother he had idolized was going to die very soon. In that letter, he called Fisher "a very good Indian" and "the best man in the world."[21] If Te Ata had any tears left, she might have shed them then. But it is likely that she did not see Otto's letter until after Fisher had passed away. On the same date that Otto wrote the letter, Fisher experienced another crisis, probably a prolonged attack of tachycardia. Margaret Ball was visiting in their apartment when this occurred. In 1995 she vividly recalled Fisher in the elevator adjacent to their apartment, "ashen faced, gasping for breath, and unable to stand on his own, being supported by Te Ata and an ambulance attendant."[22]

Fisher was admitted to Doctor's Hospital, where he lingered for nearly three days. He died at 4:20 P.M. on January 7.[23] Te Ata apparently never spoke about those last days with anyone. Among the obituaries was this remarkable summation by James P. Chapin in the *Explorer's Journal*: "This man who could name the stars in their constellation, discuss the theory of relativity, and follow the planets in their courses, was equally familiar with the flowers, insects and birds. All nature could count him as a friend."[24] In accordance with Fisher's wishes his body was cremated and the ashes interred at the Fisher cemetery plot in Sydney. Twenty years before, Fisher had eulogized the writer and naturalist Garrett P. Serviss. Much of his 1929 tribute was strikingly similar to many that were now penned about him. "As a lecturer," Fisher had written, "he was much in demand, for he had unusual ability in making his subject clear and fascinating to those who were not specialists in the field. His especial province was popular science, and in this he had rare facility. This, together with a pleasant voice, a charming personality, and a genuine enthusiasm for his subject, made him a great lecturer." And this: "He had attracted so many grateful admirers and friends, that he must have known that there is a widespread feeling that it was good for the people that he had lived. In his passing, the world has lost a real teacher, and a kind, unselfish and lovable man."[25]

The memorial service was held before a large group of mourners in the Little Church Around the Corner on January 9. Toward the end of the service, Te Ata, in obvious distress, arose and began walking back toward the front doors of the church. Margaret Ball told her husband, John, to go after her. Outside, he caught up to Te Ata and asked her where she was going. Her face was a mask of pain. "I just couldn't stand being in there another moment, " she said. With some urgency, John told Te Ata that he and Margaret wanted her to come home with them and spend a few days. He said they did not want her to be alone. Surprisingly, Te Ata accepted.[26]

Te Ata: Chickasaw Storyteller, American Treasure

Clyde Fisher was a marvelous conversationalist. He was at home talking with Einstein about relativity or with children about whatever appealed to them. Though his heart was large and caring, it wore out on January 7, 1949.

Even more surprising was Te Ata's acceptance of Dorothy Bennett's invitation to accompany her on a trip to Guatemala at the end of the month. Bennett had been skiing in Switzerland at the time of Fisher's death. When she returned and learned of his passing, she "felt crushed." To help Te Ata get through this initial period of grief, Bennett suggested that they take a trip together, to get totally away. She reminded Te Ata that ever since they had visited the Inca ruins in Peru in 1937, they had talked of visiting the ancient Maya ruins of Mesoamerica. Would Te Ata go as her guest?[27] This was an audacious offer on Bennett's part; she did not know if Ata would think that "gallivanting" through Central America would be inappropriate for a grieving widow. But the offer was very kind and selfless, because Bennett knew she might be setting herself up for a very expensive, miserable time. In her journal Te Ata wrote of her reluctance to accept. "I do not want to leave our tipi for I shall have a difficult time returning without him there to greet me. But I know it is good that I go. I must perk up and enjoy it as much as possible and make her [Dorothy] happy."[28]

They left by plane on January 28. On a layover in Miami, Te Ata met a friend who invited her to spend a few days with her there on her return trip. Te Ata did not decline then but doubted that she would accept the invitation: "There is so much to settle and I must get things straightened out so I can begin to make my living once more and I can't take too long . . . doing it."[29]

In Yucatan a tour guide took them to the ruins at Chichen Itza. Te Ata asked about the exotic flora and fauna, as Fisher would have done, but the scope of the guide's knowledge was pretty much limited to the ruins. The steps of the Warriors Temple were so narrow and steep that many in their tour group would not attempt the climb to the top. At the peak, Te Ata saw "a stirring view of the other ruins," some highly ornate, some elegant in simplicity, dramatically set off here and there against the encroaching jungle. On the two-hundred-foot-long ball court, the largest in Mesoamerica, Bennett and Te Ata stood at opposite ends, where the judges and the king sat, respectively, and talked to each other in conversational tones, so perfect were the acoustics. Seven players on a side trying to toss a ball through a ring, the game was played in deadly earnest. The captain of the losing side was sacrificed, they were told.[30]

As they visited other Maya ruins in Yucatan and Guatemala over the next week, Te Ata kept a daily journal. Though the entries were scanty, they indicate that she enjoyed being there despite her preoccupation with thoughts of C.F. One evening, as she looked up at the brilliance and clarity of the starry sky, she imagined him looking down at her through the Milky Way. She often felt like weeping but usually was able to check the urge—to keep from embarrassing Bennett.

In Guatemala the drive from Antigua to Lake Atitlán was over a winding, dusty road at eight thousand feet. On the way they passed lines of Indians wearing colorful blouses, carrying huge loads on their heads, trotting up and down the steep terrain on their way to and from the market at Antigua. Many of the women not only balanced these enormous loads in baskets on their heads, but they also carried babies in slings on their backs.[31] Such sights and experiences helped Te Ata to lose herself at intervals in a way that staying in New York City or Oklahoma could not have. On the airplane going home, while Bennett slept, Te Ata dealt with the prospect of returning home alone. She visualized entering her apartment on West 72d Street, and the thought was practically unbearable. She made a final entry in her journal: "It doesn't seem possible that CF will not be there waiting for me. I miss him so desperately[,] . . . so desperately."[32]

Te Ata did not have to return to work immediately after she got home. She received $1,175.31 as a death benefit from the AMNH and a monthly pension of almost $100.[33] She also may have had a small amount of savings, some stock dividends, and supplemental cash from Otto, who apparently wrote checks to several relatives on a fairly regular basis. The days in 1949 crept by. She wrote few letters, except to acknowledge those received from others, but was encircled by friends. One friend, a retired schoolteacher named Mildred Powell, moved into Te Ata's apartment with her for several months. Though they had been friends for some years, Powell's presumption that Te Ata needed or even wanted this type of companionship was surely off the mark, according to Dorothy Bennett. "Te Ata just couldn't say no to her friends, even when she wanted to."[34]

Te Ata spent most of the summer and fall at Loon Island with Mona Woodring and the usual visitors. She was in Manhattan in June trying to sell some of Fisher's astronomy books to the planetarium.[35] Otto tried to pry her away from the island in September by inviting her to Detroit and extending the use of a car for trips to Mackinaw or Oklahoma, if she wished.[36] In November, in Pittsburgh, she performed a special expanded rendition of "Along the Moccasin Trail," featuring segments of folklore alternating with a choral group and musicians performing Native American musical themes by Thurlow Lieurance and Charles Cadman.[37] The Russian émigré composer Vladimir Bakaleinikoff wrote, "[Te Ata's performance] belongs to the few great artistic pleasures of my life." The impression she made on him was comparable to performances of "great artists" such as the Italian actress Eleonora Duse and the Russian opera star Feodor Chaliapin.[38] Meanwhile, Ataloa had helped to secure Te Ata a guest faculty position with

Te Ata, performing in Philadelphia in 1949. She earned typical rave reviews. She was accompanied by her longtime Oklahoma Pawnee friend, Kuruks Pahetu.

the University of Southern California's Idyllwild School of Music and Arts for summer 1950. She would be introducing elementary school teachers to Indian folklore and adapting folklore of the tribes living in the San Jacinto Mountains for a pageant presented by university students. If she was inclined, she could also direct the students in other plays or programs.[39]

As 1949 was ending, Fisher's last book, *The Life of Audubon*, was published. John Kieran, wrote the foreword, which read in part: "It's too bad that every reader of this book could not have had a day with

Dr. Fisher in the open. For all the record of his scientific accomplishments and his educational honors, he carried himself in such a simple modest manner that the farmer who met him in the wood or along the brook would take him for just a quiet, smiling stranger from the next township. [The book] is filled with the whirr of wings, the lisp of leaves and ripple of rain, the lapping of water along strange river banks and the pursuit of wild things to wild places."[40]

Te Ata spent her first Christmas without C.F. with Mona and her extended family in Nashville, Tennessee. At social gatherings during that holiday season, Te Ata apparently made contact with some people who were influential in Nashville arts and education. One of them was Coleman S. Smith, who became Te Ata's unofficial agent and publicist. It was through his efforts that Te Ata got several bookings locally instead of just one or two. Included were appearances on a new mass medium, television.[41] In New York a Fifth Avenue company called Video Events, Inc., contacted two of the top nationally broadcast television shows, those of Kate Smith and Ed Sullivan, about possible appearances by Te Ata and Kuruks Pahetu, but apparently nothing came of it.[42] Mary Pritchett, an author's agent, saw Te Ata perform in 1951 and immediately wrote to propose that she write an Indian history book for a new McGraw-Hill history series. But Te Ata recommended Muriel Wright, her former Tishomingo high school teacher and editor of the history journal, *Chronicles of Oklahoma*.[43]

In the early 1950s Te Ata was again traveling as much or more than ever. Nearing 60 years old, her life, she wrote, "seems to follow the same pattern." She apparently was once again handling her own bookings, "giving programs of Folk Lore and making tracks all over the country doing it." "I am seldom at my apartment[,] . . . always busy as can be, one way or another," she wrote.[44] She was a perpetual visitor. The only place she lighted long enough to be homelike was Loon Island. Always having contributed improvements to the property, she crowned her efforts one fall day in 1953.

Waiting outside an antique shop for her friends to finish shopping, Te Ata looked up from her book and noticed a somewhat undersized totem pole leaning against the building. The sad eyes and banana-shaped nose of the owl sitting on top appealed strongly to her, and almost simultaneously she was struck by the notion that if she did not rescue the totem pole, it would share the same fate as most wooden Indians, winding up in front of a barber shop or some other unsuitable location. How much? she asked the proprietor. "For you, Te Ata, $50." It seemed fair, but she did not have $50, not having worked in some time. Still, she wanted to buy the totem pole and give it a new home on Loon Island. Later that afternoon she discussed the idea with Mona, who reminded her that she hardly had enough money to buy a can of coffee.[45]

When the mail arrived, Te Ata opened a letter from a publishing company asking permission to reproduce Te Ata's photograph of Julian Martinez, which had appeared on the April 1943 issue of *Natural History*. The company would pay her $50. She looked up from the letter at Mona and smiled. "I said, 'Mona, the Great Spirit wants me to have that totem pole.'" After it was delivered, a neighbor Te Ata called "Uncle Billy" wanted to bring the totem pole out to the island in his rowboat. Rowboat? Out of the question. She said she would come get it in her little red canoe. Te Ata sat astride the pole, which hung precariously over the canoe's bow; Uncle Billy tried to dissuade her, saying the totem pole was too heavy and could well wind up on the bottom of the lake. Would the Great Spirit deliver the means to acquire it, only to have it sink to the bottom of a lake? Extremely unlikely, thought Te Ata, and she slowly paddled the totem pole across to the island without incident. It remained a fixture there for many years until Mona, old and in ill health, sold Loon Island. Not knowing the new owners well, Te Ata gave the totem pole to some good people who ran a small trading post in nearby North Conway. For years afterward, the couple sent Te Ata a Christmas card, always mentioning that the totem pole still lived.

The year 1955 marked the one hundredth anniversary of the Treaty of Washington, in which the modern Chickasaw Nation was born. To celebrate the centennial, several prominent Oklahoma Chickasaws organized planning committees. The event would be held in the historic national capital city of Tishomingo the weekend of June 24–25.[46] The city of Tishomingo, named for the famed Chickasaw war chief who died on the Trail of Tears, was founded in 1855 and a year later designated the tribe's capital. The centennial planners were led by Chickasaw governor Floyd Maytubby, who had succeeded Douglas Johnston after his death in 1939. Maytubby, an Oklahoma

City insurance man, was ideally suited to his largely ceremonial role as governor, presenting headdresses (which Chickasaws historically never wore) and "Honorary Chickasaw" certificates to Oklahoma bigwigs and prominent or important visitors to Oklahoma City. Though he was not rich, Maytubby, a well-connected state Democrat, hobnobbed with those who were at the locally prestigious Oklahoma City Golf and Country Club. Knowing how to throw a good party, Maytubby recognized that he needed a headliner to attract publicity for the centennial.[47]

That person, everyone agreed, was Te Ata. She was the perfect choice: a nationally renowned Chickasaw raised in nearby Emet and Tishomingo and the daughter of a member of the last tribal cabinet. But would she be available? And since Maytubby was unable to pay her from the meager Chickasaw trust funds without the permission of the estimable Bureau of Indian Affairs, would she work for free?

To inform Te Ata of the event and pop the questions by telephone, Juanita Smith was selected, an astute choice.[48] As one of Uncle Doug's children, she was practically kin. When Mary Thompson was growing up in Emet, she occasionally visited Uncle Doug's dazzling home, the "Chickasaw White House," and observed the sophisticated ways and beautiful clothes of the governor's family. She probably got some of her earliest notions on the importance of bearing and poise from Juanita.

Now that very role model from so long ago was asking her to be the guest of honor at her tribe's centennial celebration. "I would be honored," she said, and she meant it. Two weeks after the centennial, she wrote that "this was as great an honor as being asked by Mr. and Mrs. Roosevelt to come to the White House and Hyde Park."[49] After Te Ata accepted the invitation, she told Juanita she would need round-trip air transportation, as she had to be back in New York on June 27. Maytubby arranged complimentary airfare with American Airlines and got Oklahoma City's Biltmore Hotel to provide Te Ata with a suite, gratis.

She arrived on June 21, the summer solstice, for precentennial publicity appearances. As her flight was quite late, the photographers had departed, but a sizable welcoming party was still on hand, including Governor Maytubby, Ataloa, who also was on the centennial program, and many of the Thompson relatives. She was taken to her hotel suite, pronounced it "something!" and was photographed there with Maytubby and Ataloa for the local newspaper. (When she saw the photo in the newspaper she said it made them all look "like *thugs!*")[50]

The next day Te Ata was up early to appear on two television programs and one radio program and attend a luncheon in her honor, escorted by Maytubby. That evening about fifty people attended a special dinner for her at the country club, filmed by another television station. On June 23, accompanied by Maytubby and a retinue, she made appearances in Norman and Ada, en route to Tishomingo.[51] When she arrived there, it probably occurred to her that she had never come into her old hometown with so much pomp and fanfare. While she was pleased and flattered, she could imagine C.F. chuckling at her.

In Tishomingo she stayed with her half sister, Selena, but the Thompson siblings, including Avis, Tom, and Snake, scarcely had a moment to themselves. About fifteen thousand people attended the centennial program.[52] A rough wooden stage was set up in front of the 1898 Chickasaw Capitol Building. During the day, Te Ata was too busy for much reflection. But late in the evenings, as she lay still in the transition from exhilaration to sleep, she immersed herself in childhood memories. She pondered her future and wondered not if but when she would return to Oklahoma to live. She and her brothers and sisters were starting to reach old age, and there might not be many more moons left them. She also felt close to the people and the land and thought she could live out her days in happiness in a variety of roles: respected tribal elder, performing artist, mentor, storyteller, teacher. That sort of life had a certain appeal to her. And there is something to say for going out on top, before skills or memory begin to erode. But should she retire while she still had the power to reach people, particularly young people, and still had the motivation and energy and desire to get behind the wheel of her car and go? Witness the hold she had on the large crowd earlier that day, under less than ideal performance conditions. People were standing windblown and hot under the blazing sun, but many seemed transfixed, some with tears in their eyes.

Moreover, it was 1955 and times were changing. Adolescents seemed more independent, even more rebellious in a good sense, she thought. Perhaps they were ready to turn away from a surfeit of postwar materialism and embrace the beauty inherent in tribal culture and folkways. Furthermore, now that the federal government's tribal termination policy had run its unsuccessful course, tribes all over the United States were clamoring for self-determination.[53] Even the Chickasaws and Choctaws had grassroots campaigns for the right to once again elect their own leaders. These Chickasaws and their Choctaw allies believed that Floyd Maytubby, an unresponsive figurehead, had to go.[54]

While Te Ata was not actively involved in these movements, she felt a revitalizing spirit. She concluded that the Great Spirit still had plans for her during the second half of the twentieth century. She drifted off to sleep in the serenity of her sister's house, in that abiding belief.

Epilogue

Te Ata did not return to Oklahoma until 1966. She continued touring, seemingly in as much demand in the turbulent sixties as she had been in the twenties, thirties, forties, and fifties. She was seldom in her West 72d Street apartment, which served as little more than a way station for trips to New England and the Southeast, particularly Nashville. Even when she was in the East and not performing, she was likely to be with the Balls in Wilton, Connecticut, or at Loon Island. Her apartment had become an extravagance, a business expense, in effect, that she could no longer afford. Simultaneously, Ataloa, who had been teaching in California since the end of the war, was growing restless. In spring 1962 they decided to relocate together to Santa Fe, New Mexico. That summer they bought a house a few blocks from the historic plaza and improved and decorated it to their liking—as they had their tiny New York apartment three decades before.[1] Ataloa lived there full time; for Te Ata, the house was more a headquarters between tours. Still, she treasured those few years in Santa Fe. This was the first and only house she ever owned, and when she was in town, she felt a part of the community and its population of artists. Her few years as a home owner ended when Ataloa developed cancer in the mid-1960s and moved back to California for treatment and to live out her final months. She died on November 11, 1967; Te Ata was the executrix of her will.[2]

Unwilling or unable to remain in the house alone, Te Ata headed home to Oklahoma for good. She had not returned to her home state sooner in part because she could get more bookings in the East where she was better known. The event that increased Te Ata's acclaim in Oklahoma more than any other during this period was her induction into the Oklahoma Hall of Fame in late 1957. Frances Davis, who herself had been inducted in 1946, probably played a role in her former pupil's selection. At any rate, following the ceremony, Te Ata embarked on a statewide tour, in which she made thirty appearances in as many days.[3] If that was remarkable for a woman nearing the then traditional retirement age, incredibly she would continue her career for more than twenty years. She arranged her own bookings, drove herself all over America, and performed, regardless of venue or how she felt physically or emotionally, at a consistently high level. Wherever she went, she always placed a small framed photo of C.F. by her bed.[4]

Te Ata's last two active decades, the 1960s and 1970s, were a period of renaissance for the Chickasaws and many other Indian tribes. Whether the progress in Indian self-government, health care, and education resulted from the well-publicized activities of activist Indians or the commitment of the larger society to atone for the sins of the past, or both, Te Ata was enormously pleased. And regardless of the political or social climate, or who was in or out, she continued to dramatize folklore. Her original purpose, to present the beauty and wisdom of Indian culture, never changed. The stories were timeless, and because the quality of her performances did not diminish, she was still in demand. She was not a national celebrity, but she was well known in the places across the country where she performed intermittently. Her best advertising had always been word of mouth. Some of the schoolchildren who wrote thank-you letters to her in the 1920s and 1930s enjoyed her performances ten or twenty years later or brought their own children, who in turn wrote her thank-you letters. In this way she affected the lives of thousands of Americans.[5]

She appeared on radio and local television several times, but her folklore performances did not translate well aurally or on small, black-and-white screens. The only time she appeared on national television was on the "Today" show in 1976, as that program highlighted all of the states in the nation's bicentennial year.[6] But by then she was in semiretirement.

Of the hundreds of thousands of Americans who saw Te Ata perform live, few left the venue unmoved. She gave dimensions to Native

Te Ata, at age 77, captivates a class of Connecticut schoolchildren. Photo by Perry Ruben studio, Georgetown, Conn. Though living in Oklahoma at the time, she often headed East to visit old friends such as Margaret Ball.

American life and thought that few non-Indians knew about. Only then were some Americans able to develop an appreciation for the immense loss that native people had sustained across the American continent. Surely, if prompted, many would remember the beautiful, dignified woman; a picture of her in her Cheyenne dress or just the distinctive name "Te Ata" would surely conjure up impressions, a few details, and a smile. Thousands of tribal members, from the Seminoles in Florida to the Salish in Washington, were proud that this Chickasaw represented them in such an artistic and honorable manner across what for them was an American wasteland from the 1920s through the 1950s. Unfortunately, admiration and even adulation rarely results in monuments, like Lake Te Ata, but through the 1970s, her reputation was revitalized at least in Oklahoma.

Te Ata: Chickasaw Storyteller, American Treasure

Te Ata's tour dates tapered off in the 1970s and stopped altogether in about 1980, when she was eighty-five. During the twilight of her career, as she became more widely respected and accumulated more honors, she lost many of her dearest friends: Mona Woodring, John Ball, Frances Davis. Her career was summarized in a 1975 documentary titled *God's Drum*, named after the Hartley Burr Alexander work she had performed for nearly fifty years and reprised in the film. Created by the Oklahoma City filmmaker Shawnee Brittain with a combination of private, state, and federal funds, the twenty-eight-minute film was produced for two reasons: to inspire young Indian people to hold on to their heritage and to raise scholarship money for Indian students. Through sales and rentals of the film, Te Ata's alma mater set up a scholarship fund named in her honor.[7]

Having moved into an apartment in Oklahoma City in 1968, she maintained her residence there for nearly twenty years, until her mind started to wander. But before the dementia worsened, while she was still aware of the significance of the honor, the Oklahoma Arts Council selected her in 1987 as the first official Oklahoma Treasure, patterned after a tradition in Japan. Te Ata was the only nominee for the award that year.[8] Since then only eight other Oklahomans have received the honor. Later she collaborated with the Oklahoma City storyteller Lynn Moroney to adapt one of her stories, "Baby Rattlesnake," for a children's book. When the book was published in 1989, the Chickasaw Nation, headquartered in Ada, Oklahoma, planned a book-signing ceremony for Te Ata and Moroney, also of Chickasaw ancestry.[9] Te Ata could not attend. She had recently been moved into a nursing home by her nephew, Hiawatha Estes, and her niece, then state senator Helen Cole. The decision had been made with great anguish, but to protect their aunt, Hi and Helen felt they had no other choice. In the late 1980s, Te Ata had been living increasingly in her memories and had been experiencing more prolonged periods of disorientation.[10]

When she became the third person to be inducted into the Chickasaw Nation Hall of Fame in 1991, she was too frail to attend the ceremony. Her sole surviving sibling, Tom, accepted the plaque for her. The induction ceremony was presided over by an emotional Chickasaw governor, Bill Anoatubby. Raised in Tishomingo in the 1950s and 1960s, Anoatubby, like virtually every Chickasaw boy and girl,

In 1975 an Oklahoma City filmmaker, Shawnee Brittain, produced a documentary on the life of Te Ata called *God's Drum*. The title came from a Hartley Burr Alexander work that Te Ata had performed for nearly fifty years.

had heard of Te Ata. But after he began working for the rejuvenated tribal government in 1975 and learned more about her remarkable achievements, his esteem for her had gradually become veneration. Governor Anoatubby told the gathering that the tribe's debt to Te Ata for her accomplishments could never be repaid.[11] After the ceremony Linda Harris, granddaughter of Te Ata's sister, Selena, gathered some pebbles from Pennington Creek, which ran by the place in Tishomingo where the Thompson family's big house had been located, and took them to Te Ata, as she had requested.[12]

Te Ata: Chickasaw Storyteller, American Treasure

Te Ata became the first official Oklahoma Treasure in 1987. Among the many family members who were with her at the ceremony at the Oklahoma State Capitol Building were her nephew Hiawatha Estes, left, and younger brother Tom. Governor Henry Bellmon presented the award.

Later that year Tom "went away." Te Ata had not attended the funerals of any of her adult brothers and sisters. Rather, she spent time alone with each of them before the service. At the funeral home, Helen Cole pushed her aunt's wheelchair into the room next to Tom's casket and left her alone for about an hour. As Te Ata gazed at her brother's face for the last time, she thought of his sweet smile, a memory that only increased her pain when she reflected on the "injustice" of her baby brother "going away" before she did.[13]

In Te Ata's one hundredth year, 1995, a Chickasaw drama professor, musician, and playwright, Judy Lee Oliva, was researching the life of Te Ata in earnest, intending to produce an ambitious biography for the stage that would include original music and choreography. By 1999 Oliva and a collaborator had developed a musical and were seeking the financial backing to bring it to the stage. A year later Oliva's play won the $10,000 grand prize in an annual competition sponsored by the Five Civilized Tribes Museum in Muskogee, Oklahoma.

Also in 1995, Te Ata's alma mater, now named the University of Science and Arts of Oklahoma, announced that a new and improved version of *God's Drum* had been made, featuring commentary from admirers.[14] Lynn Moroney said, "[Te Ata] moved traditional storytelling from folk tradition into a fine art. And she was one of the first to work in the pan-Indian area. She not only told her own tribal stories but incorporated those of many other tribes." Governor Anoatubby said that Te Ata was perpetuating Indian heritage and culture during the years when the tribes needed this the most. In 1998 the famed Chickasaw artist Tom Phillips of San Francisco accepted a commission from the Chickasaw Nation to do an oil painting of the Chickasaw Capitol Building in Tishomingo to commemorate its one hundredth anniversary. His sketch was approved by Governor Anoatubby and a committee of tribal members, save for their recommendation that the faces of two ghostly images be painted into the sky. One was the war chief, Tishomingo. The other was Te Ata. The painting is now on display in the tribe's Council House Museum, adjacent to the capitol building, along with the buckskin dress she wore at Hyde Park.[15]

Her own time to go away came on October 26, 1995, just thirty-eight days short of what would have been her one hundredth birthday. Her body was cremated, as she had requested. A memorial service was held on a sunny, windy day early in November. Though she had outlived almost all of her contemporaries, more than one hundred people paid their respects. (Margaret Ball and Dorothy Bennett were too frail to make the long trips from Connecticut and New Mexico, respectively.) Helen Cole planned the service, which was simple, elegant, and poignant. Although most memorial services are designed for the survivors, this was one that Helen believed Te Ata would have enjoyed.[16]

Te Ata, age ninety-four, listens to one of her most ardent admirers, Bill Anoatubby, governor of the revitalized Chickasaw Nation. Te Ata was the third person to be inducted into the Chickasaw Hall of Fame in 1991. Governor Anoatubby told the audience that the tribe's debt to Te Ata for her accomplishments could never be repaid. She died just thirty-eight days short of her hundredth birthday.

Te Ata would have been enormously proud of Helen's grandson, Mason Cole, dramatically reciting "Baby Rattlesnake" from memory; she would have been pleased to hear Judy Oliva reciting her poem to Te Ata and reading Te Ata's beautiful love letter to Clyde Fisher, written on the high seas in 1936, as she returned to him from Scandinavia; she would have felt honored by the presence of Governor Anoatubby, representing all Chickasaw people, and the Comanche artist and musician Doc Tate Nevaquaya playing three flute solos during the service; and she would have enjoyed and been amused by the stories and anecdotes about her that were volunteered by some of the participants. Doc Tate told the audience that he had thought about wearing his feather bonnet to honor her but decided against it because he felt he was not on the same high plane.[17] In fact, Doc Tate had been named the second Oklahoma State Treasure earlier in 1995, eight years after Te Ata.

As the mourners filed out of the chapel, each person carried a memento, a card bearing a poem written by Te Ata. Written in 1932, the poem, "My Feet Are Dancing," was especially appropriate for the occasion:

> Down the gone-away trail
> My heart walks with him.
> His strength is mine now
> His gifts are mine
> His Dancing spirit now a part of me.
> I am strong now!
> Now my spirit feet are dancing
> Now my spirit feet invade the hills
> Now my spirit feet have touched the mountains
> There in the blue they dance
> Upon the corners of the winds.[18]

There was one last thing to do. Years before her death Te Ata had given written instructions to Helen and Hiawatha about wanting to be cremated and what to do with her ashes. "Want no urn!" she wrote emphatically. The family was much amused by that admonition. But Helen knew without asking that the directive was Te Ata's way of saying that she wished always to be free. "Mix my ashes with wild-flower seeds and on a quiet day when there is very little wind, scratch the earth gently and bury them beside Mother and Dad or scatter them in Tishomingo." Helen and Hi did both, and because they are both buoy-ant and loquacious people, they filled the air along Pennington Creek with occasional laughter and good stories about Te Ata—making their ceremony more joyous than solemn.[19]

Afterword

by RAYNA GREEN AND JOHN TROUTMAN

Indian biographies have typically fallen into two categories: ethnographic accounts of "traditional" nineteenth-century Indians undergoing or resisting culture change and biographies of tribal and national political leaders engaged in diplomacy, religious revitalization, or resistance. Te Ata's life story, as constructed by Richard Green, is neither of those conventional, expected forms of Indian biography, nor is it about a conventional, "expected" Indian. It *is* a narrative biography, in the Western literary tradition, about an unusual and compelling, though seemingly prototypical individual, in the tradition of the new Indian histories presented by tribal historians. Certainly, it also provides a means to trace and explore some of the thematic strands in the larger movements in Native American history—allotment, land alienation, urbanization, relocation, assimilation, and cultural loss—and to raise questions about the effects of these policies and movements on twentieth-century native lives.

However, Te Ata's life offers us anything but a prototypical route, through biography, into prototypical issues in native history. Her life story and professional life offer a new textbook exegesis of some important theoretical and analytic questions applicable both to modern Indian life and to contemporary scholarship, such as the evolution and construction of intertribal or pan-Indian behaviors, the construction of Indian identity, performative identity, Indian agency, authenticity, cultural appropriation, cultural brokerage, boundary crossing, hybridity, the social construction of race, and the politics of gender and difference.

Often by her own account, Te Ata scripted her life as she scripted her performances; she was in control or took control, even when she appeared to accede to the persuasive forces of public demand. Repudiating victimization and refusing to fall within any particular category or stereotype of "Indianness," her agency is found in her conscious ambiguity, her success in traversing the racial, gendered, and cultural borders that shaped her experience and the expectations of everyone around her. At once a woman, a Chickasaw, a "mixed-blood," an "Indian," an Oklahoman, a world traveler, an educated socialite, an actress, a "show Indian," a daughter/wife/sister/aunt/friend, a professional colleague, an educator, and a writer, she is aware of, acting on, and at times explicitly articulate about the ambiguities and contradictions of her multivocality, on and off the stage.

Te Ata put competing versions of authenticity to the test, consciously and unconsciously sorting out the pressures and presents of a developing urban, hybridized, pan-Indian consciousness. She was the new culturally omnivorous Indian, seeking the sources of her input and the inspirations for her output from all that she encountered in her life, even while wishing perhaps vainly (and not too seriously) for a "purer," authentic, single-tribal muse. She took the sources of her stagecraft (song, dance, style, story) from the complex world she came to inhabit, yet she remained passionate in her devotion to "Indian" traditions and to the Chickasaw world she left in Oklahoma, the one she would always try to share with an audience. She occupied a stage with Indian and non-Indian partners in front of an audience as diverse as her partners in stagecraft, though often throughout the 1950s that audience was segregated by race and ethnicity.

We can interrogate these performers for their challenges to conventional wisdom about the results of land loss, language loss, and mainstream schooling. Rather than see Te Ata (and her fellow performers)— as early-twentieth-century scholars might have done—as the inevitable product of assimilation policy, the sad end result of massive culture loss, the downside of urbanization, and thus the culturally marginal antithesis of authenticity, we can see her as a remarkable woman who stood in the vanguard for modern Indians. Te Ata encapsulated this new form of fluid Indian identity, a cosmopolitan Indianness couched in modernity, agency, and authority, an identity honed in urban migration and entry into a burgeoning mass-entertainment industry in the United States. Perhaps she typifies the many native people in the 1920s and 1930s who were in fact moving to urban centers such as New York and Chicago, establishing new native communities and persisting in claiming their difference in ever new environments and changing circumstances. This innovation and movement was inconsistent with the stereotypes of native people in the popular imagination yet consistent with their histories as creative survivors who knew that moving targets were harder to shoot.

Te Ata grew up at the apex of the assimilation and allotment era of federal Indian policy. While the U.S. government sought to destroy tribal institutions and break up communally held reservation lands, native children were placed in federal Indian boarding schools to train them essentially to become good American citizens. At home, native language, music, dance, clothing, and religious and ceremonial life had been banned or thwarted by government agents and missionaries alike. At school, instructors forbid the use of native languages, separated siblings and co-tribal members, clothed children in "citizen" clothes or uniforms, and cut their hair. The schools tried to attenuate or extinguish cultural ties to native communities, to destroy any semblance of Indianness students might claim. Te Ata's second school, Bloomfield Academy, established by missionaries, was such a place.

Some could not resist the colonizing force of school, but others, such as Te Ata, created new and unique forms of resistance to cultural and historical extinction. The significance of this era of American Indian history, then is not found only in the continued assaults on native identity, native land, and native life but also in the innovative manners and tactics that so many native people employed in their insistence on survival as Indians.

Many Indian students took the musical and dramatic skills that they had honed in the schools far beyond the campus. Oratorical English skills were put into nativist political rhetoric on the lecture circuit and in Washington courts and forums, arguing the Indian case before the press, the public, and politicians. Many of the show Indians who moved on from Wild West shows to the circuses, the movies, the tourist circuit, and the popular stage had created and refined their acts at the Indian schools, or at least certainly had been introduced to the major components of it there. They learned the formal dramatic arts in the vignettes and plays and the informal dramatic arts of deception by which to persuade preachers, teachers, and Indian agents that they were both native and civilized.

As many critics have signaled in their new assessments of the Wild West shows, tourism, and the participation of native performers and artists, their interests, experiences, and motives were much more complex and different than conventional views would have it. Far from simply exploited and victimized, they were living out the satisfactions of their former lives, at once free to travel, grow, and experience the world as Indians. Virtually forbidden to do so during the first third of the twentieth century by the mandates of federal Indian policy, Te Ata and the other performers found a means to publicly perform and celebrate their Indianness, even if it meant that Malecites, Chickasaws, Kiowas, and Cherokees masqueraded as Sioux for a Plains-fetishist audience. Indians and non-Indians alike have criticized "acts" like Te Ata's for lending credibility to white stereotypes. But the acts of Te Ata, Henry (Red Eagle) Perley, Ataloa, Gertrude Simmons Bonnin, Tsianina Redfeather, Molly Spotted Elk, Princess Watawaso, Bruce Poolaw, and hundreds of other show Indians used the images of Indians that Americans demanded of them both to remain viable commercially and to testify to the survival and authenticity of real Indians.

Performing Indianness, even someone else's version of it, stretched and transcended the boundaries and burdens of strict cultural maintenance and served, almost ironically, as an act of resistance to assimilation. It became, in itself, a form of creative survival. Te Ata's life story reveals an outline of how Indians developed that form, with its interesting modernist permutations, of survival.

The continuing official and unofficial on native cultures and cultural manifestations provided for the members of these new native generations a significant impetus toward sharing and incorporating into individual "act," across tribal lines, what cultural repertoire they did retain. In addition by means of increased exposure to other Indians through social, cultural, and political interactions—in the Indian schools, on the lecture circuit, in the movies, in the Wild West shows, in intertribal marriage, and in political delegations on behalf of tribal peoples in Washington, D.C., and elsewhere—many native people began to share and adopt others' performative repertoires: songs, stories, jokes, and ceremonies. Native men and women alike adopted and adapted to these "new" behaviors, regardless of their individual and collective cultural origins or cultural stability, giving them a chance to perform an Indian identity on the stage as well as to articulate for themselves a form of Indianness consistent with their own circumstances.

In part and ironically so, the spread and popularity of this pan-Indian culture, especially the celebration of pan-Plains culture and dress, came as much from non-native demand as from intertribal exposure and interaction. In the early twentieth century urban white audiences began to flock to presentations of Indian songs and stories by native performers. Philip J. Deloria has argued that during this period the desire of non-native audiences for American Indian authenticity was rooted in antimodern primitivism, a movement in the worldwide popular imagination that still holds captive the representation of American Indians. For many non-native people, Indians in the modern era became referential symbols of "authenticity and natural purity" in an otherwise compromised and inauthentic urban industrial landscape;[1] such symbols could easily be and were regularly appropriated by non-native Americans. These symbols then fueled the attraction of white audiences to venues of instruction and entertainment by "authentic" native performers.

Federal Indian agents and missionaries had to struggle, therefore, not only against Indian people intent on perpetuating their community, tribal, and native identities but also against the yearnings of non-native people eager to witness practices of Indianness for their own edification. Having tried to stamp out Indianness, they were faced with white folks demanding a display of it. The eastern tourists, tourism industry developers, artists, arts patrons, scholars, and collectors who flooded into the Great Lakes, the West, and the Southwest were fascinated with and demanded to see those same ceremonies, dances, costumes, ceremonial arts, and objects that the government sought to destroy. They "discovered," valued, bought, traded, or took those objects for trophies, for their own collections, and for newly formed museums. When they returned home, they flocked to lecture halls and stages to see Indians. Some even collected live Indians, taking them to their museums, to department stores, and to their drawing rooms to sing, dance, and make pots. In every possible venue, there was a market for Indians. Using every means possible, Indians tried to meet that market head-on.

Indian women—Iroquois and Ojibwa basket makers, Pueblo potters, Dakota linguists and musicians, Okanogan writers, Mohawk poets, Osage and Penobscot dancers, and Chickasaw and Creek actresses—would lead the way in fitting native life into these new economic and cultural realities. In the midst of poverty caused by the ever vigorous attack on lands and cultures, many native women converted their traditional skills into artistry, often based on outsider demand, which allowed native people to participate in the new cash economy and continue to live as Indians. They would lead the way in the new necessities of cultural preservation, collecting the stories, the linguistic material, translating it into Western literary form, and "performing" it anywhere anyone would appreciate it. Native men developed dances they could do in front of tourists, songs they could sing, dramas they could act and reenact, without showing and compromising the "real" dances, songs, and ceremonies considered improper for outsiders to experience. In this way, much of the performance so critiques in retrospect as fake was in fact developed to mask the things they did not want others to see. But the new forms of performance would take on life as the real thing or at least one version of realness, of authenticity for the native people participating in it. We can see this process unfolding in the lives of Te Ata and her friends.

In the midst of the economic and cultural devastation everywhere in Indian country, Te Ata was one of the more successful native performers of her time. Still, her relative economic success compared to those left at home remains insignificant compared to her cultural successes of representation.

Ironically, most of the Indian artists and performers often found greater economic success in playing to the market and in "playing Indian" than in pursuing the assimilative policies and philosophy of the Bureau of Indian Affairs. Participating in the new tourism and mass entertainment industry as artists or performers, either at home where tourism was being developed or by hitting the road as a show Indian, offered many of them a unique if double-edged opportunity. Like those who were sent away to the boarding schools, some who left home for economic and artistic opportunities never came back to live. And they had to live with the odd contradictions inherent in their performance of this new Indian identity.

Although Te Ata performed in numerous plays as a non-native character, because of the desire of the public to witness "authentic" Indianness she did not begin to attract attention to herself until she began to perform as an Indian, dressing in fringe and buckskin, singing native songs, and telling native stories. Where did her material and dress originate, and how did they relate to popular notions of Indianness and the modern circumstances of native people? In her first public performance, the young Chickasaw woman billed herself as an Indian princess, walked onstage in a Kiowa dress, and performed "From the Land of the Sky Blue Water," a piece by the non-native and Indianist composer Charles Wakefield Cadman. She introduced her selections with lines from Longfellow's "Hiawatha." Throughout her career she continued to perform material collected from anthropologists or written by non-native composers. But the use of such sources does not suggest that she was inauthentic in her Indianness or performances as much as it demonstrates the fallacy of the concept of authenticity and the complexity of her condition.

In fashioning and using the expectation of her audience to suit her needs and circumstances, Te Ata reified many expectations of the non-native public while shattering others. She built her career around her Indianness. Her dress, her stories, her songs, her props—all represented or authenticated her Indianness while her Indianness authenticated them. But first and foremost, Te Ata was an entertainer who pitched her presentation to an audience that *expected* to see an Indian princess, that *expected* her verse and song to resemble those of popular writers like Longfellow and composers like Lieurance and Cadman, and that *expected* her to appear in pan-Plains buckskins. Te Ata, quite clearly, understood and took advantage of the non-native quest for authenticity, though she was regularly and openly dismissive of the requested play Indian cultural and material paraphernalia, for example, wearing war bonnets or referring to herself as an Indian maiden or princess. And as a native woman encountering and in fact becoming a part of the social circles of her urban audiences, she transcended the limited expectations that the concept of authenticity and its inherent stereotypes guaranteed her.

Furthermore, like her sister Oklahoma tribeswomen, the younger Osage ballerina Maria Tallchief and her contemporary, the Creek singer and actress Tsianina Redfeather, her sophistication in manipulating the ambiguities and contradictions of Indianness and Euro-American styles made her a new kind of persuasive advocate for native people. Te Ata was able to use entertainment venues and schools throughout the country as a way to reach across racial, class, and geographic barriers in demonstrating the vitality of modern native people. As Richard Green points out, "people often told her that they had met Indians before, but not like her."

But there were hundreds of native performers on American and European stages, in "new" tourist centers such as Niagara Falls, the Wisconsin Dells, the Grand Canyon, and Glacier National Park, and in Indian schools. Te Ata was one among a community of many who had begun touring urban cities and the countryside performing Indianness. The establishment of the community is well documented in this biography through her interactions in New York City. Her extensive professional and personal friendships and interactions with Mary Stone McClendon (aka Ataloa), Kuruks Pahetu (Pawnee), her accompanist, and Fred Cardin (Miami-Quapaw), among others, testifies to the reality and especially the conflicts of this new urban Indian world.

Te Ata and Ataloa were both close friends with fellow New Yorker and performer Sylvester Long (Buffalo Child Long Lance). Their friendship with him and defense of his Indianness raises, even at this earlier moment, the questions of authenticity and border and culture crossing that have been so compelling in recent scholarship and in native community debate. Long Lance, who may have been black, Indian, North Carolina Cherokee, or all or none of these, billed himself as Blackfoot (no doubt a more "authentic" and authenticating identity for the Plains-fixated audiences than whatever else he might have claimed). Ataloa, Te Ata, and Clyde Fisher accepted his representations of himself and worried that it was the burdens of a highly racialized public identity that may have killed him.

Did they worry, as well they might, about the consequences to themselves and their reputations when questions of authenticity were raised about others? Were they more concerned about the competition from non-Indians who were replacing them on the stage and film set? Did they talk about and were they thoughtful about their collaboration with popular images of Indians or the degree to which they insisted on their own de facto establishment of authenticity? We know, from her own accounts, that Te Ata questioned the silliness of her audience's demands for Plains headdresses and princess titles while holding firmly to her Chickasaw public and private presence. Nevertheless, she and her circle of performing friends reconstituted so many versions of Indianness that perhaps all those versions must have begun to seem unquestionable and normative, the very essence of postmodern ambiguity.

We also know that most of these Indian performers used their stages to become effective and persistent advocates for native people. They often took advantage of their relative celebrity and access to public forums by expressing their political views. The burgeoning mass mediums of the stage, lecture circuits, film, radio, and later television provided them with access to audiences that they otherwise probably would have never faced. While some were more openly political in their performances and stage banter than others, together this community of performers often served as a liaison between rural reservation communities and eastern reformers and polity makers.

In the interface with their extended audiences, Indian and non-Indian, policy maker and common citizen alike, these artists came to epitomize the newest versions of and reputations for cultural brokerage, formerly reserved for mixed-blood fur trade–era translators or wives and children. Te Ata's alliance with Clyde Fisher was not unusual but in fact almost predictable in the context of native women's lives everywhere. Her story and those of her contemporaries rewrites the essential story of the Indian female who befriends, marries, or collaborates with white men. Was she a traitor, hero, guide, survivor, broker, cultural diplomat? From Pocahontas and John Smith and John Rolfe, Mary Matthews Musgrove Bosomsworth and all her husbands, Sakakawea and Lewis and Clark, the wives and children of the fur trade era, the Pueblo potters and the anthropologists who joined their mutual patronage, and Suzette LaFlesche–Bright Eyes and her husband, the journalist Thomas Tibbles to the professional and personal collaboration between Maria Tallchief and George Balanchine, Tsianina Redfeather and the composer-pianist Charles Wakefield Cadman, and Humishuma and Lucius McWhorter, Te Ata fits into the paradigmatic ambiguities of native women's histories.

The complexities of continually negotiating a place for herself as an Indian while married to a white scientist and inhabiting an economic class unlike that of the Indians she met on her tours, are evident in Te Ata's and her husband's visit with the Bloods in 1946. Te Ata was at once an outsider, a tourist, the wife of a scientist, yet welcomed by the Bloods as a special guest, as an Indian, and as a celebrity Indian at that. The predicament forced her to acknowledgment the difficulties of sorting out her roles, her allegiances, and her obligations in this circumstance. We can only wish for more such entries in her journal—more on the Long Lance episode, for example—which doubtless would have documented other instances in which she had to confront the complexities of reconciling her multifaceted identity. Still, the conflicts she outlines and that we can ferret out bring up the lights on an otherwise dimmed stage.

Of course, Te Ata's success stands out among many failures by other native performers and numerous additional trials that native communities have had to face in the twentieth century. With the immense desire of the public in the first half of the twentieth century to witness authentic Indians perform or to visit and consume native homes and products, it was difficult for Indians to get jobs as anything other than Indians on the mainstream stage or in film. Even the Indian roles were often in short supply, especially in the film industry, and by the late 1930s native actors saw themselves increasingly supplanted by non-Indians who took the Indian roles in redface. There was increasingly even more competition for the role of Indian than for Indians playing non-Indian roles. While many native people toured the country from the 1920s through the 1980s and played Indian before non-native, often urban middle-class audiences, many non-native people played Indian and marketed their authenticity of knowledge and material as well. That competition for the role of "Indian" a major role in American performative history, continues today in ever new and interesting forms. Such competition had and has enormous economic and cultural consequences for Indian performers, casting further doubts on the authenticity and cultural competence of those Indians standing in the role.

Te Ata's story tells us much about how native peoples had learned to live within the contradictions of a world that removed, exiled, dispossessed, and disenfranchised them while demanding access to and lionizing many of their customs and cultural practices. Thousands of old and new Indian-made objects and hundreds of recordings of songs reside now in museums and libraries where they give testimony to the values and motives of those who both hated and loved Indians. They also give testimony to the ways in which native peoples evolved the things essential to their physical and spiritual as well as to the ways in which those things embody their spiritual, political, and social universes. These objects, old and new, these recordings and films, these dramas played out on so many stages, bear witness to the creative strategies Indians employed to live through several centuries of hate and love for their lives, their lands, and their cultures. These "performances," fixed *and* fluid, reveal what it took—the magic, the prayers, the disguises, the laughter, the creativity—for native people to preserve the old ways and means of being Indian while claiming new forms of Indianness and adapting to their new circumstances and new modes of living. If, as Alexandra Harmon has suggested, "Indianness is an ongoing creation, and Indians are chief among its creators,"[2] stories like Te Ata's hold a rich education about the creators of modern native life and its modern circumstances.

NOTES

PROLOGUE

1. Richard Green, "The Migration Legends," *Journal of Chickasaw History* 1, no. 1, (1994): 4–8.

2. Arrell Gibson, *The Chickasaws* (Norman: University of Oklahoma Press, 1971), 4–6.

3. Monte Ross Lewis, "Chickasaw Removal: Betrayal of the Beloved Warriors, 1794–1844" (Ph.D. dissertation, North Texas State University, 1981), 264–65.

4. Angie Debo, *And Still the Waters Run* (Princeton: Princeton University Press, 1940), 4.

5. Grant Foreman, *Indian Removal* (Norman: University of Oklahoma Press, 1953), preface.

6. Gibson, *The Chickasaws*, 158–59, 192, 254–55.

7. Daniel F. Littlefield, Jr., *The Chickasaw Freedmen* (Westport, Conn.: Greenwood Press, 1980), 18–19.

8. Gibson, *The Chickasaws*, 298.

9. Littlefield, *The Chickasaw Freedmen*, 40–46.

10. Francis P. Prucha, *The Great Father*, abr. ed. (Lincoln: University of Nebraska Press, 1984), 256–57.

11. Debo, *And Still the Waters Run*, 7.

12. Gibson, *The Chickasaws*, 302–3.

CHAPTER 1. LISTENING TO THE CORN GROW

1. Ancestor file, Te Ata Collection (TAC), Chickasaw Council House Museum (CCHM), Tishomingo. Several papers are included that provide sketchy genealogical details of the Thompson family and one similar paper on the Freund family. Most are in Te Ata's handwriting, but no sources are given.

2. Te Ata, with Jane Werner Watson, "Te Ata: As I Remember It," unpublished memoir, 1981, partially paginated, references contained in introduction titled "Before My Time" and in chap. 2, no page, TAC, CCHM.

3. Te Ata Oral History, Archives and Manuscripts Department, Oklahoma Historical Society, Oklahoma City; Te Ata Oral History, Chickasaw Tribal Library, Ada, Okla.

4. Testimony of William Goforth, Transcript of Citizenship Committee meeting, February 4, 1890, Oklahoma Historical Society Microfilm Roll CKN 2, Oklahoma City. This source is courtesy of Chickasaw genealogist Kerry Armstrong of Fort Worth, Texas. In one source the name is Thomas Jacob Thompson; in the others it is Jacob Thompson.

5. Helen Cole, personal correspondence, October 1999.

6. Ancestor file, TAC, CCHM.

7. In the Ancestor file, the woman is identified as Selena Bynum. However, according to Armstrong, the records reveal no daughter of Turner and Lucinda Bynum named Selena. Of their six daughters, Armstrong believes Te Ata's grandmother was most likely the one referred to as Melinne or Millenium, who was born, according to the Bynum family Bible, in 1845.

8. Marriages, births, and deaths as recorded in the Bynum family Bible and published in the *Pontotoc County* (Okla.) *Historical Quarterly*; copy provided to the author by Kerry Armstrong. According to the genealogy, James Logan Colbert's third wife was part Chickasaw. They had a son, James Colbert, who married Susan James. They had a daughter, Tennessee Robinson Colbert, who married John A. Bynum. They produced Turner Bynum, who married Lucinda Dyer. They had a daughter, Millenium, who married Thomas Jefferson Thompson, Te Ata's grandfather.

9. From these genealogical sources it is apparent that most of Te Ata's Choctaw blood came from her paternal great-grandfather's side, while most of her Chickasaw blood came via her maternal grandmother.

10. H. F. O'Beirne, *Leaders and Leading Men of the Indian Territory* (Chicago: America Publisher's Association, 1891), 285.

11. Mother's story file, TAC, CCHM. Much of what is known about Bertie's background, her courtship and marriage to Thompson, and their early years together is contained in a remarkable manuscript that she wrote at Te Ata's request in 1939, soon after Thompson's death. Unless otherwise indicated, all of the information on Te Ata's parents and early married years comes from this source.

12. Mother's story file, 14.

13. In notes for her autobiography, Te Ata says that Bertie was part Osage, but Bertie does not mention this in her handwritten autobiography.

14. Mother's story file, 14–15.

15. Ibid., 16.

16. Gibson, *The Chickasaws*, 292. All non–Indians wanting to reside and do business in the Chickasaw Nation were required to purchase $5 permits from the nation. But the vast majority of them did not bother to do so, and the federal government, which in the treaty of 1867 had promised to evict intruders, could not begin to stem the tide with the few federal marshals operating in Indian Territory.

17. Mother's story file, 17.

18. Ibid.; Te Ata, "As I Remember It," notes prepared by Te Ata for her memoir, Childhood folder, TAC, CCHM. (Hereafter, notes for Te Ata's memoir.)

19. Chickasaw Nation Roll for Thomas Benjamin Thompson, 1897, CCHM.

20. Thompson family Tree prepared by E. R. Thompson, Jr., son of Eugene "Snake" Thompson, Family Tree folder, TAC, CCHM; Helen Cole, personal correspondence, October 1999.

21. Mother's story file, 18; notes for Te Ata's memoir, Childhood folder, TAC, CCHM.

22. D. C. Gideon, *History of Indian Territory* (Chicago: Lewis Publishing Co., 1901), 541–42. Copy located at Oklahoma Historical Society.

23. "As I Remember It," chap. 2, 8, TAC, CCHM.

24. Ibid., chap. 3, 5–6.

25. Ibid., chap. 1, 17–18.

26. Mother's story file, 19.

27. Ibid., 28; "As I Remember It," chap. 1, 18–19.

28. "As I Remember It," chap. 2, 9–11.

29. Ibid., chap. 6, 6. Te Ata's version does not mention that the annual busk festival was a four–day event for conducting all sorts of tribal business. The Smithsonian ethnologist John Swanton wrote that it was diety ordained for national "renewal and the perpetuation of health." Swanton, *Indians of the Southeastern United States*, Bureau of American Ethnology Bulletin 37 (Washington, D.C., 1946), 775.

30. "As I Remember It," chap. 6, 3–4; Richard Green, "Voices from the Past," *Journal of Chickasaw History* 1, no. 2, (1995): 10.

31. "As I Remember It," chap. 6, 7.

32. Ibid, chap. 3, 1–6.

33. "White House of the Chickasaws," *Sunday Oklahoman*, May 1, 1960; notes for Te Ata's memoir, Childhood folder.

34. "As I Remember It," chap. 3, 6.

35. Ibid., chap. 3, 7.

36. Irene B. Mitchell and Ida Belle Renken, "The Golden Age of Bloomfield Academy in the Chickasaw Nation," *Chronicles of Oklahoma* 49, no. 4, (1971): 414.

37. "As I Remember It," chap. 3, 8–9.

38. Mitchell and Renken, "Golden Age of Bloomfield Academy," 419; "As I Remember It," chap. 3.

39. Prucha, *The Great Father*, 167.

40. Mother's story file, 29.

CHAPTER 2. OKLAHOMA COLLEGE FOR WOMEN

1. Mother's story file, p. 31.

2. "As I Remember It," chap. 4, 55.

3. Interview with Helen Cole, January 11, 1995.

4. "As I Remember It," chap. 4, 55.

5. Ibid.

6. These are found throughout the 1930s folders.

7. 1939 Mississippi Choctaw Trip folder, TAC, CCHM.

8. "As I Remember It," chap. 4, 2; and LeRoy Fisher, "Muriel Wright, Historian of Oklahoma," *Chronicles of Oklahoma* 52, no. 1 (1974): 8.

9. Ibid.; Muriel Wright spent only one year in Tishomingo; she went on to other teaching assignments before becoming one of Oklahoma's preeminent experts in the history of Indian Territory and the state of Oklahoma. In addition to publishing

many books, she was the editor for many years of Oklahoma's official history journal, *Chronicles of Oklahoma*.

10. Ibid., 4.

11. Ibid., 4–5

12. Ibid., 5.

13. Ibid., 8; official transcript of Mary Thompson, Oklahoma College for Women, Chickasha, OK. Now named University of Science and Arts of Oklahoma (USAO).

14. "As I Remember It," chap. 5, 63–66.

15. Ibid.

16. Ibid., 73–74.

17. Ibid., 69.

18. Ibid., 72–73.

19. "History of Artist Course," USAO, alumni office, Frances Davis folder, Chickasha.

20. "As I Remember It," 70. Having little documentation, much about their relationship is subject to conjecture. They apparently corresponded regularly for years, but curiously very few of the letters could be found. Frances Davis, like Te Ata, saved most of her personal papers, according to Davis's longtime friend and OCW colleague Louise Waldorf. Those papers included dozens if not hundreds of Te Ata's letters. Although Waldorf told me that she had Davis's papers in her house after Davis's death in 1973, she said in 1995 that she did not know where they were. She might have loaned them to someone, she said. (Ms. Waldorf has since passed away.) I checked with several officials at the college, and they knew nothing of the papers. Te Ata's voluminous collection of papers contain only a few brief letters from Davis but several lengthy original letters from Te Ata to Davis written in the early 1920s from Pittsburgh and New York.

21. "As I Remember It," chap. 6, 77.

22. Annie Kate Gilbert, "As We Remember," 1963, OCW file, TAC, CCHM. In her remembrance Gilbert does not say what the name Em Hi means or provide its origin.

23. Interview with Louis Waldorf, who later joined the OCW music faculty, 1995.

24. Mary Thompson, official transcript, OCW, 1915–19.

25. "As I Remember It," chap. 5, 75–76.

26. Te Ata rarely used dates in her memoir, probably because they had never been important to her until 1933 when she married Clyde Fisher, who never wrote anything down that was not dated. Also after Te Ata left Oklahoma she was vain about her age.

27. "As I Remember It," chap. 6, 77–79.

28. Prucha, *The Great Father*, 304–5.

29. "As I Remember It," chap. 6, 92.

30 "Princess Te Ata Presents a Programme of Indian Folk Lore," printed program, undated but in Te Ata's handwriting are the notes "Program at O.C.W. in 1919" and "Te Ata's first professional program." I think it is very likely that the idea for using the title Princess came from Davis, OCW folder, TAC, CCHM.

31. "As I Remember It," Chap. 6, 93.

32. Ibid., chap. 7, 95–98.

33. The Shepherd Manor Retirement Home was built by the Shepherd family in 1964 to function as a nursing home and to house the bulk of Nellie Shepherd's collection of paintings. Her paintings grace its walls. The painting of Te Ata is beautifully done, but because her deerskin dress lacks detail and her arms and hands lack definition, it appears to be unfinished. Since the date of the sitting is unknown, it is possible that Miss Shepherd died before the painting could be completed. Or perhaps it was the artist's intent to focus attention on Te Ata's lovely face.

34. "As I Remember It," chap. 7, 97–101.

35. Ibid, chap. 8, 106–7.

36. "Chautauqua Movement," in *The Reader's Companion to American History*, ed. Eric Foner and John A. Garraty (Boston: Houghton Mifflin Co., 1991), 158–59.

37. "As I Remember It," chap. 8 103–6.

38. Thurlow Lieurance to Mary Thompson, March 1919; Mary Thompson to Lieurance, March 10, 1919; Chautauqua folder, TAC, CCHM.

39. "As I Remember It," chap. 8, 108–9.

CHAPTER 3. CHAUTAUQUA EXPERIENCES

1. Most of these publications are no longer in print. They include *Etude, Outlook, Craftsman, Theatre Arts Monthly, Harper's Monthly*, and *The Nation*.

2. Rayna Green, *Women in American Indian Society* (New York: Chelsea House, 1992), 75–76; *The Women's Way* (Alexandria, Va: Time-Life Books, 1995), 143.

3. Susan Avery and Linda Skinner, *Extraordinary American Indians* (Chicago: Children's Press, 1992), 107–10; Dexter Fisher, forward to Zitkala–Sa, *American Indian Stories* (Washington, D.C.: Hayworth, 1921), v–xviii.

4. Natalie Curtis, "The Perpetuating of Indian Art," *Outlook* 105 (1913): 629–30; Natalie Curtis, "An American Indian Artist," *Outlook* 124 (1920): 37–40; Charles A. Eastman, "My People: The Indians' Contribution to the Art of America," *Craftsman* 27 (1914–15): 182–83.

5. Red Cloud, "Indian Musicians in the Modern World," *Etude*, October 1920.

6. Eastman, "My People," 183–85.

7. "Collectors of Native American Indian Melodies," *Etude*, October, 1920.

8. Curtis, "The Perpetuating of Indian Art," 623–24.

9. William Inglis, "Buffalo Bill's Last Trail," in *Wild West Shows*, ed. Judy Alter (New York: Franklin Watts, 1997): 40–53.

10. Ellsworth Collings, *The 101 Ranch* (Norman: University of Oklahoma Press, 1971), 143–44.

11. Alter, *Wild West Show*.

12. Charles Cadman, "The American Indian's Music Idealized," *Etude*, October 1920.

13. Tsianina Blackstone, *Where Trails Have Led Me* (Burbank, Calif.: Blackstone, 1968), 4, 34.

14. "As I Remember It," chap. 8, 104–5.

15. "Who Was Thurlow Lieurance?" Wichita State University Web site, www.twsu.edu; Thurlow Lieurance, "The Musical Soul of the American Indian," *Etude*, October 1920.

16. Ibid.

17. "As I Remember It," chap. 8, 109, 112. Te Ata gave Dowanwin's English name as Thompson, but apparently had forgotten her first name. Te Ata guessed at the spelling of Godje.

18. Ibid., 111–12.

19. Ibid., 110. Kincaide lived in Clinton, Oklahoma.

20. Ibid., 114–15; "Chautauqua," narrative made by Te Ata for Florence Pielke, Chautauqua folder, TAC, CCHM.

21. "As I Remember It," chap. 8, 113–14.

22. I assembled bits and pieces of information on the chautauqua circuit from various notes in Te Ata's collection. These notes are found in my Chautauqua folder, TAC, CCHM. According to one message she wrote to Jane Watson, she saw no reason for keeping these experiences in order. In another note, she wrote down the name of the chautauqua company and the year she thought she toured with it: 1919, Standard of Mid-West; 1920 and 1921(?), White and Myers; 1922, Chicago Redpath; 1923, Ellis and White.

23. Although Te Ata remembered the background of the stories and generally would tell her audiences the tribal origin, she did not record this information during those years and never comprehensively or systematically recorded it. The same was true for the arts and crafts she bought or was given. She could tell you that the piece was a Navajo wedding basket, but, lacking documentation, the place, year, and person she acquired it from often got blurred. Of course, at this time she was not planning her future around a career as an interpreter of Indian folklore. By 1921 or 1922 her sights were set on the Broadway stage.

24. "As I Remember It," chap. 8, 116–17.

25. "Chautauqua," Chautauqua folder, 2, TAC, CCHM.

26. Ibid., 2–3.

27. Ibid., 2; "As I Remember It," chap. 8, 115.

28. Prucha, *The Great Father*, 272.

29. Interview with Hiawatha Estes, October 19, 1995; interview with Helen Cole, Te Ata's niece, January 11, 1995.

30. Interview with Helen Cole, January 11, 1995.

31. Interview with Hiawatha Estes, October 19, 1955.

32. This comment is circumstantial because the papers of Frances Davis (including the letters she exchanged with Te Ata) were not available to me.

33. Frances Dinsmore Davis to Chairman of Committee on Admission, Carnegie Tech, Pittsburgh, Pa., April 26, 1920, Carnegie Tech folder, TAC, CCHM.

34. "As I Remember It," chap. 9, 118–19.

35. Ibid., 119, 122–23.

36. Ibid., 124–26.

37. Ibid. 126–30.

CHAPTER 4. IN TRANSITION:
CARNEGIE TECH AND THE GREAT WHITE WAY

1. "Into the Friendly Lion's Den," Carnegie Tech folder, TAC, CCHM.

2. Te Ata to Frances D. Davis (hereafter FDD), letter 5, n.d. (evidently 1920), Carnegie Tech folder.

3. Ibid., letter 9.

4. Ibid., letter 4.

5. Te Ata to Ione Ballew, letter 2, Carnegie Tech folder.

6. Te Ata to Florence Pielke (her putative biographer), n.d. (undoubtedly written in the mid-1960s), 1920s folder, TAC, CCHM.

7. Te Ata to FDD, November 1920, letter 4, Carnegie Tech folder.

8. Ibid.

9. "As I Remember It," chap. 10, 135.

10. Te Ata to FDD, Easter 1921, letter 9, Carnegie Tech folder.

11. Ibid.

12. Te Ata notes probably prepared for Jane Watson, undated and untitled, Carnegie Tech folder.

13. "Miss Davis Presents Mary Thompson in 'As You Like It,' May 4, 1922," copy of OCW program. This is the only record of the school year 1921–22 in Te Ata's papers. 1920s folder, TAC, CCHM.

14. Te Ata, "New York Days," unpublished writing probably intended for Jane Watson, her collaborator in the memoir, n.d., 1920s folder (all source material in chapter 4 from 1920s folder unless otherwise indicated).

15. Ibid.

16. "As I Remember It," chap. 10, 136.

17. Interview with Margaret (Malowney) Ball, September 27, 1995. Ball lived in the Three Arts Club with Te Ata. She used the term "housemother," but said none of the society matrons ever lived at the club.

18. "New York and the Broadway Stage," a page of notes probably made for Jane Watson, n.d. In October Thurlow Lieurance sent Te Ata a telegram asking her to reply immediately if she would be making the trip to Australia. She replied that she could not go. Lieurance to Te Ata, October 17, 1922.

19. "New York and the Broadway Stage."

20. Leo Marsh, "The Red Poppy Excellent Play," New York *Morning Telegraph*, December 21, 1922, 16.

21. Te Ata to Florence Pielke, 1920s folder.

22. Gibson, *The Chickasaws*, 80.

23. Interview with Hiawatha Estes, October 19, 1995, Hiawatha folder, TAC, CCHM.

24. Te Ata to FDD, n.d. (probably early spring 1923).

25. Marion Gridley, *Indians of Today* (Crawfordsville, Ind.: Lakeside Press, 1936), 28.

26. "As I Remember It," chap. 11, 147.

27. Interview with Margaret Ball, October 19, 1995. In her nineties, Margaret lived alone in a spacious brick house outside Wilton, Connecticut. Although frail and as she noted, "with somewhat less brainpower" than she once possessed, she still insisted on living independently and got around her home competently if slowly.

28. Ibid.

29. Te Ata, "New York Days," notes for memoir, n.d.

30. Brian Gallagher, *Anything Goes* (New York: New York Times Books, 1987), 92–93.

31. Te Ata to Florence Pielke, 1920s folder.

32. "As I Remember It," chap. 11, 136–37.

33. "New York Days," 3.

34. John Steele Gordon, "J. Pierpont Morgan," in Foner and Garraty, *Reader's Companion to American History*, 747–48. J. P. Morgan himself was not involved, however, having died in 1913.

35. "As I Remember It," 143. Unfortunately, these performances, like virtually all of them given in the 1920s, occurred before Te Ata began documenting her life, and there are no details of these two occasions. Moreover, before FDR became governor, entertaining Eleanor Roosevelt would be no more memorable than entertaining any of the other wealthy bluebloods and society matrons.

36. Although Te Ata told her niece Helen Cole that she had stopped reading her press clippings very early in her career, she was certainly saving them by the late twenties. I retained only a few in the 1920s folder, TAC, CCHM.

37. "Teata [*sic*] Presents an Interesting Program Here," *Sulphur Springs American*, August 20, 1926.

38. Interview with Margaret Ball, September 27, 1995.

39. "Bibliography of Indian Legends," Office of Indian Affairs, Bulletin 2, 1926, Bibliography and Source Material folder, TAC, CCHM.

40. H. B. Alexander, Testimonial, Septe,ber 22, 1924, 1920s folder.

41. H. B. Alexander, *Manito Masks* (New York: E. P. Dutton, 1925), 22.

42. H. B. Alexander to Te Ata, December 5, 1925, 1920s folder.

43. H. B. Alexander to Te Ata, March 5, 1926, 1920s folder.

44. "As I Remember It," 161.

CHAPTER 5. COMMAND PERFORMANCES IN ENGLAND

1. Hartley B. Alexander, "For An American Indian Theatre," *Theatre Arts Monthly* 10, (1926): 191.

2. Prucha, *The Great Father*, 275–76.

3. Mary Austin, "American Indian Dance Drama," *Yale Review* 19 (1911): 742–43.

4. Ibid., 744–45.

5. "Lew Sarett and Our Aboriginal Inheritance," *Poetry* 27 (November 1925): 88–95.

6. Laura Gilpin, "The Dream Pictures of My People," *Art and Archaeology* 4 (1918): 12–13.

7. Blackstock, *Where Trails Have Led Me*, 53–59.

8. Ibid., 157–57.

9. "Loon Island," Diary of Clyde Fisher, August 16, 1942 to November 3, 1942, Clyde Fisher Collection, Miami University Libraries, Oxford, Ohio.

10. "New York Days," 5.

11. William J. Myles, "Lake Te Ata, " Historical Papers of the Palisades Interstate Park Commission, Bear Mountain, NY 1991.

12. "New York Days," 5.

13. Ibid.

14. Te Ata note, unaddressed and undated, Family Tree folder, TAC, CCHM; in the note Te Ata says that her father and Ataloa's mother, Cousin Jo, may have been cousins, but among the Chickasaws such titles often signaled terms of endearment or clan ties.

15. Chickasaw Nation (Dawes) Roll, microfilm, Oklahoma Historical Society.

16. Unidentified and undated newspaper clipping, probably a New York paper in the early or mid-1930s, Ataloa file, TAC, CCHM. Robert Perry, Chickasaw Nation Hall of Fame Nomination Form, undated, CCHM, Tishomingo, Okla.

17. "As I Remember It," 151.

18. Buffalo Child Long Lance, *Long Lance* (New York: Cosmopolitan, 1928.)

19. Donald B. Smith, *Long Lance: The True Story of an Imposter* (Lincoln: University of Nebraska Press, 1982), 1, 206.

20. Ibid., 185.

21. Clyde Fisher, "Diary of Woodcraft Indian Trip," June 30, 1927–July 27, 1927, 19–20, Clyde Fisher Diary, 1927 folder, TAC, CCHM (hereafter CF Diary).

22. "As I Remember It," 152; "New York Days," 4.

23. Clyde Fisher, "Clyde Fisher," biographical sketch, September 1931, CF file—bio and articles about CF, TAC, CCHM.

24. Interview with Dorothy Bennett, September 26, 1995.

25. "As I Remember It," 153.

26. Ibid., 140–41; "New York Days," 3.

27. Ibid.

28. "New York Days," 3.

29. Charles Curtis to Honorable John Garrett, March 26, 1930, London Trip folder, TAC, CCHM.

30. Te Ata's memoir describes how she got the round-trip ticket from the Tuckers and the support from her other patrons but wraps up the three-month trip in a paragraph about the weather and a count's boyhood anecdote about playing Indians.

31. Gilda (Varesi) Archibald to Te Ata, April 30, 1930, London Trip folder.

32. Sir Archibald Flower to Te Ata, May 1930, London Trip folder; Te Ata, England and Scotland, London Trip folder.

33. Bladon Peake, "The Te Ata Matinee," *Stratford-Upon-Avon Herald*, July 25, 1930, London Trip folder.

34. According to the "Programme," she performed several works by Alexander and others by Cadman, Lieurance, and Sarett, as well as several native legends and songs, including "How the World Was Made," "Romance Legend," "Why Folks Die," and "Sam-A-We-No," London Trip folder.

35. "Peggy Wood's Party," (London) *Daily Mirror*, n.d., London Trip folder.

36. "Letter from Mrs. Samuel A. Tucker," *Forward*, (Three Arts Club, New York, n.d.), 12, London Trip folder.

37. J. Bradford De Long, "The Great Depression," in Foner and Garrity, *Reader's Companion to American History*, 280.

38. Owing to the number of people involved in promoting Te Ata in London in 1930, she probably received numerous such contacts. However, there are only two letters in the London Trip folder that allude to helping her promote herself in Europe; unfortunately, there were no copies of her responses.

39. Interview with Hiawatha Estes, October 19, 1995, Hiawatha folder, TAC, CCHM.

40. Debo, *And Still the Waters Run*, 388–89.

CHAPTER 6. CLYDE FISHER

1. All of the following letters, clippings, and documents are found in the 1930 folder and the 1931 folder, TAC, CCHM.

2. Te Ata to Commissioner of Indian Affairs, November 5, 1930, National Archives, Washington, D.C., RG 75, Chickasaw 1908–20, Box 2977.

3. Te Ata to Clyde Fisher (hereafter CF), n.d., 1930 folder.

4. CF to Te Ata, October 30, 1930, 1930 folder.

5. Interview with Dorothy Bennett, April 1995, Bennett folder, TAC, CCHM.

6. Interview with Dorothy Bennett, June 26, 1995, Bennett folder.

7. Ibid.

8. From her reluctance to discuss the relationship of Te Ata and Clyde Fisher, it was obvious in both interviews with Bennett that she still respected their privacy.

9. Te Ata 1932 calendar, 1932 folder, TAC, CCHM.

10. Te Ata's journal, January 1—February 15, 1932, 1932 folder.

11. Whether this journal was complete or a fragment is not known. This was the only journal found in Te Ata's papers, other than the later ones she kept to record the events of prolonged trips.

12. Te Ata's journal, January 5, 1932.

13. Program of January 31, 1932, Prologue, Theatre Guild, New York, January 31, 1932, 1932 folder.

14. Vivian Shirley, "Vivian Shirley Learns Culture of Indians," Philadelphia *Evening Public Ledger*, January 19, 1932, 1932 folder.

15. Photocopy of photo of Te Ata and Ruby Jolliffe, February 20, 1932, 1932 folder.

16. Gridley, *Indians of Today*, 16.

17. Chief Max Big Man to Te Ata, February 1932, 1932 folder.

18. Smith, *Long Lance*, 196, 207.

19. Long Lance to Te Ata, May 5, 1931, 1931 folder.

20. Smith, *Long Lance*, 228.

21. Ibid., 186.

22. "halfi" does not appear in any other correspondence; it may have been an inside joke.

23. Te Ata to CF, April 1, 1932, 1932 folder.

24. Te Ata to CF, June 6, 1932, 1932 folder.

25. Te Ata to CF, June 16, 18, 21, 1932, 1932 folder.

26. Te Ata to CF, June 21, 1932, 1932 folder.

27. D. R. Barton, "He Brought the Stars to America," *Natural History*, June 1940, CF bio folder, TAC, CCHM.

28. Henry Beckett, "The Man in the Moon—Well, Not Quite," *New York Post*, July 9, 1943, 3, CF bio folder.

29. CF biographical sketch, CF bio folder.

30. Ibid.

31. Ibid.

32. E. J. Kahn, Jr., "The Moon's Best Friend," *New Yorker*, December 28, 1940, 23, CF bio folder.

33. Barton, "He Brought the Stars to America," 59.

34. Erich M. Schlaikjer and Herbert Schwarz, "In Memory, Clyde Fisher," *Explorers Journal* (Winter 1949): 29, CF bio folder.

35. James Traub, "Shake Them Bones," *New Yorker*, March 13, 1995, 48–49.

36. Schlaikjer and Schwarz, "In Memory, Clyde Fisher," 29.

37. Henry F. Osborn to CF, December 6, 1924, CF letters, 1932 folder.

38. CF bio sketch, 3.

39. "Lectures by G. Clyde Fisher, Ph.D.," Emmerich Lecture Bureau, Inc., n.d., CF letters to 1932 folder.

40. G. Clyde Fisher, "Reminiscences of John Burroughs," *Natural History* 21, no. 2, (1921): 113–25.

41. Clyde Fisher, "With John Burroughs at Slabsides," *Natural History* 31, no. 5, (1931): 500–10.

42. Fisher, "Reminiscences of John Burroughs," 113–25.

43. Fisher, "With John Burroughs at Slabsides," 500–10.

44. Clyde Fisher, "Popular Astronomic Education in Europe," *Science*, January 22, 1926.

45. Kahn, "The Moon's Best Friend," 23.

46. Ibid., 25.

CHAPTER 7. FROM LAKE TE ATA TO THE WHITE HOUSE

1. Clyde Fisher, daily journal of Western Trip, June 29–August 26, 1932, CF 1932 Western Trip folder, TAC, CCHM.

2. Ibid., 20–22.

3. Betty Keller, *Blackwolf* (Vancouver: Douglas and McIntyre, 1984), 200–01.

4. Ibid., 209–10.

5. "Dedicates Park Lake," *New York Times*, July 12, 1932, 2.

6. Te Ata to CF, July 20, 1932, Lake Te Ata folder, TAC, CCHM.

7. CF, Western Trip journal, 41–47.

8. Ibid., 27, 51–54.

9. Four letters from Te Ata to CF, undated but likely November 1932, 1932 folder; CF to Te Ata, November 28, December 7, December 12, 1932, 1932 folder.

10. Te Ata to CF, Dec. 3, 1932, 1932 folder.

11. Eleanor Roosevelt to Te Ata, November 22, 1932, Roosevelt Presidential Library, Hyde Park, N.Y., Office of Social Entertainments folder, Box 1, Dinner April 22, 1933. I also found a Te Ata brochure, on which Te Ata had written in the margin: "Bookings now being arranged" (n.d.).

12. There are three lengthy accounts of the events leading up to and including the White House performance. Two are from Te Ata. The first, titled "Te Ata Entertains the Prime Minister," appeared in the June 1933 issue of *The Forward*, the periodical of the Three Arts Club. The second account appears in Te Ata's unpublished

memoir, previously cited. The third account, which is the most detailed, is in a letter from Corinne Breeding to her mother, April 24, 1933. All three accounts are in the 1933 White House folder, TAC, CCHM.

13. Interview with Margaret Ball, September 27, 1995, Margaret Ball folder, TAC, CCHM.

14. Te Ata to CF, April 22, 1933; "Te Ata Entertains the Prime Minister," *The Forward*, June 1933, 11; and Corrine Breeding to her mother, April 24, 1933. 1933 White House folder.

15. Ibid.

16. Te Ata to CF, April 22, 1933.

17. "MacDonalds Dined at White House," *New York Times*, April 23, 1933.

18. Te Ata told essentially the same story to Mrs. Tucker and Ms. Breeding, who had been a classmate at OCW. If she chronicled the occasion for herself, as I expect she did, it was not in her papers.

19. I read the articles on the evening in most of the Washington and New York papers.

20. Te Ata to CF, April 22, 1933, 1933 White House folder.

21. "Indian Princess Gives Recital at Philmont," *Philadelphia Inquirer*, June 30, 1933, 1933 folder, TAC, CCHM.

22. Interview with Margaret Ball, September 27, 1995, Margaret Ball folder, TAC, CCHM.

23. Margaret Ball to Te Ata, September 16, 1933; John Ball to Te Ata, September 16, 1933, 1933 folder.

24. "The History of Bacone," *Daughters of American Revolution Magazine*, February 1980, 132; Gridley, *Indians of Today*, 13.

25. According to Margaret Ball and Dorothy Bennett, the couple was always known as Clyde and Te Ata or Dr. Fisher and Te Ata, never the Fishers. Although referring to the couple as the Fishers in the pages ahead would be much simpler, I will honor the way things were.

26. "New York Scientist Is Wed to Prominent Indian Woman Here," probably *Muskogee Phoenix*, September 29, 1933; "Te Ata and Dr. Fisher Are Married at Lodge," *Bacone Indian*, October 25, 1933. (All material dated 1933 is in the 1933 folder.)

27. Telephone interview with Helen Cole, January 8, 1997.

28. "As I Remember It," 176–77.

29. After reviewing Te Ata's correspondence in her collection, it was clear that many of the letters between Te Ata and Clyde Fisher were not there. But in their correspondence there are enough references to letters sent and received to lead me to believe that they wrote to one another almost daily. They had always been prolific letter writers; they enjoyed writing and receiving letters; and they thought that the long-distance telephone rates were impossibly extravagant.

30. CF to Te Ata, October 6, 1933. Actually, they normally used Indian designations for the months, so that October 6 was written as 6th Sun of the Leaf-falling Moon.

31. CF to Te Ata, October 8, 1933.

32. Te Ata to CF, October 10, 1933

33. Evelyn Burke, "Indian Maid, Authority on Tribal Lore, Loses Heart to White Man," *Pittsburgh Press*, October 26, 1933.

34. Ibid.

35. Te Ata to CF, n.d. (probably June 1934), 1934 folder.

36. Tom Thompson to Te Ata, November 4, 1933. The letter does not say where Bertie was when the heart attack occurred.

37. Ibid.

38. Tom Thompson to Te Ata, March 6, 1934.

39. CF to Te Ata, December 27, 1933 (two letters).

CHAPTER 8. COAST-TO-COAST HONEYMOON

1. "Welcome to the Planetarium," *New York Herald Tribune*, January 6, 1934; "Funds Provided for Hayden Planetarium in New York," *Museum News*, January 15, 1934, news clips, Hayden Planetarium Library.

2. Press bulletin with no headline, American Museum of Natural History (AMNH), New York, May 28, 1934; press releases, Hayden Planetarium Library, AMNH.

3. CF to Te Ata, March 3, 1934, 1934 folder, TAC, CCHM.

4. Te Ata to CF, March 4, 1934, 1934 folder.

5. Ibid.

6. Te Ata to CF, n.d. (but March 1934), 1934 folder.

7. Ibid.

8. "Mr. Rogers Gives Advice to Classes at Harvard," "Indians Ate Bolivian Recruiting Officers as Chaco War Protect," and "Street Begging Here Called Unjustified; Public Asked to Cease Contributing Alms," *New York Times*, April 24, 1934, 1934 folder.

9. Prucha, *The Great Father*, 321–22.

10. Reese Kincaide to Te Ata, March 22, 1934, 1934 folder.

11. Te Ata to CF, n.d., (probably June 1934), 1934 folder.

12. Ibid.

13. "Start 12,000 Mile Honeymoon," *New York Sun*, n.d. (probably June 28, 1934), CF Western Trip folder.

14. CF, Western Trip diary, June 28, 1934–September 8, 1934, CF Western Trip folder.

15. Te Ata to CF, probably June 1934, 1934 folder.

16. "Pipestone, Minnesota, Rich in Indian Lore," handout in 1934 CF Western Trip folder.

17. CF Collection, AMNH photo archives, library, 282712–18.

18. Ibid., 18.

19. Interview with Juanita Byars, Chickasaw elder, Tishomingo, Okla., October 27, 1999, Author's file.

20. The existing tribal records from 1897 to 1898 reflect only the need for a new building, since the old capitol building had been declared a hazard to health and safety. Although the new building was constructed from the granite mined in quarries owned by the sitting tribal governor, Robert M. Harris, no charges of impropriety appear in the tribal records.

21. Prucha, *The Great Father*, 260–61.

22. Wilburn Cartwright Collection, letters received 1928–42, Carl Albert Collection, University of Oklahoma, Norman.

23. Michael Lovegrove, "Dissolution of the Tribal Governments and the Sale of the Chickasaw-Choctaw Coal and Asphalt Land," *Journal of Chickasaw History* 2, no. 4 (1996): 7–16.

24. Prucha, *The Great Father*, 321.

25. The name has been spelled both Seeley and Seely.

26. Douglas Johnston statement, Seely Chapel, September 18, 1934, vertical file, Chickasaw Library, Ada, Okla.

27. Debo, *And Still the Waters Run*, 368–69.

28. Dick Pearce, "State Indians Are Skeptical of New Deal," *Oklahoma City Times*, October 19, 1934.

29. Numerous such letters are found in the Johnston Papers, especially during the 1920s and 1930s, CCHM.

30. CF's Western Trip, CF Western Trip folder, 20.

31. Interview with Hiawatha Estes, October 19, 1995, Hiawatha Estes folder, TAC, CCHM.

32. CF's Western Trip diary, Western Trip folder, 19.

33. Ibid., 21.

34. Ibid., 23–27. Unless otherwise noted, Fisher's diary is the source for the remainder of the text dealing with the honeymoon trip. Pp. 27–48.

35. Memorial Service for Ataloa, Idyllwild, Calif., March 24, 1968, Ataloa folder, TAC, CCHM.

36. CF Collection, AMNH photo archives, library, 282755.

37. The photos are part of the Fisher Collection at the AMNH Library in New York; the cornfield is neg. 282775; the trading post is neg. 282776.

CHAPTER 9. TALKING LEAVES AND REPERTOIRE BUILDING

1. Te Ata to CF, n.d. (mid–January 1935) 1935 folder. Unless otherwise indicated, all material dated 1935 is from the 1935 folder.

2. Te Ata to CF, January 16, 1935.

3. CF to Te Ata, January 28, 1935.

4. Te Ata to CF, January 31, 1935.

5. Te Ata to CF, February 1, 1935.

6. Club Program, Chicago Woman's Aid, February 5, 1935, Performances folder, TAC, CCHM.

7. "For Te Ata's Programs," n.d., Performances folder.

8. Te Ata, "What We, as Indians, Have Contributed to American Culture," n.d., Source material—1930s–1970s folder, TAC, CCHM.

9. Ibid.

10. Gridley, *Indians of Today*, 118, 96–97.

11. "Ace among Indian Painters," *Christian Science Monitor*, February 8, 1941, 12.

12. Michael Hilger, *From Savage to Nobleman* (Lanham, Md.: Scarecrow Press, 1995), 20.

13. Stanley Vestal, "The Hollywooden Indian," in *The Pretend Indians*, ed. Gretchen M. Bataille (Ames: Iowa State University Press, 1980), 63–67.

14. Bunny McBride, *Molly Spotted Elk* (Norman: University of Oklahoma Press, 1995), 125.

15. Ibid., 128–35.

16. This judgment was made after an examination of the *Reader's Guide to Periodical Literature* from the turn of the century to 1950. If I had examined local newspapers, I might have found other Native American performance artists; even so, none of them would have had Te Ata's national notoriety and influence.

17. Douglas J. Preston, *Dinosaurs in the Attic* (New York: St. Martin's Press, 1986), 109–10.

18. Clyde Fisher to W. S. Campbell, July 18, 1935, Campbell Collection, Box 26, Folder 36, University of Oklahoma Western History Collections, Norman.

19. Fisher Collection, AMNH photo archives, negs. 284230–1, 284237–9.

20. Interview with Dorothy Bennett, June 26, 1995, Bennett folder, TAC, CCHM.

21. Some of her letters in the mid-1930s were datelined from Franklin, Vermont, apparently another retreat similar to Bear Mountain and Loon Island.

22. CF to Te Ata, August 7, 1935, 1935 folder.

23. Princess Alexandra Kropotkin, "To the Ladies," *Liberty*, August 17, 1935.

24. Gibson, *The Chickasaws*, 47–50.

25. Mary Ann Wells, *Native Land* (Jackson: University Press of Mississippi, 1994), 110–11.

26. Ibid., 108, 111–12.

27. Te Ata to CF, September 13, 1935.

28. Te Ata to CF, September 16, 1935.

29. "Parade of Stars in Planetarium Seems a Miracle," *New York Herald Tribune*, October 3, 1935.

30. Ibid.

31. Hans Christian Adamson, no headline, Hayden Planetarium press bulletin, September 16, 1935, Hayden Planetarium Library, news clips, New York.

32. CF to Te Ata, October 24, 1935.

33. I was told this via telephone by the head of medical records at the Johns Hopkins University Hospital. She said the appropriate roll of microfilm was unaccountably missing.

34. Interview with Dorothy Bennett, June 26, 1995, Bennett folder.

35. CF to Te Ata, October 28, 1935.

36. Te Ata to CF, October 18, 1935.

37. Te Ata to CF, n.d. (October 1935).

38. Te Ata to CF, October 31, 1935.

CHAPTER 10. SAILING BIG WATERS

1. Frede Skaarup to Te Ata, April 21, 1936, 1936 folder, TAC, CCHM.

2. Diary of Clyde Fisher, May 16–August 25, 1936. This diary, as well as several others chronicling Fisher's trips, was donated by Te Ata to his alma mater,

Miami University. They now make up the Clyde Fisher Collection in the university's Edgar W. King Library.

3. "Sails to View Eclipse," *New York Herald Tribune*, May 17, 1936.

4. Te Ata to CF, May 17, 1936.

5. CF to Te Ata, May 26, 1936.

6. Fisher 1936 diary, 43–47, TAC, CCHM; CF to Te Ata, June 6, 1936.

7. "Eclipse Expedition Installed in Soviet," *New York Times*, May 30, 1936; CF to Te Ata, June 13, 1936.

8. Clyde Fisher, "The Eclipse in Kazakhstan," *Natural History* 38, no. 3 (1936): 203–10.

9. "Scientists Ready on Eve of Eclipse," *New York Times*, June 18, 1936, Hayden Planetarium Library; Fisher 1936 diary, 54–62.

10. Fisher 1936 diary.

11. Te Ata to CF, May 27, 1936.

12. Te Ata to CF, June 5, 1936.

13. Te Ata to CF, June 18, 1936 (two letters).

14. Skaarup to Te Ata, June 23, 1936.

15. Opal Brown, "Sooner Footprints," *Sulphur Times-Democrat*, June 20, 1996.

16. Ibid.; Opal Brown, "Lushanya, Dramatic Soprano," *Sulphur Times-Democrat*, June 29, 1966; Thomas Benton Williams, *The Soul of the Red Man*, (Oklahoma City, 1937), 328; "The Chicago Opera," *Newsweek*, November 6, 1939, 32.

17. Gridley, *Indians of Today*, 90.

18. Ibid., 143–55.

19. Fisher 1936 diary, 123–29.

20. Clyde Fisher, "At Home in Lapland," *Natural History*, n.d. (ca. 1945–49), CF Articles folder, TAC, CCHM.

21. Fisher 1936 diary, 159–62.

22. Ibid., 180–85.

23. CF to Te Ata, August 15–24, 1936.

24. Te Ata to CF, September 4, 1936.

25. Te Ata to CF, August 20–21, 1936.

26. Te Ata to CF, September 2, 1936.

27. Te Ata to CF, September 4, 1936.

28. Te Ata to CF, September 2, 1936.

29. Te Ata to CF, September 13, 1936.

30. Typed transcriptions of reviews, 1936 folder.

31. Ibid.

32. Te Ata to CF, September 15, 1936.

33. Te Ata to CF, September 17, 1936, written in Copenhagen.

34. Ibid., written in Stockholm.

35. Te Ata to CF, September 28, 1936.

CHAPTER 11. PERUVIAN EXPERIENCE

1. CF to Te Ata, February 9, 1937, 1937 folder, TAC, CCHM.

2. Interview with Dorothy Bennett, June 26, 1995, Bennett folder.

3. Frank Farrell, "Princess Te Ata Refuses to Stay Cooped Up When Sun-gazing Husband Traipses Away," *New York World Telegram*, no.d. (May 7 or 8).

4. AMNH Press Bulletin, April 3, 1937; AMNH Press Bulletin, April 28, 1937, AMHN Library, New York.

5. Bennett interview, June 26, 1995.

6. Green, "Migration Legends."

7. Because they were now in the southern hemisphere, the seasons had reversed.

8. Fisher, "Eclipse in Peru," Fisher Writing folder, TAC, CCHM.

9. Gladys Baker, "Te Ata Keeps Indian Traditions Alive," *Birmingham News-Herald*, July 25, 1937, 6.

10. Bennett interview.

11. This was taken from a fragment of Te Ata's writing about her stay in Cuzco. The writing is more expository and in a format different from her diary. N.d. 1937 Peru folder, TAC, CCHM.

12. Ibid.

13. In addition to Te Ata's journal, I used an informational brochure from her papers, now part of the Peru 1937 folder. The brochure is titled "Cusco, Archeological Capital of South America," n.d., n.p.

14. Fisher, "Eclipse in Peru."

15. Te Ata, "Across the Desert to Trujillo," unpublished manuscript, n.d., Peru 1937 folder.

16. Ibid.

17. Fisher, "Eclipse in Peru."

18. Ibid.

19. Te Ata to Em Hi's, October 15, 1937, 1937 folder, TAC, CCHM.

20. Te Ata to Eva (CF's sister-in-law), October 22, 1938, 1938 folder, TAC, CCHM.

21. Ibid.

22. Urith Lucas, "Te Ata, Indian Impersonator, Addresses Woman's Club Here," *Lexington* (Ky.) *Sunday Herald-Leader*, November 13, 1938.

23. Baker, "Te Ata Keeps Indian Tradition Alive."

24. Ibid.

25. Ibid.

26. Hazel Muller to Te Ata, July 9, 1937, 1937 folder.

27. Edward Weyer, Jr., to Te Ata, August 30, 1937; Weyer to Te Ata, September 22, 1937; 1937 folder.

28. Gibson, The Chickasaws, 3.

29. Ibid.

30. Marian Lockwood, "Books and the Sky," *Sky Magazine*, AMNH periodical, December 1937, Hayden Planetarium Library, AMNH, New York City.

31. CF to Howard (CF's brother), February 12, 1938, 1938 folder.

32. CF to Howard and Eva, December 26, 1937. Unfortunately, Einstein's letter was not among Te Ata's papers.

CHAPTER 12. HYDE PARK AND THE MISSISSIPPI HOMELAND

1. There was no correspondence in Te Ata's papers for the period between 1924 and 1938, nor was there any from this period in the Roosevelt Library in Hyde Park, New York.

2. Doris Kearns Goodwin, *No Ordinary Time*, (New York: Touchstone, 1995), 91.

3. Te Ata to Eleanor Roosevelt, January 16, 1939, Roosevelt Library, 1939 White House, folder T.

4. Mrs. James Helm to Te Ata, January 18, 1939, Roosevelt Library, 1939 White House folder T.

5. Sarah Knott to Te Ata, January 17, 1939, 1939 folder, TAC, CCHM.

6. Leland Stowe to Te Ata, May 5, 1939, 1939 folder; Te Ata to Leland Stowe, n.d., 1939 folder.

7. Oliver La Farge to Te Ata, February 24, 1939, 1939 folder.

8. Bob Bartlett to Te Ata, n.d., 1939 folder.

9. John Ball to Te Ata, April 29, 1939, 1939 folder.

10. Interview with Hiawatha Estes, October 19, 1995, Estes folder.

11. Mrs. James Helm to Te Ata, April 22, 1939, Roosevelt Library, 1939 White House, folder T.

12. Te Ata's mother's illness is alluded to in several letters exchanged between Te Ata and CF and others, but no diagnosis is provided. The death of her husband probably exacerbated Bertie Thompson's already frail status.

13. Mrs. Helm to Junge, May 6, 1939, Roosevelt Library, 1939 Hyde Park folder, TAC, CCHM.

14. CF to Te Ata, May 2, 1939, 1939 Hyde Park folder.

15. CF to Te Ata, May 10, 1939, 1939 Hyde Park folder.

16. Junge to Mrs. Roosevelt, May 10, 1939, 1939 Hyde Park folder.

17. Te Ata to CF, May 17, 1939, 1939 Hyde Park folder.

18. Part of news clipping (no headline available), *Chicago Daily Tribune*, May 23, 1939.

19. Mrs. Helm to Junge, May 23, 1939, 1939 Hyde Park folder.

20. Junge to Helm, June 4, 1939, 1939 Hyde Park folder.

21. Te Ata to Mamma, June 5, 1939, 1939 Hyde Park folder.

22. "Morning Bearer," *New Yorker*, undated but certainly the first week of June 1939.

23. Emma Bugbee, "Modern Pocahontas to Recite for Royal Couple at Hyde Park," *New York Herald Tribune*, June 5, 1939.

24. Program, 1939 Hyde Park folder.

25. This decision is found in a paper titled "Questions to be answered on Hyde Park Picnic Program" and was undoubtedly written by Mrs. Helm to June; 1939 Hyde Park folder.

26. "As I Remember It," chap. 13.

27. Papers found in Roosevelt Library, now included in 1939 Hyde Park folder; interview with Margaret Ball, September 27, 1995, Ball folder.

28. When I visited Hyde Park in September 1995, an employee of the U.S. Park Service, which cares for the Roosevelt mansion, told me that the Hill Top Cottage had been sold by the Roosevelt family several years before to a private owner. That owner had recently put the cottage up for sale. Asking price: $600,000.

29. Seating arrangements, 1939 Hyde Park folder. Oddly, Eleanor Roosevelt's name does not appear at any of the seven tables on the porch.

30. Paper titled "Persons who will sit at tables on porch at Hyde Park." 1939 Hyde Park folder.

31. Hartley B. Alexander, *God's Drum* (New York: E. P. Dutton, 1927), 14.

32. Bugbee, "Modern Pocahontas."

33. Interview with Margaret Ball, October 26, 1995, Ball folder.

34. Goodwin, *No Ordinary Time*, 73.

35. Eleanor Roosevelt to Te Ata, June 14, 1939, 1939 Hyde Park folder.

36. "Dr. Alexander, a Philosopher and Poet, Dead," newspaper clipping, July 27, 1939, 1939 folder, TAC, CCHM.

37. Te Ata to Mama and Gladys, September 3, 1939, 1939 folder.

38. Prucha, *The Great Father*, 78–79.

39. Te Ata to Mother, October 12, 1939, 1939 trip to Mississippi folder, TAC, CCHM.

40. Clyde Fisher, Diary of Trip to Mississippi, September 22–October 2, 1939, 10–11, 1939 Trip to Mississippi folder.

41. Richard Green, "The Claim on Our Past," *Journal of Chickasaw History* 1, no. 1 (1994): 13.

42. Printed Program of Choctaw Council Meeting, September 26–27, 1939, 1939 Trip to Mississippi folder.

43. Te Ata to Mother, October 12, 1939, 1939 folder.

44. "As I Remember It," 181–82.

45. Te Ata journal to Mother, 1939 Trip to Mississippi folder.

CHAPTER 13. HEART LOADED DOWN AND HEAVY

1. Clyde Fisher, "Lecture Trip into N.Y. and Pennsylvania," March 2–April 8, 1941, Clyde Fisher Diaries, Special Collections, University Libraries, Miami University, Oxford, Ohio.

2. Colston Leigh To Te Ata, June 14, 1941, Te Ata Collection, Western History Collections, University of Oklahoma, Norman, Box 7, folder 4.

3. Bertie Thompson, autobiography, 1940, Mother's story file.

4. "Story of the Turkey, Seminole," retold by Te Ata, n.d., Stories & Legends folder, TAC, CCHM.

5. Bertie Thompson, autobiography. According to her grandson, Hiawatha Estes, her manuscript was typed verbatim from her hand-written pages. It filled thirty-six, single-spaced pages and only punctuation was added. Almost everything we know about Bertie's life came from this document. For an uneducated and by then chronically ill woman living in pain, her effort was incredible.

6. Perhaps she did not count the ferry rides across the Red River (from Texas to Indian Territory and vice versa) as boat trips.

7. Verde M. Whiting, "Tribal Career Women," *Independent Woman*, December 1940, 382–84.

8. Elizabeth Blomquis Symonds to Te Ata, January 19, 1941, 1941 folder, TAC, CCHM.

9. Helen Cole, interview, January 25, 1995, Helen Cole folder, TAC, CCHM.

10. Ibid.

11. Prucha, *The Great Father*, 272–73.

12. Podine Schoenberger, "Indian Princess Tells How Tribesmen Helped Win War," *New Orleans Times–Picayne*, February 7, 1941, 1941 folder.

13. Te Ata to CF, February 10, 1941, 1941 folder.

14. Dorothy M'Aulay, "Silver and Turquoise Adorn Lecturer–Princess Te Ata," probably *Fort Worth Star-Telegram*, February 24, 1941, 1941 folder.

15. CF lecture trip, March 2–April 8, 1941.

16. CF, "Lecture Trip into N.Y. and Pennsylvania," March 2–April 8, 1941.

17. Interview with Helen Cole, January 1995, Helen Cole folder, TAC, CCHM.

18. Interview with Dorothy Bennett, June 26, 1995, TAC, CCHM.

19. Te Ata to CF, June 3, 1941, 1941 folder, TAC, CCHM.

20. CF to Te Ata, June 7, 1941, 1941 folder.

21. Te Ata to CF, June 3, 1941, 1941 folder.

22. Te Ata to CF, June 9, 1941, 1941 folder.

23. "Astonomy Curator Ends 28 Years with Museum," *New York Times,* August 1, 1941, 17.

24. Clyde Fisher, Journal of Trip to Southwest, August 1–September 14, 1941, Special Collections, University Libraries, Miami, University.

25. Ibid.

26. Te Ata to CF, October 25, 1941, 1941 folder.

27. Te Ata to CF, October 27, 1941, 1941 folder.

28. Death Certificate, November 3, 1941, Nebraska Department of Vital Statistics, Lincoln.

29. Josephine Fisher to Te Ata, November 12, 1941, 1941 folder.

30. Te Ata to Em Hi Girls, December 15, 1941, 1941 folder.

CHAPTER 14. LOON ISLAND

1. Photo, *Daily Oklahoman*, January 30, 1942, 1942 folder, TAC, CCHM.

2. Richard Green, "The Chickasaw Capitol Building of 1898," *Journal of Chickasaw History* 4, no. 2 (1998): 6, 37.

3. W. W. Short to U.S. Senate Indian Affairs Committee, October 14, 1942, Carl Albert Center, University of Oklahoma, Norman, W. G. Stigler Collection, Box 5, Folder 95.

4. Ibid.

5. Te Ata to CF, February 22, 1942, 1942 folder.

6. Te Ata to CF, February 23, 1942, 1942 folder.

7. Te Ata to CF, February 25, 1942, 1942 folder.

8. Te Ata to CF, March 1, 1942, 1942 folder.

9. Te Ata to CF, March 3, 1942, 1942 folder.

10. Te Ata to CF, March 5, 1942, 1942 folder.

11. Kahn, "The Moon's Best Friend."

12. Ibid.

13. Interview with Helen Cole, January 11, 1995, Helen Cole folder.

14. Ibid.

15. Diary of Clyde Fisher, "Loon Island," August 16–November 3, 1942, Loon Island folder, TAC, CCHM.

16. Te Ata, untitled, reminiscences of Loon Island, transcript of a recording made when she was in her early nineties, Loon Island folder.

17. Ibid.

18. CF, Loon Island diary, Loon Island folder.

19. Ibid., 22.

20. Ibid., appendix.

21. There are numerous references to sunbathing and sunlamp-like devices in her letters, but she never wrote why she preferred to have a tan.

22. Te Ata, book review, Angie Debo, *The Road to Disappearance, Natural History,* October 1942, 239–40; CF, book review, Oliver La Farge, ed., *The Changing Indian, Natural History,* October 1942, 1942 folder.

23. CF, review, October 1942, 1942 folder.

24. CF Loon Island diary, 66–67, Loon Island folder.

25. Ibid., 82.

26. Kahn, "The Moon's Best Friend," 24.

27. Fred Whipple reviewed *The Story of the Moon* by Clyde Fisher in *Natural History,* February 1943.

28. Edward Weyer, Jr., editor, *Natural History,* to Te Ata, May 29, 1943, Te Ata Collection, Box 7, folder 7, Western History Collections, University of Oklahoma, Norman. The magazine's pay rate was one and one–half cents per word and $2.50 per photograph.

29. Te Ata, "The Creation of an Indian Jar," *Natural History,* April 1943, 180–85.

30. Kenneth Chapman to CF, May 15, 1943, 1943 folder, TAC, CCHM.

31. CF to Te Ata, August 22, 1943, 1943 folder.

32. John Kieran, *Not Under Oath* (Boston: Houghton Mifflin, 1964), 96–98. Chapter 8, "Adventures with an Astronomer," is mainly about Kieran's friendship with Fisher.

33. CF to Te Ata, October 12, 1943, 1943 folder. Unfortunately for us, Fisher told Te Ata that he would fill her in on all the details of the meeting when she got home.

34. Te Ata to Dorothy Bennett, n.d., 1943 folder.

35. Kieran, *Not Under Oath,* 96–98.

36. CF Diary of Trip to Mexico, November 5–29, 1943, CF Diaries, Special Collections, University Libraries, Miami University.

37. Ibid.

38. CF to Howard Fisher, December 21, 1943, 1943 folder.

CHAPTER 15. FINAL JOURNEYS

1. Clyde Fisher, "American Museum Expedition to Volcano Paricutin in Mexico," Explorers Club Records, n.d., 1944 volcano folder, TAC, CCHM.

2. Frederick H. Pough, "Paricutin Comes of Age," *Natural History,* October 1944, 342.

3. Clyde Fisher Journal, Paricutin Expedition, February 21–March 24, 1944, Special Collections, University Libraries, Miami University, Oxford, Ohio.

4. Pough, "Paricutin Comes of Age," 342.

5. Ibid., 345.

6. Ibid., 346, 348.

7. Ibid., 348.

8. Te Ata, "A Race from Molten Lava," unpublished manuscript, n.d., 1944 volcano folder.

9. Ibid.

10. Pough, "Paricutin Comes of Age," 348.

11. Te Ata "Race from Molten Lava," 3.

12. Ibid., 4–5; Pough, "Paricutin Comes of Age," 348.

13. Pough, "Paricutin Comes of Age," 348.

14. Te Ata, "Race from Molten Lava," 5; Pough, "Paricutin Comes of Age," 348.

15. Ibid.

16. Te Ata, "Race from Molten Lava," 6–7.

17. Ibid., 7.

18. Pough, "Paricutin Comes of Age," 348.

19. James B. Pond to Te Ata, June 29, 1944; and Roxanna Wells to Te Ata, January 25, 1944, 1944 folder, TAC, CCHM.

20. In separate 1995 interviews with two of her best friends, Dorothy Bennett and Margaret Ball, they repeatedly attested that Te Ata did not discuss highly personal details or aspects of her life and rarely discussed subjects she considered unpleasant. For example, she avoided prolonged discussions of World War II. Why? Because war represented what she deplored: violence and killing. And while she realized that humans of all races were maiming, degrading, and killing one another in the most barbarous ways, she insisted on concentrating on beauty.

21. To cite only one, CF to Howard (CF's brother) and Eva, December 22, 1944, 1944 folder.

22. Lucille Ogle of Artists and Writers Guild to CF, September 7, 1944, 1944 folder.

23. Otto Fisher to CF, September 1944, 1944 folder.

24. Ibid., July 10, 1944, 1944 folder.

25. Ibid., September 20, 1944, 1944 folder.

26. CF journal, "To Alberta, Canada," June 14–September 5, 1946, University Libraries, Miami University, 1, 106 (hereafter CF 1946 journal).

27. Te Ata journal, no title, no page, June 14–September 5, 1946, 1946 Blood Indian folder, TAC, CCHM (hereafter Te Ata 1946 journal).

28. CF 1946 journal, 6–7.

29. Te Ata 1946 journal.

30. Ibid.; CF 1946 journal, 8.

31. CF 1946 journal, 10.

32. CF 1946 journal, 13–17; Te Ata 1946 journal.

33. CF 1946 journal, 20–29.

34. Te Ata 1946 journal.

35. Ibid.

36. Ibid.

CHAPTER 16. SUN DANCE OF THE BLOODS

1. CF 1946 Blood Indian journal, 35, Special Collections, University Libraries, Miami University.

2. CF 1946 Blood Indian journal, 32; Te Ata 1946 journal, Blood Indian folder, TAC, CCHM.

3. Marlene Martin, Blackfoot culture summary, Culture.7833@lucy.ukc.ac.uk, 3, 1946 Blood Indian folder, TAC, CCHM.

4. Mountain Horse, *My People the Bloods*, 57.

5. Ibid., 152, 155.

6. CF 1946 Blood Indian journal, 50.

7. Martin, Blackfoot culture, 3; Mountain Horse, *My People the Bloods*, 58.

8. Adolf Hungry Wolf, *The Blood People* (New York: Harper and Row, 1977), 285–86.

9. Te Ata 1946 journal.

10. Ibid.

11. Martin, Blackfoot culture, 2.

12. CF 1946 Blood Indian journal, 35.

13. Te Ata 1946 journal, July 10.

14. "As I Remember It," 192–93.

15. Te Ata 1946 journal, July 12.

16. "As I Remember It," 96–97.

17. Te Ata 1946 journal, July 17.

18. Ibid.

19. Ibid.

20. "As I Remember It," 198; Te Ata 1946 journal, July 18.

21. Te Ata 1946 journal, July 19.

22. Mountain Horse, *My People the Bloods*, 58

23. Te Ata 1946 journal, July 20.

24. Eagle Speaker to Te Ata, December 14, 1946, 1946 Blood Indian folder.

25. "As I Remember It," 199–200.

26. Ibid., 200.

27. Mountain Horse, *My People the Bloods*, 61.

28. Ibid., 62–63; Te Ata 1946 journal, July 20.

29. Eagle Speaker to Te Ata, December 14, 1946, 1946 Blood Indian folder.

30. Te Ata 1946 journal, July 21.

31. Ibid.

32. CF 1946 Blood Indian journal, 57–58.

33. Mike Eagle Speaker to CF, December 14, 1946, 1946 Blood Indian folder.

34. CF 1946 Blood Indian journal, 56.

35. Te Ata 1946 journal, July 22.

36. Te Ata, Notes on Fisher and Te Ata at Blood Indian Sun Dance, n.d., 1946 folder, 8; Te Ata 1946 journal, July 24–26.

37. Te Ata 1946 journal, August 2.

38. CF 1946 Blood Indian journal, 94; Te Ata 1946 journal, August 21.

39. "As I Remember It," 204.

40. CF 1946 Blood Indian journal, 91; Te Ata 1946 journal, July 20.

41. "As I Remember It," 204.

42. Te Ata 1946 journal, August 22, 28.

43. Te Ata to Middleton, handwritten copy of an undated letter, Te Ata 1946 journal.

44. Eagle Speaker to Te Ata, December 14, 1946, 1946 Blood Indian folder.

CHAPTER 17. ALONE

1. Te Ata to Em Hi's, June 3, 1947, 1947 folder, TAC, CCHM.
2. Bonnie Pride, "Te Ata Thrills Audience with Chants, Legends"; "Our Messengers Are Meteorites, Says Dr. Fisher," clips from the OCW student newspaper, May 7, 1947, 1947 folder.
3. Ibid.
4. J. H. Belvin, "Negotiations for the Sale of the Choctaw–Chickasaw Coal and Asphalt Lands," May 13, 1947, Carl Albert Center, University of Oklahoma, Stigler Collection, Box 6, Folder 22.
5. Lovegrove, "Dissolution of the Tribal Governments," 16.
6. Prucha, *The Great Father*, 343.
7. Lovegrove, "Dissolution of the Tribal Governments," 18. Tabulation of the two tribes' ratification vote shows that 6,100 voted to sell the lands while only 400 opposed the sale.
8. CF to Walter, June 19, 1948, 1948 folder, TAC, CCHM.
9. Most of these letters (mainly 1947–48) are in the custody of Audrey Gregory, one of Otto's children by his first wife. She graciously sent me the letters, and I made copies of the pertinent ones, which are in the Otto Fisher, 1947–50 folder, TAC, CCHM.
10. Otto to children, July 10, 1947, 1947 folder, TAC, CCHM.
11. Ibid.
12. Otto to children, December 22, 1947, 1947 folder.
13. Otto to folks, December 30, 1947. I cannot be more specific about the operation because the head of medical records at Johns Hopkins University Hospital informed me by telephone in summer 1996 that the microfilm containing CF's medical record (and presumably the records of many others) was unaccountably missing.
14. Otto to folks, January 14, 1948.
15. Ibid.
16. Otto to folks, March 1, 1948.
17. Dr. J. A. Colston to Mrs. Clyde Fisher, April 20, 1948, 1948 folder.
18. Otto to folks, July 21, 1948.
19. Otto to relatives, August 18, 1948.
20. Otto to folks, December 27, 1948.
21. Otto to Te Ata, January 4, 1949, 1949 folder, TAC, CCHM.
22. Interview with Margaret Ball, September 27, 1995, Margaret Ball folder.
23. Certificate of Death, Clyde Fisher, City of New York Bureau of Records and Statistics, January 11, 1949, 1949 folder.
24. James P. Chapin, "In Memory," *Explorers Journal* (Winter 1949): 29–30.
25. Clyde Fisher, "Garrett P. Serviss," *Popular Astronomy* 37, no. 7 (August–September 1929): 2, 5.
26. Interview with Margaret Ball, March 16, 1995, Margaret Ball folder.
27. Interview with Dorothy Bennett, June 26, 1995, Dorothy Bennett folder.

28. Te Ata, "Guatemala Trip," a daily journal, January 28–February 7, 1949, 1, 1949 folder.

29. Ibid., 1.

30. Ibid., 2.

31. Ibid., 3–4.

32. Ibid., 5.

33. Sandra Kitt, AMNH, to author, AMNH archives, New York, September 4, 1997.

34. Interview with Dorothy Bennett, June 26, 1995, Dorothy Bennett folder.

35. Te Ata to Gordon Atwater, June 29, 1949, 1949 folder.

36. Otto Fisher to Te Ata, September 6, 1949, 1949 folder.

37. Program, Tuesday Musical Club, November 22, 1949, 1949 folder.

38. Vladimir Bakaleinikoff to Mrs. Lewis Young, November 29, 1949, 1949 folder.

39. Max T. Krone, Dean, USC, to Te Ata, October 25, 1949, 1949 folder.

40. Clyde Fisher, *The Life of Audubon* (New York: Harper, 1949), introd.

41. Coleman S. Smith to Te Ata, September 24, 1953, 1950s folder.

42. Julienne Dupuy to Te Ata, April 30, 1950, 1950s folder.

43. Mary Pritchett to Mrs. Clyde Fisher, May 16, 1951, 1950s folder.

44. Te Ata to Em Hi's, October 26, 1954, 1950s folder.

45. Transcription of an audiotape featuring Te Ata's reminiscences of Loon Island, 8–10. Made around 1990, Loon Island folder, TAC, CCHM.

46. Nita to Te Ata, June 7, 1955, 1955 Centennial folder, TAC, CCHM.

47. Richard Green, "The Grassroots Movement in the 1960s," *Journal of Chickasaw History* 2, n. 1 (1996): 24–25.

48. Nita to Te Ata, n.d., 1955 Centennial folder.

49. Undated and unaddressed letter from Te Ata about the 1955 centennial, 1955 centennial folder. Looks like a background piece she did for a news reporter.

50. Te Ata to Loons, June 26, 1955, 1955 Centennial folder.

51. Ibid.

52. Ibid.

53. Prucha, *The Great Father*, 357.

54. Green, "The Grassroots Movement in the 1960s," 3.

EPILOGUE

1. Te Ata to Ataloa, June 10 and June 14, 1962, 1960s folder, TAC, CCHM.

2. John M. MacGregor to Edward Amschel, February 2, 1968, Ataloa folder, TAC, CCHM.

3. "Te Ata Will Tour State," *Daily Oklahoman*, November 7, 1957, 1956–59 folder, TAC, CCHM.

4. Interview with Helen Cole, March 17, 1995, Helen Cole folder, TAC, CCHM.

5. Ibid.

6. Marcia Norman, "Te Ata Captivates Palefaces with Indian Lore," Wilton, Conn. *Fairpress*, Wilton, January 21, 1976, 22, 1976–79 folder, TAC, CCHM.

7. "World Premier of Film Will Be Here Saturday," *Chickasha Daily Express*, April 9, 1976, God's Drum folder, TAC, CCHM.

8. Program, Twelfth Annual Governor's Arts Awards, September 18, 1987, Oklahoma Arts Council, Oklahoma City, Okla.

9. Lynn Maroney, interview with author, October 18, 1995, Lynn Maroney folder, TAC, CCHM.

10. Helen Cole, interview, March 17, 1995.

11. Governor Bill Anoatubby, interview, 1995, Governor Anoatubby folder, TAC, CCHM.

12. Interview with Linda Harris, March 18, 1995, Harris folder, TAC, CCHM.

13. Helen Cole interview, March 17, 1995.

14. "New film gives fresh approach to 'God's Drum,'" *The Trend*, USAO, February 20, 1995, 9, God's Drum folder.

15. Interview with Tom Phillips, 1999, Author's file.

16. Interview with Helen Cole, December 13, 1999, Author's file.

17. I attended the memorial service.

18. "In Memoriam," the memorial service of Te Ata, November 11, 1995, 1980s and 1990s folder, TAC, CCHM.

19. Helen Cole wrote a special remembrance of Te Ata at my request, 1980s and 1990s folder.

AFTERWORD

1. Philip J. Deloria, *Playing Indian* (New Haven: Yale University Press, 1998), 103.

2. Alexandra Harmon, "Wanted: More Histories of Indian Identities." In *The Companion to American Indian History*, ed. Philip Deloria and Neil Salisbury (London: Blackwell, 2001), 261.

BIBLIOGRAPHY

ARCHIVES AND LIBRARIES

American Museum of Natural History Library, New York, New York.
Bizzell Library, University of Oklahoma Libraries, Norman.
Carl Albert Center, University of Oklahoma, Norman.
Chickasaw Nation Library, Ada, Oklahoma.
Clyde Fisher Collection, Miami University Libraries, Miami, Ohio.
Historical Papers of the Palisades Interstate Park Commission, Bear Mountain, New York.
National Archives, Washington, D.C.
National Archives, Southwestern Branch, Fort Worth, Texas.
Oklahoma Historical Society, Oklahoma City.
Franklin Roosevelt Presidential Library, Hyde Park, New York.
Te Ata Collection, Chickasaw Council House Museum, Ada, Oklahoma.
Western History Collections, University of Oklahoma Libraries, Norman.

BOOKS

Alexander, Hartley B. *God's Drum*. New York: E. P. Dutton, 1927.
———. *Manito Masks*. New York: E. P. Dutton, 1925.
Alter, Judy, ed. *Wild West Shows*. New York: Franklin Watts, 1997.
Avery, Susan, and Linda Skinner. *Extraordinary American Indians*. Chicago: Children's Press, 1992.
Bataille, Gretchen M. *The Pretend Indians*. Ames: Iowa State University Press, 1980.
Bird, S. Elizabeth, ed. *Dressing in Feathers: The Construction of the Indian in American Popular Culture*. Boulder, Colo.: Westview Press, 1996.
Blackstone, Tsianina. *Where Trails Have Led Me*. Burbank, Calif.: Blackstone, 1968.
Buffalo Child Long Lance. *Long Lance*. New York: Cosmopolitan, 1928.
Clifton, James. *Becoming Indian: Biographical Studies of Native American Frontiers*. Chicago: Dorsey Press, 1989.
Collings, Ellsworth. *The 101 Ranch*. Norman: University of Oklahoma Press, 1971.
Debo, Angie. *And Still the Waters Run*. Princeton, N.J.: Princeton University Press, 1940.

Deloria, Philip J. *Playing Indian*. New Haven: Yale University Press, 1998.

Fisher, Clyde. *The Life of Audubon*. New York: Harper, 1949.

Foner, Eric, and John A. Garraty, eds. *The Reader's Companion to American History*. Boston: Houghton Mifflin, 1991.

Foreman, Grant. *Indian Removal*. Norman: University of Oklahoma Press, 1953.

Gallagher, Brian. *Anything Goes*. New York: New York Times Books, 1987.

Gibson, Arrell. *The Chickasaws*. Norman: University of Oklahoma Press, 1971.

Gideon, D. C. *History of Indian Territory*. Chicago: Lewis Publishing Co., 1901.

Goodwin, Doris Kearns. *No Ordinary Time*. New York: Touchstone, 1995.

Green, Rayna. *Women in American Indian Society*. New York: Chelsea House, 1992.

Green, Rayna, with contributions by Melanie Fernnandez. *The British Museum Encyclopedia of Native North America*. London, Bloomington, Toronto: British Museum Press, Indiana University Press, Groundwood Books, 1999.

Gridley, Marion. *Indians of Today*. Crawfordsville, Ind.: Lakeside Press, 1936.

Hilger, Michael. *From Savage to Nobleman*. Lanham, Md.: Scarecrow Press, 1995.

Hungry Wolf, Adolf. *The Blood People*. New York: Harper and Row, 1977.

Kartunnen, Frances. *Between Worlds: Interpreters, Guides, Survivors*. New Brunswick, N.J.: Rutgers University Press, 1994.

Keller, Betty. *Blackwolf*. Vancouver: Douglas and McIntyre, 1984.

Kieran, John. *Not Under Oath*. Boston: Houghton Mifflin, 1964.

Lewis, Monte Ross. "Chickasaw Removal: Betrayal of the Beloved Warriors, 1794-1844." Ph.D. dissertation, North Texas State University, 1981.

Littlefield, Daniel F., Jr. *The Chickasaw Freedmen*. Westport, Conn.: Greenwood Press, 1980.

McBride, Bunny. *Molly Spotted Elk*. Norman: University of Oklahoma Press, 1995.

Moses, L. G. *Wild West Shows and the Images of American Indians, 1883–1933*. Albuquerque: University of New Mexico Press, 1996.

Mountain Horse, Mike. *My People the Bloods*. Calgary: Glenbow Museum, 1979.

O'Beirne, H. F. *Leaders and Leading Men of the Indian Territory*. Chicago: American Publisher's Association, 1891.

Preston, Douglas J. *Dinosaurs in the Attic*. New York: St. Martin's Press, 1986.

Prucha, Francis Paul. *The Great Father*. Abr. ed. Lincoln: University of Nebraska Press, 1984.

Smith, Donald B. *Long Lance: The True Story of an Imposter*. Lincoln: University of Nebraska Press, 1982.

Swanton, John. "Indians of the Southeastern United States." *Bureau of American Ethnology, Bulletin 37*. Washington, D.C., 1946.

Te Ata, with Jane Werner Watson. "As I Remember It." Manuscript, 1981.

Weigle, Marta, and Barbara Babcock, eds. *The Great Southwest of the Fred Harvey Company and the Santa Fe Railway*. Phoenix: Heard Museum, 1996.

Wells, Mary Ann. *Native Land*. Jackson: University Press of Mississippi, 1994.

Williams, Thomas Benton. *The Soul of the Red Man*. Oklahoma City, 1937.

The Women's Way. Alexandria, Va.: Time-Life Books, 1995.

Zitkala-Sa. *American Indian Stories*. Washington, D.C.: Hayworth Publishing House, 1921.

ARTICLES

"Ace among Indian Painters." *Christian Science Monitor*, February 8, 1941, 12.

Alexander, Hartley B. "For an American Indian Theatre." *Theatre Arts Monthly* 10 (1926): 191–202.

"Astronomy Curator Ends 28 Years with Museum." *New York Times,* August 1, 1941.

Austin, Mary. "American Indian Dance Drama." *Yale Review* 19 (1911): 740–45.

Baker, Gladys. "Te Ata Keeps Indian Tradition Alive." *Birmingham News Herald,* July 25, 1937, 6.

Barton, D. R. "He Brought the Stars to America." *Natural History,* June 1940.

Beckett, Henry. "The Man in the Moon—Well, Not Quite." *New York Post,* July 9, 1943, 3.

Brown, Opal. "Lushanya, Dramatic Soprano." *Sulphur Times-Democrat,* June 29, 1996.

———. "Sooner Footprints." *Sulphur Times-Democrat,* June 20, 1996.

Bugbee, Emma. "Modern Pocahontas to Recite for Royal Couple at Hyde Park." *New York Herald Tribune,* June 5, 1939.

Burke, Evelyn. "Indian Maid, Authority on Tribal Lore, Loses Heart to White Man." *Pittsburgh Press,* October 26, 1933.

Chapin, James P. "In Memory." *Explorers Journal* (Winter 1949): 29–30.

"The Chicago Opera." *Newsweek,* November 6, 1939, 32.

Curtis, Natalie. "An American Indian Artist." *Outlook* 124 (1920): 37–40.

———. "The Perpetuating of Indian Art." *Outlook* 105 (1913): 629–30.

"Dedicates Park Lake." *New York Times,* July 12, 1932, 2.

De Long, J. Bradford. "The Great Depression." In *The Reader's Companion to American History,* ed. Eric Foner and John A. Garraty, 279–83. Boston: Houghton Mifflin, 1991.

Eastman, Charles A. "My People: The Indians' Contribution to the Art of America." *Craftsman* 27 (1914–15): 179–86.

"Eclipse Expedition Installed in Soviet." *New York Times,* May 30, 1936.

Farrell, Frank. "Princess Te Ata Refuses to Stay Cooped Up When Star-gazing Husband Traipses Away." *New York World Telegram,* n.d.

Fisher, Clyde. "American Museum Expedition to Volcano Paricutin in Mexico." Explorers Club Records, 1944.

———. "At Home in Lapland." *Natural History,* n.d. (ca. 1945–49).

———. "The Eclipse in Kazakhstan." *Natural History* 38, no. 3 (1936): 203–10.

———. "Garrett P. Serviss." *Popular Astronomy* 37, no. 7 (August–September 1929): 2–5.

———. "Popular Astronomic Education in Europe." *Science,* January 22, 1926, 29.

———. "Reminiscences of John Burroughs." *Natural History* 21, no. 2 (1921): 113–25.

———. "With John Burroughs at Slabsides." *Natural History* 31, no. 5 (1931): 500–10.

Fisher, Dexter. Foreword to Zitkala-Sa, *American Indian Stories,* v–xviii. Washington, D.C.: Hayworth, 1921.

Fisher, LeRoy. "Muriel Wright, Historian of Oklahoma." *Chronicles of Oklahoma* 52, no. 1 (1974): 49.

Gilpin, Laura. "The Dream Pictures of My People." *Art and Archaeology* 4 (1918): 12–19.

Gordon, John Steele. "J. Pierpont Morgan." *In The Reader's Companion to American History,* 747–48. Boston: Houghton Mifflin, 1991.

Green, Rayna. "More Than Meets the Eye: Gertrude Kasebier's 'Indian' Photographs." Special issue of *The History of Photography* 24, no. 1 (Spring 2000): 58–60.

———. "The Pocahontas Perplex: Images of American Indian Women in American Culture." *Massachusetts Review* 16 (Autumn 1976): 698–714.

———. "Repatriating Images: Indians and Photography." *Rendezvous* 28, nos. 1–2 (1993–1994): 151–58.

———. "Rosebuds of the Plateau: Frank Matsura and the Fainting Couch Aesthetic." In *Partial Recall: Photographs of Native North Americans*, ed. Lucy Lippard, 46–53. New York: New Press, 1992.

———. "The Tribe Called Wannabee: Playing Indian in Europe and America." *Folklore* (1988): 30–45.

———, curator. "Survival/Art/History: American Indian Collections from the Hood Museum of Art." Hood Museum of Art, Dartmouth College, Hanover, New Hampshire, 2000–2001. Printed script booklet.

———, producer and director. *From Ritual to Retail: The Fred Harvey Company, Tourism and American Indians*. Color video, 20 min. Produced for the Heard Museum, 1998.

Green, Rayna, and John Troutman. "By the Waters of the Minnehaha: Dance and Music, Princesses and Pageants." In *Remembering Our Indian School Days*, ed. Tsianina Lomawaima, Brenda Child, and Margaret Archuleta, 60–83. Phoenix: Heard Museum, 2000.

Green, Richard. "The Chickasaw Capitol Building of 1898." *Journal of Chickasaw History* 4, no. 2 (1998): 4–18, 37.

———. "The Claim on Our Past." *Journal of Chickasaw History* 1, no. 1 (1994): 13–24.

———. The Grassroots Movement in the 1960s." *Journal of Chickasaw History* 2, no. 1 (1996): 12–29.

———. "The Migration Legends." *Journal of Chickasaw History* 1, no. 1 (1994): 4–8.

———. "Voices from the Past." *Journal of Chickasaw History* 1, no. 2 (1995): 3–12.

Harmon, Alexandra. "Wanted: More Histories of Indian Identities." In *The Companion to American Indian History*, ed. Philip Deloria and Neil Salisbury, 2468–65. London: Blackwell, 2001.

Hinderaker, Eric. "Translation and Cultural Brokerage." In *The Companion to American Indian History*, Philip Deloria and Neil Salisbury, 357–75. London: Blackwell, 2001.

"The History of Bacone." *Daughters of American Revolution Magazine* (February 1980).

"Indian Princess Gives Recital at Philmont." *Philadelphia Inquirer*, June 30, 1933.

"Indians Ate Bolivian Recruiting Officers as Chaco War Project." *New York Times*, April 24, 1934.

Inglis, William. "Buffalo Bill's Last Trail." In *Wild West Shows*, ed. Judy Alter, 40–53. New York: Franklin Watts, 1997.

Kahn, E. J., Jr. "The Moon's Best Friend." *New Yorker*, December 28, 1940, 23.

Kropotkin, Princess Alexandra. "To the Ladies." *Liberty*, August 17, 1935.

"Lew Sarett and Our Aboriginal Inheritance." *Poetry* 27 (November 1925): 88–95.

Lieurance, Thurlow. "The Musical South of the American Indian." *Etude*, October 1920.

Lockwood, Marian. "Books and the Sky." *Sky Magazine*, December 1937.

Lovegrove, Michael. "Dissolution of the Tribal Governments and the Sale of the Chickasaw-Choctaw Coal and Asphalt Land." *Journal of Chickasaw History* 2, no. 4 (1996): 7–16.

Lucas, Urith. "Te Ata, Indian Impersonator, Addresses Woman's Club Here." *Lexington Sunday Herald-Leader*, November 13, 1938.

"MacDonalds Dined at White House." *New York Times,* April 23, 1933.

Marsh, Leo. "The Red Poppy Excellent Play." (New York) *Morning Telegraph,* December 21, 1922, 16.

M'Aulay, Dorothy. "Silver and Turquoise Adorn Lecturer–Princess Te Ata." *Fort Worth Star-Telegram,* February 24, 1941.

Mitchell, Irene B., and Ida Belle Renken. "The Golden Age of Bloomfield Academy in the Chickasaw Nation." *Chronicles of Oklahoma* 49, no. 4 (1971): 412–26.

"Morning Bearer." *New Yorker,* n.d. (first week of June 1939).

Moses, L. G. "Performative Traditions in American Indian History." In *The Companion to American Indian History,* ed. Philip Deloria and Neil Salisbury, 193–208. London: Blackwell, 2001.

"Mr. Rogers Gives Advice to Classes at Harvard." *New York Times,* April 24, 1934.

Myles, William J. "Lake Te Ata." Historical Papers of the Palisades Interstate Park Commission, Bear Mountain, N.Y., 1991.

"New Film Gives Fresh Approach to God's Drum." *The Trend* (USAO), February 20, 1995, 1–2.

"New York Scientist Is Wed to Prominent Indian Woman Here." *Muskogee Phoenix,* September 29, 1933.

Norman, Marcia. "Te Ata Captivates Palefaces with Indian Lore." (Wilton, Conn.) *Fairpress,* January 21, 1976.

"Parade of Stars in Planetarium Seems a Miracle." *New York Herald Tribune,* October 3, 1935.

Peake, Bladon. "The Te Ata Matinee." *Stratford-upon-Avon Herald,* July 25, 1930.

Pearce, Dick. "State Indians Are Skeptical of New Deal." *Oklahoma City Times,* October 19, 1934.

"Peggy Wood's Party." *London Daily Mirror,* n.d., 1930.

Pough, Frederick H. "Paricutin Comes of Age." *Natural History* (October 1944): 342–49.

Pride, Bonnie. "Te Ata Thrills Audience with Chants, Legends." *The Trend,* May 7, 1947.

Red Cloud. "Indian Musicians in the Modern World." *Etude,* October 1920.

"Sails to View Eclipse." *New York Herald Tribune,* May 17, 1936.

Schlaikjer, Erich M., and Herbert Schwarz. "In Memory, Clyde Fisher." *Explorers Journal* (Winter 1949): 29–30.

Schoenberger, Podine. "Indian Princess Tells How Tribesmen Helped Win War." *New Orleans Times-Picayune,* February 7, 1941.

"Scientists Ready on Eve of Eclipse." *New York Times,* June 18, 1936.

Shirley, Vivian. "Vivian Shirley Learns Culture of Indians." (Philadelphia) *Evening Public Ledger,* January 19, 1932.

"Start 12,000 Mile Honeymoon." *New York Sun,* June 28, 1934.

"Street Begging Here Called Unjustified; Public Asked to Cease Contributing Alms." *New York Times,* April 24, 1934.

Te Ata. "Across the Desert to Trujillo." Manuscript, 1937.

———. The Creation of an Indian Jar." *Natural History* (April 1943): 180–85.

———. "A Race from Molten Lava." Manuscript, 1944.

———. "What We, as Indians, Have Contributed to American Culture." Manuscript, n.d.

"Teata [*sic*] Presents an Interesting Program Here." *Sulphur Springs American,* August 20, 1926.

"Te Ata Will Tour State." *Daily Oklahoman*, November 7, 1957.

Traub, James. "Shake Them Bones." *New Yorker*, March 13, 1995, 48–49.

Tucker, Anne. "Letter from Mrs. Samuel A. Tucker." *Forward* (Three Arts Club, New York), n.d., 12.

Vestal, Stanley. "The Hollywooden Indian." In *The Pretend Indians*, ed. Gretchen M. Bataille, 63–67. Ames: Iowa State University Press, 1980.

"Welcome to the Planetarium." *New York Herald Tribune*, January 6, 1934.

Whiting, Verde M. "Tribal Career Women." *Independent Woman* (December 1940): 382–84.

"World Premier of Film Will Be Here Saturday." *Chickasha Daily Express*, April 9, 1976.

SOURCES AND ACKNOWLEDGMENTS

Te Ata saved a sizable portion of the memorabilia from her sixty-year career, which until recent years was contained in twenty or so boxes of varying sizes stored in Oklahoma City. These included hundreds of newspaper clippings, brochures, and other promotional material, as well as a treasure trove of personal correspondence, primarily between her and her husband, Clyde Fisher. She also collected a large number of Indian stories and folklore.

Her urge to save so much memorabilia may have been innate, but as far back as the 1930s friends had been suggesting that she tell her story. At least three people had accepted the challenge to help her do that. Florence Pelke began the task in the early 1960s, but relatively early in the project she became too ill to continue. Jane Werner Watson spent several days with Te Ata in the early 1980s and completed what amounted to an oral history of her life mainly before she married Fisher in 1933. Although Te Ata liked Jane Watson and collaborated with her, she did not much care for the manuscript, and it was never published. However, it contained information not available elsewhere on Te Ata's formative years, and I drew freely on that manuscript.

In the early 1990s Mary Ann Thacker, a University of Texas at Arlington graduate student in history was beginning the research phase of her Ph.D. dissertation, a biography of Te Ata, when she was murdered in her Fort Worth antique store. I began this project after Thacker's untimely death. I had met her in Tishomingo and listened one afternoon as she talked about Te Ata and described her planned dissertation. Just before that conversation, I had taken the job as tribal historian of the Chickasaw Nation and was developing and would later edit a quarterly history journal for the tribe's new historical society. Since

Chickasaw governor Bill Anoatubby and I agreed that this would be a part-time job, I would have time to do research on my own for a book-length manuscript. I had several topics in mind. But after Thacker's death, I felt strongly that I should write Te Ata's biography—that it was meant to be.

Still, it would have been impossible without the cooperation of Te Ata's family, and I am indebted especially to former Oklahoma state senator Helen Cole and Hiawatha Estes, Te Ata's niece and nephew, and Linda Harris, the granddaughter of Te Ata's half sister, Selena. Helen and Hi gave me complete and unrestricted access to Te Ata's papers. I hope they feel that I have honored their trust.

I am grateful to Governor Anoatubby for providing my travel expenses so that I could interview two of Te Ata's oldest and dearest friends, Dorothy Bennett of Taos, New Mexico, and the late Margaret Ball of Wilton, Connecticut, and do research at the American Museum of Natural History in New York. I also owe a debt of gratitude to Bill Welge, Rodger Harris, and Judy Mitchener of the Archives and Manuscript Division of the Oklahoma Historical Society; Chickasaw storytellers Glenda Galvan and Lynn Moroney; Sandra Kitt of the Library of the American Museum of Natural History; Randy Talley of the University of Science and Arts of Oklahoma (formerly the Oklahoma College for Women); LaDonna Brown, formerly of the Chickasaw Council House Museum; Jack Focht of the Trailside Museum at Bear Mountain, N.Y.; C. Martin Miller, head of the Library's Special Collections at Miami (Ohio) University; the staff of the University of Oklahoma's Western History Collections; and the staff of the University of Oklahoma Press, especially Jo Ann Reece, Marian Stewart, and Shelia Buckley. My excellent copyeditor, Sheila Berg, spared me from embarrassment countless times. I also am grateful to three early readers of the manuscript, Wendy St. Jean, Michael Lovegrove, and Rose Marie Smith, for their insights and enthusiasm for the project.

Last, but by no means least, I thank my wife, Gail Fites. Her love, patience, and support enabled me to devote a substantial part of four years to complete this project. We gave up significant income, and there were intervals when the work seemed to be going nowhere, but she never once complained. Also, when the manuscript needed cutting, she performed the task in a ruthless but beneficial manner.

After Te Ata's retirement in the late 1970s, she attempted to put her large collection of papers into a coherent framework, but she always got bogged down with the attendant memories and was unable to focus on the task at hand. When the family gave me access to these papers, I photocopied the ones I thought I needed, roughly one-half of the collection. I placed my copies in file folders, appropriate to subject or chronology, and after the manuscript was completed, I donated my copies to the Chickasaw Council House Museum (CCHM), located in Te Ata's hometown, Tishomingo, Oklahoma. The bulk of Te Ata's correspondence remains with her family. There are a few video-taped and audiotaped interviews with Te Ata at the Oklahoma Historical Society and Chickasaw Nation Library. Unfortunately, the sessions came very late in Te Ata's life and offer very little useful information.

When I decided to do the biography in January 1995, Te Ata had just turned ninety-nine. Accompanied by Helen Cole, I visited her a few times to pay my respects. I never got to know her and be captivated, as the other writers had been, by a gifted artist and storyteller. On the other hand, I felt I was freer to write a more balanced account of her life. Although I was always mindful of being a free agent, I realize now that somewhere along the line I had become a fan. While it was not my job, as biographer, to make the reader follow suit, if I have told Te Ata's story the way I understand it, there should be a new generation of devotees.

Index

*in Te Ata's repertoire

Fisher, Josephine (Otto's wife), condolence to Te Ata, 230
Fisher, Ora (Clyde's sister), 235, and breast cancer, 274; death of 277
Fisher, Otto (Clyde's brother), 140, 230, 252, letters about Clyde's bad health, 274–78; at Paricutin volcano, 245–52
Five Civilized Tribes, 6
Fletcher, Alice, 48–49
"Floor culture," 88
Flower, Sir Archibald, 94
Foreman, Grant, 4
Fretwell, Ernest, 84, 90
Freuchen, Magdalene, 170, 179–82, 184
Freuchen, Peter, 170, 179–80
Freund, Daniel and Mary (Bertie Thompson's parents), 10–13
Freund, Lucy Alberta "Bertie" (Bertie Thompson's maiden name), marriage to T. B. Thompson, 9
"From the Land of Sky Blue Water,"* 40

Gardner, Belle, 9
Geronimo, 49
Gilbert, Annie Kate, 36
Gilbran, Kahlil, 105
Gilpin, Laura, 83
Gimble Ellis, 126
Godje (Hanging Flower), 51, 56
Godowsky, Leo, 104
"God's Drum":* 1995 remake of documentary, 294; 1975 documentary, 291; performance piece, 99, 153, 211
Good Spring (capital of Chickasaw Nation, later Tishomingo), 5
Göteberg, 178
Great Depression, 97, 100, 103
Great White Way, 67
Green Corn Dance (busk festival), 20–21, 196–98, 311n.29
Green Sky, Mrs., 140
Grosvenor, Gilbert, 114
Guatemala, Te Ata's trip to, 280

Hako ceremony of the Pawnee, 40
Harkins, Mary (aunt who gave Mary Thompson name, Te Ata), 17
Harris, Linda, 292
Hayden, Charles, 135, 170
Hayden Planetarium, 160, 175, 198; Fisher at opening of, 166
Helm, Edith, 201, 205
He Who Always Has a Good Day, 136, 150
Hiamovi (Cheyenne chief), vision of,* 103
"Hiawatha,"* 41, 65, 303
Hind Bull, Jack (Blood Indian): led Pipe Ceremony, 263; danced with Te Ata, 265
Hippolytus, 65
"Hollywooden Indians," 158
Horn Society, 262–63, 265–66
"How Death Came into the World,"* 79, 103
Hyde Park performance: list of guests, 208; Te Ata's program, 208–210
Hyde Park Hill Top Cottage, 326n.28
"Hymn to the Sun"* (Zuni chant), 273

Incas, of Peru, 187
Indian Artists Company, 70
Indian authenticity, 303
Indian boarding schools, 299
Indian calendar, 320n.30
Indian ceremonial dances at Gallup, 149, 229
Indian churches, 141–42
Indian Recovery Act, 144
Indian Removal Act, 1830, 4
Indian self-determination, 287
Indian sign talkers, 224
Indianness, 307; and creative survival, 300
"Indian's Contribution to America,"* 155
Ish-ti-Opi (Wesley Robertson), at Hyde Park, 204–205, 207, 209